ISRAEL/PALESTINE.

A 4000 YEAR HISTORY OF THE
CONFLICT IN THE MIDDLE EAST.

BY IAN CARROLL.

To DAVID
'THE ORACLE'
BERRYMAN.

BEST WISHES.

Ian Carroll.

1

Published 2006 by Ian Carroll Publications.

ISBN 0-9554709-0-0
ISBN 978-0-9554709-0-5

Cover design by Ste Mason.

Printed in Great Britain by Antony Rowe Ltd, Chippenham, Wiltshire

ACKNOWLEDGEMENTS.

Thanks to my mum and dad for their support, Carole for the company, and Marcus for the help. Thanks also to friends, family, and colleagues, the Entrepreneurs, and everyone at Peter Kavanagh's, whose constant refrain of 'How's the book coming along?' sustained me in this endeavour. I hope it was worth the wait.

To All The Girls I've Loved Before,
And To Those Who'll Put An End to War.

PROLOGUE.

In April 2002, at the height of the Second Intifada or uprising of the Palestinian people against the Israeli Occupation, images of stone-throwing youths confronting tanks flashed nightly across my television screen. And I, a 36 year old surveyor, resident in Liverpool, with no affinity in either direction, wondered why they were fighting and how it would end. I wanted to get involved somehow, but I understood that a little knowledge was a dangerous thing, and I did not know enough about it to take sides. Instead, I resolved to go back to the beginning of time, to find out who was there first and EVERYTHING that had happened since. Only then would it be possible to decide where Right lay in this complicated issue.

The following history represents the evidence I have gathered along the way. It is my attempt to promote peace through understanding. I hope you'll come with me.

It promises to be some journey.

IN THE BEGINNING.

Our story begins with the birth of man, somewhere in Africa, some sixty thousand years ago. There, possibly in the region of Ethiopia, the first modern man was born. His genes, namely the Y chromosome, live on in every male alive today.

Prior to this, human beings inhabited earlier forms of evolution: Palaeolithic, Neolithic, Neanderthal, and the like, and are not important here. We are only concerned with the last 4000 years of habitation in the Middle East.

Look at an atlas of Africa, Arabia, and Asia and one thing stands out: the only way that man could have migrated out of Africa to eventually populate the world is through the narrow strip of land where Egypt and Arabia meet, between the Red and Mediterranean Seas.

Approximately one hundred miles wide, this crucial juncture afforded the only land bridge out of Africa, and was to become an essential migratory route and an avenue of trade long before it become a focus for religion and one of the most disputed areas on earth.

There are other possibilities for dispersal from the first continent: Ethiopia to Yemen is a short trip of fifty miles across the Red Sea at its narrowest point, as is the journey from Morocco to Spain, but it seems certain that early man would have learned to walk before he discovered the art of seafaring, and would therefore have trekked rather than sailed out of Africa.

Leaving the dusty plains and deserts behind, following the lush, verdant valley that accompanied the Nile, migratory man would then have crossed the Sinai Desert and emerged in the ancient land of Canaan, as the area of Israel/Palestine was then known. The eastward sweep of the Mediterranean coast here earned the name of the Fertile Crescent.

South East of this delicious landscape are two great rivers, the Tigris and the Euphrates, located in modern Iraq, then known as Mesopotamia. It was in this land, fed by these two rivers, that civilisation began.

The use of the wheel, the earliest forms of writing, the first cities, and the beginning of society and state, all originated here some 6000 years ago.

As populations began to emerge in the far flung corners of the globe, two great civilisations emerged either side of the Fertile Crescent: that of Egypt and Mesopotamia.

As a land bridge, for trade or for warring parties, the route through Canaan was the one and only choice.

Also, as the demand grew for Arabic spices, pottery, and precious metals, the ports of the Fertile Crescent on the Mediterranean Sea gave access to the known and unknown world.

Is it any wonder then that this sought-after land has been much fought over, and conquered, for thousands of years, or that it should have drawn inhabitants from far and wide; a mixture of peoples. The name Canaan means merchant, and the population was related by virtue of entrepreneurial skills, and was not necessarily homogenous with everyone from the same race.

Like the Swiss throughout the Second World War, you might expect a certain sanctuary for these beneficial locals, yet the land was subject to a flux of invaders, who all left their mark and their men in the area.

Egypt, emerging as the triumphant power in the region, would station battalions here in order to stake its control, or would appear at times of unrest to reinstate the rule of law.

Similarly, invading forces, such as the Hykksos, circa 1500 BC, would also mingle, marry, and maintain a presence that would echo down the generations.

At a time when the world became a home for many races; African, Asian, Arabic, and Hellenic, the land of Canaan must have been the most cosmopolitan place of all.

According to the Old Testament of the Bible, this land was promised by the Lord, the one God, to Abraham, who lived in the town of Ur in old Mesopotamia.

The Lord instructed Abraham to travel to Canaan 'Where the Canaanites live', and there he would become father to a great nation: God's Chosen People.

Abraham did as instructed, and with his son, Isaac, and Isaac's son Jacob, who fathered the twelve tribes of Israel, they became known as the Patriarchs, the founding fathers of the Chosen People in the Promised Land.

Many scholars have sought to place the age of the Patriarchs according to the chronology included in the Bible. Faith-based sources, endorsing a literal translation, point to the 480 years between Exodus and the destruction of the state of Israel by the Assyrian empire in a non-disputed 722 BC, and the 430 years of slavery prior to the flight of the Israelites from Egypt. This then gives the age for the founding fathers of God's own people, including their own recorded life spans, as somewhere around the first century of the third millennium BC, around about 2100 years before the birth of Jesus Christ.

Add to this the Bible's own chronology, from Adam to Abraham, the first Patriarch, at 1946 years, and we have a date for the first human being of approximately 4000 BC.

I, for one, do not accept the literal translation, and adopt instead a more practical reading, and I like the theory espoused in the Discovery Channel's Genographic series of 60,000 years for the first modern man.

So, if there is to be no literal reading of the Old Testament's ancestry, should we believe in the content at all?

Archaeology cannot place the early biblical characters anywhere between that stated chronological date, or anywhere else in the next 1000 years, for we are simply going too far back in time to ever really know.

What we have, instead, is the faith-based belief in their existence by the Israelites, who emerged not only as a race, but also from a particular place.

Egypt, the greatest civilisation of early history, formed the dominant regime in the Middle East, and as such drew a variety of immigrants and traders across its borders.

These would appear to have been a mixture of captives from the various wars and conquests being conducted as far away as Mesopotamia, merchants bringing their wares from subjugate territories, or starving neighbours drawn in during times of famine or drought.

The story of the Exodus can be dated to approximately 1500 BC using the Bible chronology, and archaeology and Egyptian texts from that era point to one chapter of history from the time that accords with the idea of an immigrant population being expelled from Egypt: that of the invading Hykksos Empire.

Egypt was defeated by this army of the Aegean, and was subject to their rule for more than one hundred years, before the Pharaoh Ahmose eventually roused his people and expelled the occupying force from the country.

One interesting fact about this ancient time is that it coincides with the eruption of Santorini, a volcanic island in the Mediterranean that exploded, destroying the Minoan civilisation on the island of Crete, and caused a huge Tsunami that reached the shores of Egypt.

As we have seen with the Boxing Day Tsunami of 2004, off the coast of Indonesia, to feed the crest of the approaching wave, the waters ahead of the body of water are drawn back, draining the territory in advance of it, and adding to the liquid mass that will eventually be delivered with such force and magnitude.

Such a strange phenomenon would have reverberated down the generations, even centuries, through myth and legend.

Could that explain the story of the parting of the Red Sea and the subsequent deluge that overwhelmed Pharaoh's pursuing forces in Exodus?

That is not to say that I believe the Hykksos to be the ancestors of Israel. I do not. It could be, though, that the story has been appropriated by what are, most definitely, a people of a later time.

The first mention of Israel, as a race, comes in the victory stele, or monument, of the Pharaoh Merneptah, dated 1207 BC. Recording an invasion of Canaan and the decimation of the tribes of that region, the inscription declares that

'Israel's seed is not', after his army had finished with them.

The verse reads:

The princes are prostrate, saying "Mercy!"

Not one raises his head among the Nine Bows.

Desolation is for Tehenu; Hatti is pacified;

Plundered is Canaan with every evil;

Carried off is Ashkelon; seized upon is Gezer;

Yanoam is made as that which did not exist;

Israel is laid waste, his seed is not;

Hurru is become a widow for Egypt!

All lands together, they are pacified.

This is the first recorded mention of Israel anywhere in history and, crucially, they are identified by the hieroglyphs as a people, not a place.

Therefore, they had not yet completed their conquest of Canaan. Instead, they merely had designs to, and were waiting in the terrain above, until they had sufficient numbers to invade the lowlands and coastal plain below, where the best fishing, trading, and fertile land could be found.

But who were these hilltop inhabitants? They were not mentioned in an earlier comprehensive census of the region. They were definitely an emerging presence, and they may well have been exactly who they have claimed to be: refugees from Egypt with their own unique identity.

The truth, I believe, lies in the spiritual revolution that took place more than a century earlier, with the arrival of a new Pharaoh in Egypt.

Born in the early fourteenth century before Christ, Amenhotep IV came to the throne in 1367 BC at a time when Egypt's ascendancy over the entire region of the Middle East was unquestioned and unchallenged.

The neighbouring states had long been subjugated, the wars had been won, and there was little to be done except to sit back and accept the tributes that came rolling in.

The seat of power, established at Thebes, close to the border with modern Sudan, was a strong one. Courtiers and priests enjoyed an opulent lifestyle, inhabiting palaces and owning slaves. They were respected, there was law and stability, and life was good.

Then, Amenhotep IV underwent a spiritual transformation, in one of the earliest examples of Monotheism. The belief in one God had never had a more powerful advocate than that of the Pharaoh, who took the new religion to his heart.

His power base was moved from Thebes to a new capital at Tel-el-Amarna, some 250 kilometres further north. He dispensed with the other ancient Egyptian gods, of which there were an abundance, and therefore rendered redundant all the priests of these other religions.

Osiris, Anubis, Horus, Isis, and the pantheon of gods were now replaced by one, the Sun God, known as the Aten.

Amenhotep IV completed the makeover by changing his own name to Akhenaten, meaning 'Beloved of the Aten'. One can imagine the outrage caused by this fiercely independent Pharaoh, who has been called the world's first individual.

All of those in previously powerful positions were now removed from the decision-making arena, or were left raking over the ashes of defunct idols.

The new capital attracted many followers, yet the discontent the Pharaoh had left behind in the former government seat and in the priestly corridors became a festering wound, and thoughts of a coup began to gather apace.

Akhenaten was busy establishing his new religion and blissfully happy with his beautiful wife, Nefertiti, 'She-For-Whom-The-Sun-Doth-Shine', as she was lovingly called by her devoted husband. He was isolated in his temple, and vulnerable.

Eventually, the experiment, as it must have seemed to the frustrated former establishment, became too much to bear for the old guard. Egypt's hard won territories, the respect from her defeated foes, the tribute due, all began to slip from her grasp.

Something would have to be done about Akhenaten.

A plot may well have been hatched to remove him from the throne. His brother, Semenkhare, his leading general, Aye, and even his son-in-law, Tutunkhaten, later known to the world as Tutunkhamun, could all serve the political cause with greater responsibility than the recalcitrant Pharaoh.

One can imagine the news reaching him in his citadel of Tel-el-Amarna of the imminent uprising, and then him fleeing for his life along with his religious followers, pursued by the army of Egypt, heading for a safe haven.

The tomb that had been prepared for Akhenaten was smashed, and every temple image of him was destroyed.

As no Mummy has ever been found for Akhenaten, it has been suggested, in a book by Ahmed Osman for one, that the Pharaoh and Moses may have even been one and the same.

Looking down a list of early Egyptian monarchs, we have Ahmosis, Tuthmosis, and Ramoses, or Raamses, so Moses, it would seem, would be in keeping with a name from the Royal household.

Also, in the Bible, when Moses approaches the new Pharaoh, he is carrying a staff, which he turns into a serpent. A staff topped with a serpent's head was as much a part of a Pharaoh's attire as a crown is for a king.

And what of Moses' request to 'Let my people go'?

The converts at Tel-el-Amarna could definitely be said to be Akhenaten's 'people'. They stood alone from the remainder of the Egyptian population, who were still worshipping the old gods.

We know nothing of Moses except what the Bible tells us, that he was raised in the royal household after being found in a basket amongst the bull-rushes of the Nile and taken in by a princess.

It is a wonderful story, pointing to humble beginnings, but the point, nevertheless, is that Moses grew up in the palace.

And of his people, what do we know?

It may be that the band of followers he had drawn to him were related more by religion than race at this point, but through the experience of the Exodus, and their desire to remain separate from the followers of other religions, they became a different entity and a tribe apart.

The hot pursuit would account for the years spent wandering in the Sinai Desert, and the interim would allow their number to grow to the point where they might make their presence felt in the region of Canaan, which they hoped to eventually colonise for themselves.

The forty years in hiding and the time required for their numbers to increase fits nicely into the gap between the end of Akhenaten's reign in 1350 BC and the first recorded mention of a new people who called themselves Israel in the stele of 1207 BC.

These followers of Moses and Monotheism would emerge from the wilderness to contest a land that they occupy, yet still fight for, today.

EARLY DAYS.

Moses led the Chosen People to the Promised Land, but he did not get to see it himself. As one of the generation that had known slavery, it would be their descendants alone who would enter Canaan.

The biblical conquest, of the land they had left Egypt to trek to, is said to have occurred at a time when there is much evidence to the contrary.

Until the middle of the twelfth century BC, Egypt was the dominant force in the region, and the land of Canaan was pacified.

Raamses II, one of the greatest of all pharaohs, reigned from 1279 to 1213 BC, and he was followed by Merneptah, and then came Raamses III and IV.

This was a time of stability. Egyptian strongholds existed throughout Canaan, and anyone wishing to conquer the area would have to defeat not only the native population but the army of the Egyptian governors too.

Israel would have to wait until this era of security came to an end before the opportunity arose to colonise the land. When the opportunity eventually arrived, it was as a result of someone else's war.

Living in the high plateau above the coastal plain, planting vines, grazing their livestock, and raising their families, life must have seemed pretty promised anyway. But all that was about to change.

Two great empires, Egyptian and Mesopotamian, had dominated the civilised world since early times. There were other occasional contenders, such as the Hittites from Anatolia who had plagued both parties, but even their 100 year hiatus could not prepare the Near East for the commotion that was to come.

The Mycanneans, modern Greeks, were at war with the residents of the kingdom of Arzawa in what became known as the Trojan War.

No one can be sure, but it is possible that veterans of this conflict, rather than return home when the fighting subsided, set sail for the southern Mediterranean and became known as the Mysterious Sea-People.

According to a temple inscription of the reign of Raamses II, the Sea-People were a confederation of the Tjeker, Shekelesh, Denyen, Weshen, and Peleset united.

These invaders sacked the Fertile Crescent, toppling the major ports of Tyre and Sidon and destroying the native Canaanite communities. Eventually, they would come up against Egypt.

Artwork left by Raamses III shows a fierce naval battle between the two sides, and it is a frantic picture of hand to hand fighting, on boats, with swords.

Egypt claimed victory, but the assault on their shores inflicted enough damage that from there on in, the great Empire was happy to stay behind its own borders, leaving the rest of the Middle East to fend for itself.

The vacuum of power left in Egypt's wake was soon to be filled, both by the Peleset, better known as the Philistines, who settled down to enjoy their spoils, and by the Israelites who were resident in the hills above awaiting an opportunity to take control of the Promised Land.

Pottery types dating to this period point to an Aegean origin for the Peleset people. They quickly established communities throughout the region, though sticking mainly to the coast.

The Israelites seized the remaining Canaanite villages, rebuilding and putting down roots of their own.

There must have been considerable tension between the two sides, as they considered who had the best farm land, watering holes, vantage points and therefore defences.

Other factions of the Sea People settled in Phoenicia, at the north eastern end of the Fertile Crescent, known as the Levant, which is modern day Lebanon.

Egypt stood strong in the West, Arabia proved impenetrable to the south, and Mesopotamia and Phoenicia dominated the east. To the north lay the Mediterranean, leaving Canaan boxed in between these superpowers and the deep blue sea.

The population of the contested region would have consisted of original Canaanites who had survived the recent invasion, the traders who were perennially drawn here from neighbouring lands, and the two new arrivals; the Israelites and the Philistines.

As war veterans, who had sailed hundreds of miles to get here, and who had fought and conquered their way in, the Philistines were not about to go anywhere.

The Israelites had a date with destiny, they had departed from Egypt, and they had waited patiently for their opportunity. They were also, most importantly, on a mission from God.

This narrow band of terrain, eighty miles wide and forty miles deep, would be home to both, but the argument as to whom it belongs rages to the present day.

As learned a man on the subject as Lawrence of Arabia has said that the question of who was here first is academic. Meaning?

Well, either the question is so complicated that it requires a great deal of knowledge to answer it and it is therefore an academic problem, or, the question is unanswerable and is rendered academic.

It seems to me that, to all intents and purposes, especially going so far back in time, the two groups of people arrived at the same time.

One claim to the territory was built on conquest; the other was built on faith. Both took advantage of the opportunity presented by the Egyptian withdrawal from the region.

The Israelites had lived in the highland region for a hundred years of more, after they had wandered in the desert for forty years after Exodus. They could also claim to be originally Canaanite, having moved to Egypt in a time of famine and then been enslaved by the Pharaoh.

In Egypt, they had adopted Akhenaten's religion and carried it with them to the land of their forefathers.

They had followed Moses to a land that they already knew well. Their roots were there, and their future too, but it seemed that they would have to share their homeland with another.

Still, they would remain a tribe apart and maintain their unique identity, and by following the code set down in the Ten Commandments and keeping faith with the Lord they hoped that one day they would inherit the Promised Land and that their Philistine neighbours would be vanquished.

But whose vision was this? The founding father of the Israelites was Abraham, who came from Ur, moved to Canaan, and then went on to Egypt in a time of famine.

The descendants of Abraham, led by Joseph, were also drawn through necessity to the land of the Pharaohs, and there they were put to work building the great temples and cities of the age.

And what of Moses? I have voiced the opinion that Moses may have been the Pharaoh Akhenaten himself. In his book 'The Origins of Religion', Sigmund Freud poses a similar theory, believing that Moses was an Egyptian, and possibly a high-ranking official in pharaoh's court.

Freud believes that every emerging nation fashions a legend of its own origins, and that there is a pattern to all of these founding myths.

Firstly, the hero comes from the royal household, is cast out and raised in humble surroundings, before eventually resurfacing to claim the throne.

The story of Moses is a variation on this theme. From humble Hebrew beginnings, Moses is raised in the royal house, before returning to lead his people. Freud's analysis of this twist in the tale is that, if it complied with the classical structure, Moses would therefore have been an Egyptian, and you can't have the Jewish people claiming a foreigner for their prophet.

Also, when we get to Canaan, the Bible concerns itself with the battle between the pious southern Hebrew territory of Judah and the frivolous northern kingdom of Israel. Here, Freud applies his analysis to argue that the two peoples being talked about are not two Israelite identities engaged in sibling rivalry but that the reference is to the two distinct communities resident in Canaan at this time: the Hebrews and the Philistines.

It would seem that neither had the resources to extinguish the other, with one battle-hardened and the other emboldened by faith. Converting one to the religion of the other might be the easier option, but one thing is clear, both from the Bible stories and the archaeological evidence, there were two nations resident in Canaan, and neither was about to go away.

TWIN STATES.

There were now two distinct groups of people in Canaan. Bordered by powerful neighbouring states; Egypt to the west, Assyria to the south, and Phoenicia in the east, the land inhabited by the Israelites and the Philistines would be theirs to contest for the next two hundred years.

According to the Bible, we are now in the age of Saul, who gave way to David, who was followed by Solomon.

It must have seemed to the tribe of Israel that the journey that began in Egypt had finally delivered them to the Promised Land. They had given up their homes and, along with their families, they had followed Moses, surviving on their faith for more than a hundred years.

Now, what must have seemed an elusive dream during the darkest days in the desert wilderness had finally come true, for here they were, resident in the towns of Beersheba, Jericho, Jerusalem, and Gezer.

The only blot on the landscape, literally, was the Philistine community that inhabited the coastal plain, with major cities at Ashkelon, Ashdod, Gaza, Ekron, and Gath.

This warring tribe, now settled, must have been a thorn in the side of the religious community that descended from the hills. Their presence presented an obstacle to the fulfilment of the Lord's covenant, but there was little the Israelites could do about it.

It would be far better to attempt to win the hearts and minds of these new arrivals on the shore. The Philistines had something that the Israelites wanted, namely, the northern territory. Did the Hebrews have something to exchange in return? They had religion, and they had belief. Could they convince the Philistines to come on board and accept the way, the truth, and the light?

Despite the Biblical tales of great victories along the way, leading to the capture of Jerusalem under David and the construction of the Jewish Temple under

Solomon, the archaeological evidence points instead to an uneasy truce between the two sides.

The greater cities and the more robust and established society was that of the northern kingdom. Having moved down from the hills only when there was an opportunity to do so, the Israelites had shown that they did not possess the military might to conquer the region, but that they had only seized what they could and rebuilt the ruins of towns sacked in the earlier campaign by the Sea-Peoples.

They did possess one powerful weapon though, and it would not be long before they put it to use. The way the Hebrews carried and conducted themselves, their self belief, and their fortitude and piety, must have impressed all who came into contact with them.

Still, it is no small thing to convert a nearby nation, and it would have to be done over generations, perhaps even a century or two.

All the while, the territory of Israel remained a backwater compared to Philistia; a collection of sparsely populated towns, villages, and hilltop outposts.

For all their zealous preoccupation, they must have wondered just how they were going to convince their rival to come on board and cede the land that they coveted.

About 1030 BC, the Israelites appointed their first king, Saul. This raised the profile of a community still seeking to establish itself in the region.

Saul fought many battles against the Philistines, all to no avail. He could not conquer them, nor convert them, and he died trying.

His successor, David, had a little more luck, although probably not as much as claimed in the Bible.

With his slingshot, David slew the mighty Goliath, pride of the Philistine army, instantly becoming a hero to his people, and he eventually rose to the throne.

Expanding his kingdom to the northern borders, establishing his capital in Jerusalem, David united the two regions known as Judah and Israel in the land of Canaan that had been split under Saul.

Going back to Freud's interpretation of the two kingdoms, he believes that the reference is not so much to Judah and Israel but to the distinct communities of the Hebrews and Philistines.

Therefore, the Davidic expansion and reunification probably points to a time of growth and prosperity under his leadership that, rather than conquering the Philistines, propelled Israel onto the international stage as an equal to its powerful nemesis and neighbour, or at least a nation worthy of their respect.

The reign of David is confirmed by outside sources in texts from Syria and from the Arameans, and points to a date around 950 BC.

When David died an old man, a new and widely respected leader would take his place. Solomon created an empire from the Egyptian border to the Euphrates River and became a revered figure for the people of Israel. He went on to build a magnificent temple in Jerusalem, the first, and helped to put the state on the map.

Israel also had an eye on expanding into Philistia to complete the journey begun under Moses, and would strengthen its position over the next two hundred years. With the Hebrew community striving for unity, they would inhabit the region with little thought to the outside world, but this mentality would soon be shattered.

There had been occasional incursions from the Egyptian side, but this had not adversely affected the status quo. Alliances had been formed with the Phoenicians to the east, not least when the Philistines threatened to trample the Hebrews underfoot.

With peace on either side, Israel could concentrate on fighting for the Promised Land and fulfilling the Covenant, but all of her hopes and dreams were about to be crushed.

From the south, the empire of the Assyrians, which had previously ended at the River Jordan, came rushing forward to seize all of the land to the Mediterranean Sea.

In 722 BC, all of the major population centres in Israel were conquered, its residents spirited away, and only the underdeveloped southern region escaped the calamity.

The dream of God's Chosen People inheriting the Promised Land came to a sudden halt. What had begun in Egypt 600 years earlier, and had still not quite come to fruition, now looked like it never would.

Having established a foothold in the region and created a state, when they were so close to convincing their neighbours of the righteousness of their cause, they were caught between the devil and the deep blue sea.

They had made gains, for sure, but if they were not able to drive out the infidels occupying a land they believed the Lord had ordained for them, what hope would the Israelites have against a much superior force?

When the Assyrians arrived, the result was near devastation. The land of Canaan was put to the sword, and the Israelites were banished into exile.

BEFORE EXILE.

The hills above the coastal plain of Canaan are part of a mountain range that runs parallel to the Mediterranean. To the east, there are plateaus ripe for grazing, traditional farming, and for inhabitation. To the west, it is an undulating landscape, with steep valleys in between, and much more difficult to traverse.

As the rain rolls in from the sea, these high ridges trap the rainfall on the hillside, producing a dense woodland and fertile soil. Grain and barley was grown on the flatland above, while the hillside was used to plant both olive and grape vines, to produce oil, wine, and food.

The settled Israelites grazed their sheep and goats and lived on a well-rounded diet.

Some 250 sites have been identified by archaeologists from this era, each home to an average of one hundred people, so the Israeli population can be estimated at around thirty thousand people in total at this time.

Most of these settlements were self-contained and self-sufficient, having their own agricultural fields and their own grazing pastures.

This collection of villages all shared a common goal to inherit the land below. These communities were each self-contained, and shared no public buildings or administrative centres between them.

The abundance of agriculture raised on their land gave rise to trade with their neighbours, the Philistines and the Egyptians, and the Edomites and Moabians in the Syrian Desert, across the Jordan River. Also, being productive meant the community could increase the size of their own families, and that is what happened, with the population growing exponentially in just a few generations.

One thing not on their diet though, despite the fact the animal was present in the region, was pig. No trace of such a thing was ever found in excavations of early Iron Age Israeli sites, although the remains of the animal were found amongst nearby Philistine villages. Already, the Israelites were observing strict dietary discipline, living apart from the remainder of the local populace, and maintaining their uniqueness.

The idea of the two states referred to in the Bible being that of the Israelites and the Philistines, rather than Judah and Israel as the Good Book would have it, is informed by Sigmund Freud and his work, 'The Origins of Religion: Moses and Monotheism.' It is an idea that I like, but it is not the only possibility.

The highland region had always been divided into a northern and southern section, even in much earlier periods of inhabitation.

As far back as 3500 BC, there were settlements in the hills above Canaan, and the northern territory was always the more densely populated. In fact, ninety percent of the residents would live in the more accessible north, with only ten percent in the south.

It seems a realistic proposition that the twin states of the Bible were two different peoples living side by side in the former region of Canaan, especially when we add another important detail to the mix.

I have said that, following the devastation wrought by the Sea-Peoples, the Israelites in the hills seized an opportunity to occupy the ruins left in the marauders wake, and took over areas of the lowlands and the coastal plain.

If we accept the biblical record, the two states of Judah and Israel are still resident in the hills at this point, but both Freud and I agree this could not have caused the level of discontent, the split personality almost, that dominates this era in the Bible.

The Bible talks of the idolatrous northern kingdom that turned away from the Lord and destroyed the covenant that they had made with Yahweh, God of the Hebrews, and brought about its own destruction.

This seems to me representative of one or two possibilities. Either, the northern kingdom was being reprimanded for not doing as the south had done, namely, capturing the land from the Jordan River to the Mediterranean coast, therefore failing to keep its half of the bargain, or it is purely aimed at the

Philistine community for refusing to adopt the religious observance of the Israelites. Unable to move this fighting nation by force, for the Israelites, it had almost been a case of 'If we can't beat you, join us!'

That the Philistines had failed to grasp the monotheistic idea and were standing in the way of the Lord's promise to the children of Israel must have been frustrating.

There is evidence of an invasion by the Assyrians that is repelled by a collection of Levantine communities, Phoenicians, Philistines, and Israelites, around 850 BC. This would be a precursor to the conquest 130 years later that would divide Canaan and see a great number of Israelites scattered to the far corners of Mesopotamia, some never to return.

For the time being, though, the Israelites can be said to have fulfilled, in some way, a portion of their goal. They were resident in half, maybe three quarters of the land the Lord had promised them, and they were an established community in the region.

The dark ages were behind them, yet they were still trying to realize the prophecy in its entirety, and it must have seemed that one day they still might. They had shaken off the yoke of Egypt which, despite a solitary incursion under Pharaoh Shishak in 935 BC, saw that once mighty kingdom remain largely behind its own borders.

A kingdom of Israel existed, with a royal lineage of the House of David. And, let us not forget, they were still beloved of God, His Chosen People.

Things are never usually that simple though, and so it would prove. External forces were at work, these were dangerous times, and this crucial piece of land, fought over for aeons, was to become a focus for the most powerful empires of the world once more.

There was something in the air, and in order to rally the populace behind the flag of Israel, something unique and special would be required in order to sustain them through the dark days ahead.

Calling on the leading scholars, prophets, and priests of the day, a manifesto to reassert their aims and uniqueness needed to be drafted, and the product of their efforts became the richest document the world had ever known. That rallying call produced a work they called the Bible.

THE BIBLE.

The name Hebrew is said to derive from an ancient tribe, the Ibiru. Scholars point to the similar sound of the two. The word means 'wanderer'.

The Ibiru existed around 1500 BC and were said to be an unsavoury band of Bedouin. Once, when a king was asked what had happened to a rival of his, he replied contemptuously, 'He has run off to join the Ibiru!'

Abraham, the Patriarch, or founding father, of the Jewish people was certainly a wanderer. Originally from Ur, in modern-day Iraq, he moved to Canaan and then on to Egypt. A nomadic tradition would have prepared the Israelites for their forty year stay in the desert with Moses.

Akhenaten, in the 14th century BC, received word from King Abdi Hepa, a Hurrian, of the Phoenician Canaanites, that he was being besieged by the Habirus. So, the Hebrews, Habirus, or Ibiru came from Canaan into Egypt, and that's where our story begins.

We can't be sure that the Hebrews and the Ibiru are one and the same, nor can we prove that the early figures in the Bible really existed, for there are no external sources to support their existence. What we have are traditional stories that were written down centuries after the events being described. No doubt there was embellishment, and the inclusion of myth and legend, but the fact remains that the only document to describe the early history of the Jewish people is the Bible.

So, what does the Bible say on the subject?

I have spent some time reading the Old Testament in order to find out, and what surprised me about the Good Book is what a good book it really is!

The first book of the Bible is Genesis, where God created heaven and earth and all the things within in just six days. On the seventh day, He rested.

He formed man from the slime of the earth, and when his creation, Adam, was sleeping, He took a rib from his chest and made of it a woman, whom Adam called Eve.

27

The Lord told the pair that they could eat anything in their earthly paradise, except the fruit of the Tree of Knowledge of Good and Evil.

Along came the Serpent and asked Eve why the fruit of that tree was forbidden, 'Because', he said 'if you eat it, your eyes will be opened and you will be a god.' So Eve ate, and Adam ate, and when the Lord found out He was not happy, and He cast them out of Paradise to till the soil for all their lives and then die the death, for dust they were and dust they would become.

Then Adam knew his wife, and she gave forth children, Cain and Abel. Cain grew up to be a farmer, Abel a shepherd, and they both offered their produce to the Lord. God was not impressed with Cain's fruit and vegetables, but He appreciated the firstlings of Abel's flock. Jealous, Cain slew Abel.

When God found out what Cain had done, he cast him out to the east of Eden. In recompense for Abel, the Lord gave Adam and Eve another son that they named Seth.

And Adam lived 930 years before he died. And the descendants of Adam came to populate the earth.

Seth lived to be 912, and when he was 105 he had a son, Enos. At 90, Enos had Cainan. At 70, Cainan had Malaleel. At 65, Malaleel had Jared.

Aged 162, Jared's wife gave birth to Henoch. At 65, Henoch had Mathusala. At 187, Mathusala had Lamech, and at 182, Lamech had a child he called Noah.

Now the earth was becoming overcrowded and, with an average lifespan of 900 years, something had to give.

The Lord decided to cap life expectancy at 120 years. But He also saw that man was wicked and He regretted creating him. It was time to start again.

Only Noah and his family would be spared the destruction, for he was a perfect man and just. God instructed Noah to build an ark for himself, his wife, and sons Sem, Cham, and Japheth and their wives, too. Also, two animals of every kind were to be placed in the ark: one male, one female.

The flood gates of heaven then opened and it rained for forty days and forty nights, so that the waters covered the whole world and the highest mountain, and it stayed like that for 150 days.

When the waters finally receded, Noah's family and all the animals and birds went forth and began to repopulate the earth.

Sem had Arphexad, who had Sale, who had Heber. Heber had Phaleg, who was the father of Reu, who in turn had Sarug, who had Nacher, who had Thare. Thare had Abram, and it is with Abram that our story really starts.

The Lord appeared to Abram and instructed him to leave his home in Ur and travel to Canaan, 'Where the Canaanites live', and He made a promise to give the land to Abram and his descendants from the Jordan River to the Mediterranean Sea. And He changed his name to Abraham.

Abraham married Sarah and in their old age they were blessed with a child, Isaac. To test his faith, God asked Abraham to sacrifice his son upon an altar. He was just about to do it when an angel appeared and told him to put down his sword. He'd passed the test.

When Sarah died, she was buried in a cave near Hebron in Canaan. When Abraham died, aged 187, he was buried alongside Sarah.

Isaac had two sons, Esau and Jacob, and even though Jacob was the younger of the two, he inherited the birthright. And Jacob came across an angel of the Lord and, not knowing who he was, Jacob fought him. When they had finished fighting, the angel said, 'From now on, your name shall no longer be Jacob but Y'sra el, meaning 'He who wrestles with God.' The name of Israel had been born.

And Jacob loved a woman called Rachel, but in order to marry her, he also had to take her older sister, Lia, too, for it was not the custom to allow the younger sister to wed first.

Lia bore Jacob six sons, Rachel bore him two, and their handmaids each bore him two more. The twelve children of Jacob became the twelve tribes of Israel, and one child, Joseph, was very successful indeed.

Being Rachel's son, Joseph was Jacob's favourite, and he gave him a coat of diverse colours. One night, Joseph had a dream that he explained to his brothers.

'I was the moon', said Joseph, 'and I was being worshipped by eleven stars, who bowed down before me.'

His brothers were not amused.

One day, while tending to their flocks, far from the family home, the brothers decided to cast Joseph into a well and leave him to die. Then, noticing a camel train, they sold Joseph into slavery instead to the Bedouins for twenty pieces of silver.

Joseph was taken to Egypt, where he went to work for a eunuch named Putiphar, a captain of Pharaoh's guard.

JOSEPH.

Joseph lived in his master's house, and the Lord blessed the house, and therefore Putiphar was pleased with the slave's contribution, and put him in charge when he was away on Pharaoh's business.

Now the eunuch's wife had eyes for Joseph, and one day called him indoors and asked him to lie down with her, but Joseph refused. Another time, Joseph was doing some work around the house and the lady asked him again, but Joseph turned her down once more and made a dash for it, but not before she managed to grab a piece of his many-coloured coat.

When Putiphar came home, his wife said 'Your slave came in to the house and tried to lie down with me. I screamed and he ran out, but I grabbed his coat. Look, here is the proof of the thing', and she produced the piece of cloth.

Aggrieved, the eunuch went to Pharaoh and had Joseph put in gaol. Soon, he was joined in the prison by Pharaoh's chief butler and chief baker, both having somehow upset the boss.

Tasked with serving their meals, Joseph was doing the rounds one day when he perceived both men in deep thought. He asked the nature of their contemplation, and they said they were sad because they had both had a dream the night before and they could not interpret them.

'Tell me your dreams', said Joseph.

The chief butler began.

'I saw a grape vine that had three branches on it, abundant with fruit. I took the grapes, pressed them into a cup, and gave the wine to Pharaoh'.

'The three branches are three days', said Joseph, 'after which, Pharaoh will remember your good service and set you free.'

The butler was pleased with the reading.

'Just remember', added Joseph, 'when Pharaoh lets you out, put in a good word for me'.

He then turned to the chief baker and said 'Tell me your dream'.

'I dreamt that I had three baskets of food that I was carrying to Pharaoh, but the birds flew down and ate it all', said the baker.

'Your three baskets are also three days,' said Joseph, 'after which Pharaoh will remember what you did, chop off your head, and feed you to the birds!'

Three days later, Pharaoh had a feast, and he remembered his butler and baker and he made their dreams come true!

Now, the chief butler was restored to his former position and he prospered and forgot all about Joseph until, two years later, Pharaoh had a dream. He called all the wise men in Egypt to him, but none could interpret it for him. Then, the chief butler remembered Joseph and said 'There is a Hebrew in the gaol very good at this sort of thing', and so Pharaoh called for Joseph.

'I saw seven fat cows, full and fair, and seven lean cows, and the thin cows ate the fat cows yet they were still lean. Then I saw seven ears of corn, blooming lovely, and seven ears of corn that were thin and blasted, and the seven thin ears consumed the seven that were fat', said Pharaoh.

'Both dreams mean the same thing', Joseph explained. 'The repetition is merely for emphasis. There will be seven years of good harvest in all of Egypt, followed by seven years of famine. What you want to do is put someone in charge of collecting a fifth of everything grown in the good years and put it into storage for the bad times.'

'What a good idea', said Pharaoh. 'And I think I've found just the man.'

So Joseph was made governor over all of Egypt, second in command only to Pharaoh. He put away one fifth of the harvest into store houses during the years of abundance and, after seven years, when the famine came, Egypt alone in the whole Middle East had food to spare.

Back in Canaan, Jacob instructed ten of his remaining eleven sons, all save the youngest, to go to Egypt to buy some grain. So off they went to speak to Pharaoh's governor in order to buy their meal.

Joseph recognised his brothers, but they did not know him, and he did not reveal his identity.

Joseph accused them of being spies, come to assess the strength of Egypt, but they said that they were ten of eleven brothers, sent by their father to purchase necessaries.

'If that is true,' said Joseph, 'I will keep one of you here, and you can take your corn and go and get the other so I can see the truth of what you're saying.'

So one brother was put in the prison, while the others returned to their home to fetch the youngest sibling.

When they returned with Benjamin, Joseph released the man in jail, but as they prepared to exit Egypt, Joseph framed the youngster for theft, in an attempt to keep him with him.

Benjamin was Joseph's only brother to Rachel and he did not want to let him go. But the eldest of the brothers refused to leave him behind, saying 'He is our father's favourite, the only remaining son of his beloved Rachel, and I will take his place in the gaol so that he might go free, for our father is old and this will otherwise kill him.'

At this point, Joseph broke down and revealed his identity to his brethren. They were full of remorse for selling him into slavery, but Joseph forgave them, saying 'It was God's will. The Lord sent me ahead of you to save you from the famine.'

Joseph was soon joined in Egypt by his brothers and his father, Jacob, and they all lived together in the land of Goshen in the north of the country.

When Jacob died, an old man, he was buried alongside Rachel in the Hebron caves. Then, aged 110, Joseph also passed away. His last wish was that, when the people of Israel eventually returned to the Promised Land to fulfil the Lord's covenant with Abraham, they should carry Joseph's body out with them to bury alongside his people.

EXODUS.

The children of Israel multiplied in Egypt, and there came a new Pharaoh who hadn't known Joseph. He was afraid of this immigrant population. To occupy them, he put them to hard work building the store-cities of Pithom and Raameses.

But the more Pharaoh oppressed the Hebrews, the more they multiplied, so he instructed his midwives to kill any Hebrew child born male. The midwives, however, could not bring themselves to do it. So Pharaoh told all the people of Egypt to kill any Hebrew child born male. And it was done.

Now a child was born to the house of Levi, one of the twelve sons of Jacob. At three months old, the child was placed in a basket made of bulrushes and pitch and hidden amongst the reeds at the river's edge.

A daughter of Pharaoh found the baby and gave him to her maid to raise. When the child was grown, Pharaoh's daughter adopted him into the royal palace and named the young man Moses.

One day, Moses was out walking when he saw an Egyptian hitting a Hebrew. Moses killed the bully and buried his body in the desert, but Pharaoh heard about the murder so Moses went to hide in the Arabian Desert.

After a long reign, Pharaoh died, and the Lord appeared to Moses from within a burning bush and told him it was safe for him to return to Egypt, where he should go and ask the new Pharaoh if he can take the Israelites into the wilderness to give a sacrifice to the Lord.

So Moses went to Egypt and did as the Lord had commanded, but Pharaoh refused, and put the people to even harder work.

Moses returned to his place of commune with the Lord and told Him he had failed in his task: Pharaoh would not let the people go and pray.

God empowered Moses to perform miracles in order to sway Pharaoh, so Moses headed off to the palace with his little bag of tricks, but the magicians of Egypt matched Moses' minor miracles, and Pharaoh would not relent.

An angry Lord then sent down the first plague, turning the waters of the Nile blood red. The magicians repeated the feat. Then a plague of frogs descended on the land, and Pharaoh backed down and said he would let the people go and pray, but as soon as the curse was lifted, Pharaoh changed his mind.

So the Lord sent a third plague, of small flying insects, troublesome to man and beast, but Pharaoh wouldn't give in. Then came a plague of flies that covered all of Egypt except for Goshen, where the Hebrews lived. Pharaoh said that to end the plague, he would allow Moses to go and pray but not his people.

This wasn't good enough, and a fifth plague ensued, where disease befell all the horses, cattle, sheep, and camels in Egypt, except the Hebrews' livestock. Annoyed, Pharaoh refused to let the people go and pray.

There followed a plague of boils on all the men, and then came a plague of hail. Having had enough, Pharaoh agreed to let the people go, but as soon as the hail stopped, Pharaoh changed his mind yet again and rescinded the offer.

A plague of locusts then assailed Egypt, devouring all the crops in the land, then darkness fell for a full three days, everywhere apart from Goshen. Still Pharaoh wouldn't back down.

Finally, the first-born child of every Egyptian died in the night, at which point, Pharaoh called for Moses and told him to take his people and go and pray.

Moses gathered the Israelites beside the Red Sea where they camped in preparation for their departure. But again Pharaoh has second thoughts, and rather than see his workforce disappear, he sent his army in hot pursuit.

The Lord then parted the Red Sea, and after the Hebrews crossed safely, the waters returned with a vengeance to overwhelm the approaching Egyptians, drowning every one of them.

The Israelites then wandered in the Sinai desert, between Egypt and the Promised Land, and they moaned to Moses that they had no food, so the Lord sent down, bread, quails, and Manna from Heaven. When they needed water, Moses struck a rock with his staff and water appeared.

The Hebrews were attacked in the desert by a Bedouin outfit, the Amalec, but the Lord saw to it that His Chosen People prevailed.

Then Moses was called up the Mountain of God, where he stayed for forty days and forty nights. The Lord issued the Ten Commandments, which he gave to Moses on tablets of stone, written by the finger of God.

Thou shalt not have strange Gods before me.

Thou shalt not make a graven image of God.

Thou shalt not serve false Gods.

Thou shalt not take the name of the Lord in vain.

Thou shalt not labour on the seventh day.

Thou shalt honour thy father and thy mother.

Thou shalt not kill.

Thou shalt not steal.

Thou shalt not bear false witness.

Thou shalt not covet thy neighbour's house, wife, servant, handmaid, his ox, his ass, or anything else that is his.

Moses headed down the mountain with the new laws, but when he got there, he found his followers worshipping a golden calf. Angry, Moses smashed the tablets. He returned to speak with the Lord and the tablets were renewed.

God then told Moses that the land of Canaan would be given to the people bit by bit, over time, and that they must not join with the Canaanites, but must remain a band apart; and they should destroy the Canaanite groves: a practice that continues to the present day.

The Lord then took Moses to a vantage point overlooking the Promised Land, but He would not let him enter, for he was of the generation that had known the bitterness of slavery.

After forty years of wandering in the wilderness, Moses died, and the Israelites entered the land of milk and honey, as was promised to Abraham.

The conquest of Canaan could begin.

THE CONQUEST OF CANAAN.

The Lord God appointed Joshua, a long-serving lieutenant of Moses', to lead the Israelites into the Promised Land. The River Jordan miraculously dried up to allow the Hebrews to cross into Canaan, and the conquest could begin.

The first city to be taken was Jericho. The Israelites surrounded the fortified walls and for seven days laid siege. Finally, with a blast of their trumpets, the walls of Jericho came tumbling down.

Next up was the city of Ai, which Joshua defeated by means of a cunning military plan. Then, the kings of Jerusalem, Hebron, Jarmuth, Lachish, and Eglon united against the new foe. Again, Joshua's men emerged triumphant.

The southern cities all captured, the Hebrews headed north to the largest city in Canaan, Hazor. There, a confederation of kings united in opposition to the Israelites but again there was only one winner; the Lord's anointed.

Hazor was burnt to the ground, and with this last bastion of resistance removed, God's covenant with His Chosen People was fulfilled.

The land was divided amongst the twelve tribes of Israel, but Judah, controlling Jerusalem, couldn't eliminate the Jebusites from his midst, and the two peoples dwelt together.

And while Judah's children controlled the hill country in the south, they weren't able to destroy the inhabitants of the valley below, and the Canaanites began to share their cities.

Before Joshua eventually retired to the heavens, he reminded the Israelites of their special relationship with God, and he forbade them to marry or mix with the Gentiles, as the non-Jews were known.

But the conquest of Canaan, though swift, was not lasting. The kings of Moab and Ammon, across the river Jordan, seized control and ruled for eighteen years. Then the old desert foe, the Amalec, along with tribes of the Midian lands of Arabia, ruled for seven years, leaving Israel awash with tent and camel.

The Lord then turned to Gideon, the least of men, and made him strong in order to drive out the Arab invaders.

And Gideon succeeded, and the Israelites wished to appoint him to rule over them, but Gideon refused, saying 'The Lord shall rule over us'.

When Gideon died in old age, the Israelites turned to idolatrous ways, and they worshipped Baal, the Canaanite god.

The Lord God saw fit to punish Israel for this sin, and he gave them Abimelech to rule over them. Abimelech proved a treacherous leader, slaying seventy of his Hebrew brethren in order to assume power, and the people of Israel opposed his rule.

After three years in charge, Abimelech and his soldiers attempted to quell an uprising. After chasing a group of rebels up a tower, Abimelech was struck on the head by a piece of millstone dropped by a female protester.

Rather than have it be said that he'd been killed by a woman, Abimelech fell on his own sword. And still the Lord was not with the Israelites.

Thola then ruled the Hebrews for twenty three years, and Jair ruled for twenty two. Afterwards, Jephte the Galaadite was in charge for seven years, Abesan of Bethlehem took control for a similar period, and then Ahialon, a Zabulonite, judged Israel for ten years.

After him came Abdon, a Pharathonite. He had forty sons and thirty grandsons, mounted on seventy ass colts. He judged for eight years and then he died. He is buried in Pharathon, in the land of Ethraim, in the mount of Amalec.

The Philistines then ruled Israel for the next forty years, and that must have been hard to bear.

The Lord heard the suffering of the Israelites and an angel visited Manue and his wife and foretold that they would have a son that would deliver Israel from the Philistine yoke. The child of Manue they named Samson.

SAMSON AND DELILAH.

Samson grew up strong, and the spirit of the Lord was with him. At the time, the Philistines were in charge of the Hebrews.

One day, Samson spotted a woman that he wanted to wed. His father begged Samson to choose someone from his own race, for the woman who had caught his eye was a Philistine, but Samson would not be swayed.

It was the Lord's will that Samson should choose this foreign lady, for He had a plan.

So the woman and Samson started courting, and while the young man was on his way to visit his fiance one day, he came upon a lion, which he killed with his bare hands.

A few days later, making the same journey, as Samson passed the carcass of the slain animal, he saw in its mouth a swarm of bees and a honeycomb.

Now the happy couple's big day was drawing near, and there was to be a seven day stag-do before the wedding and a seven day feast to follow.

There were thirty Philistine men with Samson for his party, and he decided to have a bet with them. He said, 'I will set you a riddle, and if you solve it by my wedding day, I will give each of you a shirt and a coat, but if you don't, you will give me thirty shirts and coats, one from each of you.'

His Philistine friends accepted the wager, and Samson set forth the puzzle.

'What', he said 'is strong yet gives forth sweetness?'

Well, the guests pondered for the entire week, and then, on the wedding day, they cornered the bride and said to her 'Soothe thy man and persuade him to tell you the answer to the riddle, or we will burn you and your father's house down. I mean, do you want to strip us?'

So the bride-to-be wept before Samson saying 'You hate me and you do not love me.' And Samson caved in.

Then, when Samson asked for his answer, the guests replied 'What is stronger than a lion, and what could be sweeter than honey.'

Samson immediately knew how they had come to their answer and, decidedly angry, he went off to Ashkelon, a Philistine city on the Mediterranean coast, and killed thirty men there and took their shirts and coats and then gave them to his wedding guests.

He then went off to stay with his parents for a little while to cool off.

When Samson had calmed down, he went to see the woman he was supposed to wed, but her father looked surprised to see Samson and said, 'I thought you hated her, so I gave her to one of the other guests to marry.'

Samson was not pleased, and he said to the man, 'From this day forward, whatever I do to the Philistines, I shall be blameless, and', he threatened, 'I will do you evils.' And so he did.

After catching 300 foxes, Samson tied torches of fire to their tails and let them run hither and thither, so that they destroyed all of the Philistines' cornfields, grapevines, and olive yards.

The Philistines wondered what had driven Samson to commit such an act, and when they heard the reason for his anger, they went to his former fiance's house and killed both the woman and the father who had given her away. Then they went and told Samson what they had done.

Samson, though, was not to be appeased, and he replied to them 'Although you have done this, I will still have my revenge on you, and then I will be quiet.' And Samson butchered a great many of them and then went off to hide in a cave.

The Philistine hordes went up to Judah, where the Israelites lived, and threatened a slaughter for what Samson had done, but the Judeans promised to deliver the fugitive to them.

Three thousand men of Judah went and found Samson and asked him to give himself up, saying 'Why have you done this? You know the Philistines have dominion over us.'

So Samson agreed to be delivered to the Philistines, and when this had happened, and his kinsmen had departed, Samson took up the jawbone of an ass and with it slew a thousand men.

For the next twenty years, Samson ruled over Israel, which was still under Philistine control. Samson remained a fugitive, and his enemies sought to capture him at any opportunity.

When Samson went to visit a harlot in Gaza, the soldiers surrounded her house, hoping to catch Samson as he left in the morning.

But Samson slept all the next day, and did not leave until midnight, under the cloak of darkness, taking the gates to the city with him, so that nothing could stand in his way.

Soon, Samson fell in love again. This time, like the last, she was a Philistine. Her name was Delilah.

Now the Philistine princes, hearing of the blossoming relationship, each offered Delilah 1100 silver pieces if she could find out where Samson's strength lay.

One night, Delilah asked the question.

Samson replied, 'If I were bound with cords made of sinews not yet dry, still moist, then I shall be weak like other men.'

While Samson lay sleeping, Delilah put the theory to the test, and then cried out 'Samson, the Philistines are upon you!'

And Samson jumped up, and the cords fell away from him.

'You have mocked me', said Delilah. 'Won't you tell me where your strength lies?'

'If I were bound with new ropes that were never in work, then I would be weak like other men', Samson replied.

So the next time Samson went to sleep, Delilah tried again, and then called to him that the Philistines were upon him, and Samson jumped up, and the ropes all snapped.

'How long must you deceive me?' cried a frustrated Delilah, so Samson said 'Plait my hair with seven locks, tie it with a lace, and nail it to the floor, and I shall be weak like other men.'

Again Delilah tried and again she failed.

'How can you say you love me?' she appealed. 'You have lied to me three times.' And then she pressed him much and hung upon him many days, giving him no time to rest, until his soul fainted and he was wearied almost unto death.

'Okay', sighed Samson eventually, 'I will tell you', and he opened up the truth.

Believing him, one night Delilah gathered the Philistine princes, and while Samson lay sleeping with his head in her lap, she called in a barber who cut off all his hair, wherein his strength did lie.

The Philistines then came rushing in, plucked Samson's eyes out, and led him off to the prison in chains, and there they made him grind.

And his hair began to grow again.

When the Philistine princes had a feast to Dagon, their god, they called for Samson to be brought to them for their amusement.

Samson claimed to be weary and, being blind, he asked a boy to place him between the pillars of the house, so that he might rest a while.

There, he began to shake the pillars, until he brought the whole place down around him, and he killed even more Philistines at his death than he did in his life.

THE KINGS OF ISRAEL.

The judges ruled over Israel, and war with the Philistines went on. At one point, the Ark of the Covenant, containing the tablets of stone that Moses brought down from the mountain, was seized by the enemy. For seven months, misfortune rained down on the Philistines until, wearied, they returned the Ark to its rightful owners.

In the mean time, the Hebrews had begun to worship Baalim and Astaroth, pagan idols, then the Lord anointed Samuel to be his prophet, and he urged the Israelites to abandon these false gods.

As Samuel aged and grew close to death, the Jewish people asked him to appoint them a king, like other nations had. Samuel chose Saul to become the first royal monarch of Israel, but he also said that the Lord was angry that they should require an earthly master, and he reminded the people who was boss.

The new king, Saul, was tasked by God to destroy, once and for all, the Amalec, and to spare nothing of theirs.

Saul led the Israelites to victory, but salvaged the best of the Amalec herd for his own people. God was unhappy that Saul has disobeyed Him, and His affection turned away from the king towards a young man, David.

David was fair of face and played a beautiful harp. Whenever Saul was depressed because the Lord had forsaken him, he called for David to play for him to lighten his mood.

Then Saul went off to do battle with the Philistines, and the two armies were camped on opposing hills, with a valley between them.

Goliath, a giant of the Philistine army, clad in chain-mail and carrying a staff the size of an oak beam, went every day into the valley and threw down a challenge.

'Choose one man amongst you to do battle, and if he beats me, we will be your slaves, but if I beat him, you shall be ours.'

No one would accept the invitation, and the stand off continued.

David had three older brothers in the army, and he was sent by his father to deliver them some food and to see how they were doing.

When he got to the battlefront, David heard the summons of Goliath, and decided to take him on.

Saul tried to dissuade David, but the young man knew that the Lord was with him, and he would not back down.

Eventually, Saul allowed David to go and confront Goliath, armed only with a slingshot and five stones.

The giant was unimpressed when he saw a mere lad before him, but as the two raced to meet each other in the valley, David fired his slingshot, and the stone hit the Philistine between the eyes and embedded in his forehead, and Goliath fell down dead.

The opposing army then ran off, and David was a hero to all of Israel, but this made Saul jealous. David was offered Saul's daughter in marriage, but he was set a challenge by Saul before he could take her hand. The test was designed to see David fail, but instead he excelled and became son-in-law to the king.

As the people continued to admire the giant slayer, Saul's anger grew, and he pursued David with the aim of killing him.

The youngster went into hiding, and the king eventually tracked him down to a cave. When Saul and his men entered the dark dwelling, they scoured the grotto but could not find their prey.

David was hiding in the shadows, and he crept up behind Saul, took his knife, and cut a piece of cloth from the king's coat.

David then turned himself in and showed the cloth to Saul, saying 'I could have killed you in the cave but I did not. Look, see how close I came?'

Saul realised that David was far more just than he himself and broke down and cried and promised that David would rule Israel one day.

And so it came to pass. Saul was killed in battle with the Philistines, and David was ordained king.

For forty six years, David ruled Israel from his capital in Jerusalem, and he defeated the Philistines from Gabaa to Gezer.

When David grew old, he appointed his son, Solomon, to rule in his wake.

Now Solomon was famed throughout the Middle East. He built a magnificent temple in Jerusalem to the Lord, and he married a daughter of the Egyptian Pharaoh. But that was not all. He took for himself a further 700 queens and 300 concubines of different nationalities.

He also entertained the Queen of Sheba, who came to see this powerful ruler of Israel, bearing gifts of unimagined opulence, arriving in a caravan laden with gold and precious things.

And these foreign women led Solomon into idolatry.

After a reign of forty years, in 931 BC, Solomon passed away and, for his sins, the Lord divided the Promised Land north and south, with ten tribes in the north known as Israel, and two in the south known as Judah.

Two of Solomon's sons took the reins in these two kingdoms: Rehoboam ruled Judah, and Jeroboam ruled Israel.

Judah was pious, obeying the Lord and keeping His commandments and avoiding interaction with the Gentiles.

Israel was the more advanced culture, heavily populated, with a great deal more activity taking place.

As such, there was greater intercourse with the native Canaanites, with trading and marriage between them.

According to the Bible, it is the forsaking of the covenant that brought about the destruction of Israel in 722 BC by the Assyrians.

The children of Israel were carried off into exile, to the cities of Hala and Habor, by the river of Gozan, in the cities of the Medes, in present day Syria.

Judah survived the Assyrian invasion. Less populated, less conspicuous, and less desirable, the land was not in the way of the emerging empire's expansion.

The Bible has it that their salvation was due to their keeping the faith.

Judean luck was not to last though, for in 587 BC, another power emerged in the region. The Chaldeans, ruled by Nebuchadnezar, sacked Jerusalem, destroyed Solomon's temple, and carried off the remaining Hebrews to Babylon. There, the slave army were put to work constructing the famed Hanging Gardens, one of the seven wonders of the ancient world.

Now, both Israel and Judah, no matter how pious, had disappeared. The Lord's covenant that was given to Abraham, restated to Moses, and achieved under Joshua, was now no more.

Israel ceased to be, and the Hebrews, having escaped from Egypt, were exiled once again. The dream of a Promised Land for God's Chosen People was over.

THE HISTORY BOOKS.

The history books may not accord with the version in the Bible. There are points of convergence, yet the only real detail is in the Old Testament, and there is much that relies on faith.

Saul was the first king of Israel, and he was followed by David, who was succeeded by Solomon. Israel, by this point, at the turn of the millennium, about 1000 BC, was a nation and not just a race of people.

Allied on occasion with Phoenicia, at the northern end of the Fertile Crescent, Israel sought to drive the Philistines from the coveted land of Canaan.

Under Solomon, the Israeli map grew large, encompassing Edom, across the Jordan River, and moving into Syria.

Post-Solomon, the kingdom split, with Judah in the south and a capital at Jerusalem home to two of the original twelve tribes. In Israel, to the north, the other ten tribes lived with their capital at Samaria.

The 200 year footprint that Israel had created was not to last. Their high profile existence, their alignment with foreign powers, brought them to the attention of the giant empires waiting in the wings.

From southern Syria and eastern Mesopotamia, led by Sargon II, the Assyrians rose to conquer the Levant. After taking control of Babylon in 729 BC, it wasn't long before they turned their attention north, attracted by the Mediterranean Sea ports and the bustling economy.

In 722 BC, after a siege lasting three years, Israel fell, its inhabitants either slaughtered at the scene or, if they were lucky, one of 20,000 carried off into exile and slavery, with new communities brought in to replace them.

Judah wasn't in the way of the conquering army and escaped unscathed. Living in the less hospitable terrain of the southern hills, it was easy to go unnoticed. They had little to offer an outsider, not much to steal, and posed no threat. They could be left alone.

But it must have appeared to the Judeans that they'd had a lucky escape. Eternally faithful, it seemed the Lord had spared them because they practised the Hebrew religion with orthodoxy, while their sibling state had cavorted with foreigners, diluted their covenant, and were therefore abandoned by God.

It was at this time, breathing a sigh of relief for escaping from the Assyrians, and knowing they could well be next, that the Bible came to be written.

Using the most learned scholars, the priests, high officials, and the best scribes, the Bible created a unifying history for the Hebrew people, which served as a manifesto in a time of need.

As well as pointing out the errors that had led to the Israeli downfall, it also served to rally the southern tribes in order that they might not suffer a similar fate. It was a call to arms, to faith, and to unity for this fragile infant nation.

The Assyrian empire continued to hold sway over the region, but not all of their achievements were so brutal.

Ashurbanipal, who ruled the Assyrians from 668 to 629 BC, compiled a vast library that contained original copies of some the earliest writing known to man. He also gave a universal language to the melting pot of tribes, people, and places that they controlled: Aramaic, the language that would later be spoken by Jesus Christ.

This pervasive language allowed for loyalty to the Assyrians and created unity amongst the nations they had conquered. It also diluted any lingering patriotism for the old order.

After the death of Ashurbanipal, two new forces arose to wrest control of the Fertile Crescent and other Assyrian-controlled land.

The Scyths came from the Caucasus mountain region, while the Medes came from Persia. These two armies united to defeat the Assyrians, and ruled Syria and Canaan for 100 years.

The expulsion of the Assyrians created a vacuum of sorts in Mesopotamia, but there was soon a new Babylonian empire to fill the void.

Nebuchadnezar, king of the Chaldeans, commanded an empire from Egypt to Syria, including the Fertile Crescent. His war of conquest would not spare the Judeans, and when they rose up in revolt, they were crushed, the temple of Jerusalem destroyed, and the last remaining Hebrews in the biblical land of Israel were transported to Babylon.

Of all of this, especially the early stuff, there is very little proof. We have no record, except the biblical text, for anything from Abraham to Saul. Of David and Solomon, there is one proclamation from an Assyrian king from 835 BC claiming to have killed the king of Israel and also the king of the House of David, and a stele found at Tel Dan in Judah, written in Aramaic, that confirms the existence of King David.

For the original temple in Jerusalem, archaeology can find no trace of it. It may be that subsequent construction on the site has destroyed all the evidence but, again, it seems that belief in its existence must rely on faith.

Solomon's wealth, his marriage to a daughter of an Egyptian Pharaoh, his famous mines, could all be expected to throw up some sort of identifiable trail, but there is none.

These characters, these events, are all vivid enough that they would have caught the imagination of the storytellers of the time, and the memory of what they achieved would have lingered long after the events being described.

The Egyptian empire was waning, the Assyrian one short-lived, so we cannot expect to find comprehensive supporting material for the biblical text from external sources.

Still, without additional documentation, it is possible to see that the Bible was created at a time when the Israelites had been carried off to exile and when, more than ever, they would need a reminder of their special relationship to God. Otherwise, their conviction might desert them while abroad, and the unique identity they had been carving out for themselves over five centuries might be lost forever.

It takes a great deal of faith to believe in the Old Testament, to accept that there are one people especially chosen by God, and that He promised them a land to call their own. It is much easier to see the Bible as the literary expression of the needs of a people at a certain point in time.

A written testament to their faith would inspire the Hebrews in exile and provide a practical way of practising their religion. You could take the Good Book anywhere, and therefore never be far from the Lord or succour.

The Bible was written in the seventh century BC, after the Israelites were transferred to Assyria, and before the Judeans suffered a similar fate. In the 150 year period between these two events, when the Bible came into being, the message contained within, that forsaking the Lord leads only to destruction, must have made the Israelites pine for their brethren and the last bastion of their faith in Judah.

To express their kinship, the Israelites of exile began referring to themselves as Judeans, for Israel was no more. They were no longer Israelites, they ceased referring to themselves as Hebrew, for they now had a new collective term for themselves. An abbreviation of Judeans, they began to call themselves Jews.

THE PERSIANS.

After exile, came liberation.

'He is my shepherd, and shall perform all my pleasure: even saying to Jerusalem, Thou shalt be built; and to the Temple, thy foundation shall be laid.' So says the Bible about their saviour, Cyrus the Mede, the king of Persia.

Earlier invasions had produced devastation, cities burned, populations massacred, but the Persian Empire was one of civilisation. There would be stability in the Fertile Crescent not seen since the days of Egyptian control.

The messiah who delivered the Hebrews out of slavery was Cyrus II, who came to the throne in 549 BC. He went on to conquer the territories of modern Turkey, Syria, and the Fertile Crescent.

Ten years later, in 539 BC, the Persians overran the empire of Nebuchadnezzar, adding Babylon to their conquests and creating a fiefdom as large as any seen in the world up to that point.

The Persian government practiced tolerance and celebrated diversity. The Jews were allowed to resettle in the Holy Land, where they congregated in a region they named Yehud.

The temple in Jerusalem was rebuilt at tax-payers expense, such was the benevolence of the new regime. The Philistines, also exiled by the Babylonians, now returned to their former cities on the Mediterranean coast.

Both sets of subjects could be said to be grateful to the new empire, but over on Persia's eastern border, things were not so secure. The Scyths were putting up an effective fight to stop any territorial encroachment in their direction, and the Mesopotamians were attempting to reclaim their land and make good their losses.

Cyrus ruled from 559 to 530 BC before he was eventually killed in battle on the eastern frontier. He was succeeded by his son, Cambyses, who in 525 BC deposed the last Pharaoh in Egypt and who was later to perish along with 5000 men while attempting to take a short cut across the desert to Egypt.

It is believed that Cambyses and his entire entourage perished in a sandstorm and were buried alive.

It was left to another ruler, Darius the Great, to finally put paid to the eastern uprising and to cement Persian power throughout the region.

Darius, king of kings, ruled from 522 to 486 BC. He continued the good work of Cyrus, secured stability for all of his subjects, and furthered the cause of peace.

This would be the last empire of Middle Eastern origin to control the Arabian peninsular in the ancient historical period. For the next 1000 years, the rulers of the region were all of European descent.

The Persian Empire stretched as far as India, introduced rice to the Middle East, and created a road network to rival that of the Romans centuries later. One such highway stretched for 1600 miles and was called the Royal Road. It ran from Sardis in Asia Minor, in what would now be Turkey, to Susa near the Persian Gulf. There was also a canal to link the Nile and the Red Sea.

Unlike under previous occupations, Egyptians, Asian Indians, Greeks, Jews, and Phoenicians were all free men, operating according to their own beliefs and customs under Persian suzerainty.

Tribute, in the form of taxation, was but a small price to pay for the freedom and security that flowed from the Iranian overlordship.

As was seen with the treatment of the Jews and the rebuilding of the temple, there was also a commendable degree of religious tolerance too. This despite the fact the Persians already had a state religion of their own.

Zoroastrianism is the belief in the power of good and evil as forces in the world. There are angels and devils as disciples of these causes, but there is no such thing as God. There is just good and bad. This was the religion of Persia, but it was not forced on the subordinate states, and being confined to a specific territory, it did not catch on elsewhere, although some of its ideas were later adopted by Christianity.

The Persians did not impose their religion on others, but they did insist on its subjects adopting the Aramaic language.

Based on the Phoenician alphabet, containing only twenty two letters, Aramaic became the common tongue of empire, providing a means of communication between the divergent subject states.

The Persians gave a voice to the people and provided security for almost two centuries in the Near East.

In all, there were three kings named Darius. Another king, Xerxes, invaded Greece, but was repelled, and only succeeded in stirring up a young prince in Macedon.

The last two kings named Darius would each do battle with the rising young Grecian who was soon to take the world by storm.

The losses that Xerxes had inflicted on the Hellenic empire would have to be avenged, and Persia would soon be attacked in order to do just that.

In 330 BC, the Persian Empire and the last king Darius fell before the charismatic, the indomitable rising star, Alexander the Great.

ALEXANDER THE GREAT.

On the day that Alexander was born, the temple of Diana, at Ephesus, one of the seven wonders of the ancient world, burnt to the ground. It was said by the fortune-tellers that this signalled that the force that would destroy Asia had now entered the world.

Alexander was the son of King Phillip II of Macedonia, a country the latter had founded, and which lay at the northern end of the Greek mainland.

The Macedonians thought of themselves as Grecians but the compliment was not returned. The Greeks thought the Macedonians inferior, even barbarian.

King Phillip invaded his superior southern counterparts in order to seize the respect that he desired, hoping to create a united kingdom of the two nations.

Phillip was an excellent military man. He devised new techniques of battlefield strategy that proved decisive when put into use, including the use of spears, twice as long as those used by any opposing forces, that allowed his men first strike in combat.

But that wasn't all. Phillip also had another devastating weapon at his disposal: his son, Alexander.

Born in Pella in 356 BC, Alexander was a fearless and precocious child. Aristotle, the great Greek philosopher and teacher was chosen to tutor the young prince. The student had a love of literature and the arts, with his favourite story being Homer's Iliad, the account of the Trojan Wars, featuring Achilles, reputedly an ancient ancestor of Alexander's. This heroic tale seemed to inspire him, and he wished to emulate the feats within.

At the age of sixteen, when Phillip went off to fight a war in Byzantia, Alexander was left in charge of the kingdom. With the monarch out of the country, one group of disgruntled subjects, the Maedi, began an uprising. Alexander immediately moved against the dissenting voices and succeeded in defeating the rebel state.

Having proven himself, Alexander was placed in charge of the cavalry, and his bravery in battle soon made him a favourite of the troops.

When Phillip was assassinated in 537 BC, Alexander, then aged just twenty, became king. The Greeks hoped that the change of leadership might allow them an opportunity for autonomy, but Alexander ruthlessly enforced Macedonian rule over the Hellenic world. He slaughtered 6000 rebels in the city of Thebes, demolished the city, and sold the surviving inhabitants into slavery. The surrounding cities soon pledged their allegiance to the new king.

Alexander's next task was to tackle the Persians, whom Phillip had been preparing to do battle with before his untimely demise, using the army that had been readied for that purpose.

In 334 BC, approximately 40,000 foot soldiers and 4000 cavalry followed Alexander into Asia Minor.

The Persian army was positioned next to the Granicus River, and consisted of 20,000 infantry and the same number of cavalry.

The river was deep, the hill opposite steep, but Alexander was persistent. He stood out from the ranks with his shock of blond hair, and he led the charge himself. He was wounded by a battle-axe, but rescued before a further fatal blow could be delivered.

The entire Persian infantry was wiped out in the battle, along with 2500 of their cavalry, while the losses on Alexander's side were reputedly less than forty men!

Darius, the king of Persia, had not fought in the first battle, but he soon led an army of 600,000 men from Susa to confront Alexander's army.

At first, the Persians camped in a flatland, in order to give the advantage to their superior numbers, fighting in open terrain. But Alexander had been struck ill, and was confined to his bed, incapacitated for several weeks. This led Darius to believe the Greeks were afraid of him, and he moved his army to Issus in order to cut off any retreat towards Macedonia.

Unfortunately, just as Darius arrived at the new location and saw how unsuitable it was for his foot soldiers, a series of hills that would be difficult to traverse and would split the ranks, Alexander's own army stirred and came to do battle.

In November 333 BC, the Persians were routed, with more than 100,000 of their number left dead, while Darius escaped to Persepolis, his capital city.

Rather than pursue Darius, Alexander headed south towards Syria and the Fertile Crescent. The Persians still controlled the Aegean Sea, and Alexander's supply lines were threatened. He needed to acquire ports of his own to operate from, and he managed to do this at Aradas, Tripolis, Byblus, Beirut, and Sidon.

At another Phoenician coastal city, Tyre, the Greeks were held at bay for seven months. The city was built on an island just off the mainland. The moat needed to be filled in before the city could be attacked. A bridgehead was formed and when they eventually managed to bypass the fortifications, 500 of Alexander's men were killed in the narrow city streets, along with 6000 Tyrians. For their resistance, Alexander crucified a further 2000 men along the beach in a line that stretched along the Mediterranean all the way to the next place to defy him, the Philistine city of Gaza.

Another siege ensued, this time for four months. Built on a steep hill, surrounded by strong walls, Gaza eventually succumbed to the onslaught. Every man was killed, and the Governor of Gaza, Batis, for his defiance was dragged behind Alexander's chariot until dead, echoing the example of Achilles and Hector in the Illiad.

The next stop for the Greeks was Egypt, where Alexander founded his most magnificent city, complete with the greatest library ever assembled, at a place he named after himself: Alexandria.

Meanwhile, Darius had assembled another army, consisting of a million men. The Greeks rushed to meet them and arrived one evening, ready to do battle with the huge Persian contingent.

The Greek generals urged a night attack. They were severely outnumbered and thought this was their only hope for victory, but Alexander would not hear of it.

Darius had blamed his previous defeat on the terrain, bemoaning the fact he had followed ill advice and given up the ground that would have brought victory. Alexander therefore wanted to wait until daylight rather than 'steal' victory, and to fight Darius on ground he had chosen, so that this time there could be no excuses.

Alexander went to bed and got a good night's sleep, as did his men. They woke up late the next morning, refreshed, and ready to do battle.

Unfortunately for the Persians, they had expected the Greeks to attack in the night, and they had spent the previous twelve hours standing in formation, nervously awaiting the onslaught. By the time morning came, they were knackered.

The result was another stunning defeat for the Persians and, once more, Darius deserted his army and fled the battlefield.

Alexander then moved on to the Persian capital of Persepolis, which he destroyed, and then Babylon, so that he was soon ruler of Persia, Egypt, and Arabia, to add to the Greek and Macedon thrones that he already held. He then turned his attention to India.

After securing several victories and crossing the Indus River into the Punjab, his men baulked when they reached the Ganges River. They were far from home, they had defeated an Indian army consisting of 200 war elephants and 22,000 men, but it had not been an easy victory.

The prospect of facing another Indian force, featuring 200,000 men and 6000 elephants was not an attractive one, and the Greek soldiers urged Alexander to turn back.

The unremitting leader was reluctant to oblige his men their request, but eventually he backed down.

Alexander returned to Babylon, his new seat of power, where he presided over a wedding between 10,000 of his own men and 10,000 Asian women, in a literal marriage of east and west. Alexander also participated, taking Roxanne, a Bactrian princess, for his bride.

Later, he sank into depression. He is once said to have cried when he reached the end of the known world, for there were no more worlds to conquer. Now, he began drinking heavily and contracted a fever. After twelve days of illness, on June 10th, 323 BC, Alexander the Great succumbed. He died, aged just thirty two years of age.

Alexander's only son was born posthumously, but both child and mother were killed in the upheaval that followed his death, as his generals fought for control of his empire.

Eventually, two of these generals would rise to prominence and found dynasties in their own names. The Ptolemies controlled Egypt and the Fertile Crescent, and the Seleucids controlled Persia.

Overall, a Hellenic influence was felt throughout the region. They were, after all, champions and victors and admired for their culture as much as feared for their prowess.

These 'successor' states though were but a shadow of the greatness of Alexander's empire, and they soon came under pressure from a new force that appeared on the world stage: the Romans.

THE FERTILE CRESCENT UNDER ROMAN OCCUPATION.

The Fertile Crescent has always had a magnet-like quality for attracting different nationalities. Each conquering empire left its mark, drawn to its unique location at a junction of continents, while trade and access to the Mediterranean ports were other reasons to come here.

Pressed between two dynasties of Hellenic origin, the Ptolemic and Seleucid successor states to Alexander's reign, the Greek influence was noticeable throughout the region.

The nomads of Arabia crossed the River Jordan with their spices to trade with the merchants on the coast, or to intercept with the Silk Road from Egypt to China.

The Philistines would have felt quite at home in this world. Of Aegean origin, and therefore closely related to the Greeks, they would have appreciated the new world order. By this point, they had been resident in the region for a thousand years.

Their make up reflected integration with the original Canaanites, and with subsequent settlers, such as the Persians, and later the Greeks, bringing their gene-pool full circle.

The Jews were also resettled after the nightmare of exile but, as always, they remained distinct and aloof.

We are almost out of the dark ages of history, and we can recognise more of our modern selves in the characters, people, and lifestyles that we encounter.

Greek thought is pervasive. We still revere these men of philosophy to the present day: Plato, Aristotle, who was Alexander's teacher, and Socrates to name a few.

But, despite these dandy thinkers throwing their intellectual weight around the Middle East, there was still a great deal of upheaval going on, with territorial battles raging all around.

In the East, the Seleucids were at war with the Parthians, eventually losing out and ceding Persia to them. The defeated nation concentrated their footprint in Syria, yet recovered to seize Palestine from their Ptolemic cousins.

The Phoenicians, seafarers par-excellence, were fighting to seize control of the Mediterranean trade routes to southern Europe.

Crossing the Levant, Egypt, and along the North African coast, the Phoenicians founded Carthage, in Tunisia, in order to do battle in the Mediterranean with the rising Roman Empire and the mainland Greeks in what became known as the Punic Wars.

The most famous of the Carthaginian generals was Hannibal, who led an army of elephants across the Alps in a series of successful campaigns against Rome in 218 BC.

The Romans, though, were gaining in strength and emerged victorious from the Punic Wars in 149 BC, and the Empire was soon on the march again.

The Ptolemies, veterans of Alexander's conquests, were established in Egypt for almost three centuries, in the most successful of the successor states. They controlled the nearby Fertile Crescent until the Seleucid dynasty eventually crossed the Jordan River and took control.

The Hellenic influence, introduced most forcefully under Alexander, now became the norm. Many in the Jewish community embraced this liberated lifestyle and, as always had been the case, there was a split between those that honoured the religious motifs, and those that wanted to explore and share a way of living with the wider community.

The Jews were resident in Samaria, to the north of the former kingdom of Israel, and Judea, formerly known as Judah. There were also significant Jewish communities at Alexandria, where the Torah was first translated into Greek, and at Carthage, where old allies the Phoenicians had migrated.

The Seleucid emperor Antiochus IV had little time for this religious community and, in 167 BC, attempted to sack the temple in Jerusalem and replace it with an offering to the Greek god, Zeus.

A religious leader named Judas Maccabeus led a rebellion to halt this infidel act, and then signed a treaty of protection with the emerging Roman Empire. Maccabeus founded a dynasty that ruled in Jerusalem for eighty years until, in fact, the Romans rolled into town.

The republic of Rome, having dispensed with the idea of a monarchy around 500 BC, was governed by a senate, voted for by its citizens.

The Roman Empire borrowed much from Greece in terms of its civilisation, its architecture, and its entertainment, such as the gladiatorial games.

The territory they controlled included Germany, Belgium, and France, but there were constant battles with the Barbarians, and even the capital at Rome was under constant threat.

The leader of the senate was known as the consul, and in 90 BC, under a certain Marius, Rome entered an era of unparalleled brilliance.

Rome was a republic, represented by the letters 'SPQR', a Latin abbreviation for 'the Roman senate and people', but this form of government only served to fragment the empire. Army generals were often in direct competition with the state and each other, acting as warlords, and overall leadership was lacking.

The strands eventually began to converge under Marius, and were further assimilated under the Roman general Pompey in 70 BC.

Pompey fought several wars in Asia, and in 63 BC he arrived in Canaan where he divided the land between the Jewish community, giving them Jerusalem, Judea, and Galilee, and the former kingdom of Israel he gave to the remainder of the local population.

In 59 BC, Pompey was replaced as consul by a brilliant young general, who returned from Gaul to challenge the establishment when he crossed the Rubicon River with his army in 49 BC, sparking civil war. His name was Julius Caesar.

Caesar installed himself as emperor of Rome, and chased his predecessor from the Fertile Crescent to Egypt.

There, Pompey was killed, and Caesar then fell for the queen, and the last leader of the Ptolomies: Cleopatra.

In 45 BC, Caesar returned to Rome to prepare an army to rout the Parthians and avenge a defeat under General Crassus when 40,000 Romans were killed in Persia in 54 BC.

In Rome, Caesar became the victim of a plot to assassinate him. On the Ides of March, the senators surrounded their illustrious leader and stabbed him to death.

The senators had feared that Caesar, if he were to defeat the Parthians, would become even greater and rise to the level of dictator, undermining their position. They decided to have done with him in a pre-emptive strike.

Unfortunately for them, they had underestimated the popular support for Caesar, and the senators were run out of town by the mob, and a nephew of Caesar's was chosen to succeed the man the public had declared a god.

Octavian was the chosen successor. Mark Anthony, who had been Caesar's right hand man, performed the same role for Octavian.

Mark Anthony soon embarked on the war against the Parthians that Caesar had intended to wage. The result, as with Crassus, was a grim defeat, with 35,000 men lost on the Roman side.

Mark Anthony went to Egypt to recuperate and, while he was there, he too fell in love with Cleopatra.

Octavian feared, despite the defeat, that Mark Anthony might regroup and return to Rome in order to seize the emperor's role for himself, especially now that he was allied with the Ptolomies.

A Roman army set forth for Egypt, and the two sides met at the battle of Actium in 31 BC. After tasting defeat, rather than be captured, Anthony and Cleopatra took their own lives, star-crossed lovers, just like Romeo and Juliet.

The Roman army expanded, under a regime that replaced conscription with a salary, and this swelled the ranks and allowed the empire to consolidate in Western Europe and to move into Britain. Its hold on Egypt and the Fertile Crescent was maintained, while the Parthians were left alone. There had been far too many Roman losses to make any attempt to take Persia worthwhile.

This uneasy truce left one small problem for the Romans: the Jews. Religious zealots, unique and unbending, this supposedly subject people were known allies of the Parthians. After all, it was the Persians who had liberated the Israelites. This made the Jews an unknown quantity for the Romans, who weren't sure where their allegiance lay. Suspicion existed between the two sides.

Into this volatile mix would come another incendiary element, for in the town of Bethlehem, a new messiah was born. His name was Jesus of Nazareth.

THE BIRTH OF JESUS CHRIST.

'From amongst you there will come a prophet to follow Moses.'

So it says in the Old Testament. Christ, the messiah, had been expected. He would be Jewish, of the House of David, and he was born to be king.

His prophesised arrival caused consternation at the court of King Herod, the Hebrew governor.

Herod was an Arab by birth but Jewish by religion, and the Romans had appointed him in the hope he might have influence over this intransigent community.

Herod did not prove a popular choice though, despite his spiritual allegiance, for he was decadent and enjoyed a Hellenised way of life, much given to pleasure.

When word reached the king of the birth of a messiah, the infamous 'massacre of innocents' took place, where all the male children under the age of two years were put to death.

Luckily, Jesus was removed from harm's way by his family and survived the genocide.

Jesus was a prophet, soon given to challenging the rabbis at the synagogue, re-interpreting the scriptures as he saw fit.

He gathered to himself disciples, and preached to the masses in a sermon on the mount. He proved popular: too popular.

Jesus was Jewish, and he practised their religion, but with one fundamental difference.

It seems that Jesus believed in the scriptures except for one important detail. He did not accept that the Jewish people should be the only ones to have a relationship with God. Why not open up the books, let everybody join the club and take the love that the Lord had for His Chosen People and share it with the whole world?

This, to the Hebrews, was sacrilege. They hadn't made twelve hundred years of sacrifices; eating only Kosher food, adopting circumcision, forsaking all the other gods, foregoing foreign women, to let just anybody become one of God's children. That, they said to Jesus, was heresy. And they turned against him.

When the teachings of Jesus could be said to infer an anti-Roman sentiment, this might be whispered to the occupying army. When Jesus appeared on Pontius Pilate's podium seeking salvation, the community did not save him.

Despite the prophesy of a messiah from their ranks, and despite the fact that Jesus could claim to be directly descended from the Royal House of David, the Jewish People would not recognise him as the second prophet, and they didn't like what he had to say, so they ignored him.

On a cross, Jesus died. His idea, to take the relationship with God to a wider audience, lived on in the religion founded in his name: Christianity.

In the mean time, the Jews were still under Roman dominion and viewed with suspicion by their rulers.

The Emperor Octavian died in 14 AD and was succeeded by his son-in-law, Tiberius. The dynasty eventually fell with the Emperor Nero in 67 AD.

The Galileans frequently rose up against their governors, confirming Roman suspicions about their loyalties, and in punishment, Judea was annexed to Syria.

When Rome burned while Nero fiddled, the Jews revolted in their homeland, sensing an opportunity for autonomy.

They were to be disappointed, for a general named Vespasian led 50,000 troops from Syria to put down the uprising, and it was his son, Titus, who exacted the fiercest retribution by destroying the second temple of Jerusalem in 69 AD, which had been rebuilt under Persian rule in 515 BC.

Then, in 70 AD, at a hill top fortress in the town of Masada, 1000 Jews committed suicide rather than surrender to the Roman soldiers laying siege to their encampment.

This all but did for Jewish resistance for a couple of generations, until 135 AD when Simon Bar Kochba led a further rebellion.

Again, the Romans had the might to crush the rebels and, this time, the punishment was to wipe the Jewish territory off the map. Jerusalem was renamed Aelia Capitolina and a shrine to Jupiter was built where the Jewish temple had stood. The names of Judea and Samaria, synonymous with the Jewish presence, were abolished and the area renamed Aelia Palestina.

Many Jews fled to the hills of Galilee, and they were forbidden from entering Jerusalem and were not allowed to recruit to their religion. They had no place to pray, they were banned from the Holy City, and their homeland had been renamed after their greatest enemies, the Philistines.

Israel, having endured so much and survived even exile, now had no comfort, no temple, no home. It would remain that way for almost two thousand years.

THE ARABS IN ISRAEL/PALESTINE.

Of all the people we have put under the microscope that we have placed over the region of old Canaan, every race that has entered our kaleidoscope, one has almost entirely escaped our attention: the Arabs.

Given their close proximity to the area of interest, it is surprising that they have taken so long before putting in an appearance. Eventually, of course, they will do so with a vengeance, but I think it's time for an introduction.

When we say 'Arab', we are talking about the inhabitants of that vast desert plain between the Red Sea and the Persian Gulf. This inhospitable terrain, containing very little water to sustain life, had managed to defeat all but the most dogged of people.

The Bedouins are nomadic Arabs, moving from place to place, waterhole to waterhole, always on the move, rarely settling down. This was the tradition that the Arabs grew up with.

It is around 850 BC that the Arabs start to appear in our picture, coming to trade with the merchants of the Fertile Crescent, arriving on the camels they had domesticated about 500 years earlier.

The first Arab cities appear hundreds of years later, with one of the first and most important being Petra, in modern-day Jordan. These northern-dwelling Arabs were known as Nabateans.

The Arabs were fluent in Aramaic, but as they sensed their unique identity and began to realise themselves a nation, they adopted their own language: Arabic.

Following the latest Jewish exile, instigated by the Romans, the Arabs were encouraged to enter and occupy the sparsely-populated Canaanite cities.

The Arabs soon took control of the trade routes from Egypt to Asia and onward to China. In the south of the region, in what would now be Yemen, it was possible to sail across the Red Sea to East Africa, or to use the port as a setting-off point to India.

For a while, Rome was interested in the bustling trade being conducted by the Arabs and hoped for a slice of the action, but despite a string of small cities appearing along the trade route from northern to southern Arabia, it was still difficult terrain for an outsider, and the Romans soon lost interest.

Left to their own devices, the Arabs slipped back into their Bedouin ways, Arabic culture stagnated and entered the Jahiliyya, the Muslim age of darkness, which ran from 384 to 502 AD.

Elsewhere, the Roman Empire split into two areas of influence, with a western empire ruled from Rome and an eastern empire ruled from Byzantia.

The emperor Constantine renamed the capital of Byzantium Constantinople. The Vikings called it the Great City and it would be the greatest city on earth for 1000 years. From there, the Roman Byzantine Empire ruled all of modern-day Turkey, the Fertile Crescent, and Egypt.

The Byzantines were at war with the Barbarians in the northern territories, and with the Parthians, then the Scyths, and later the Sassanids in Persia.

As if all these battles weren't enough, Rome was at war with itself when the emperor Constantine converted to Christianity in 331 AD. Not only would this lead to the eventual division between the Roman Catholic Church and the Greek Orthodox, for Byzantium was Hellenised despite being Roman, but it also led to renewed interest in the Fertile Crescent, such was the emperor's influence.

At every site associated with Jesus, shrines were built, including the Church of the Holy Sepulchre at the place where Christ was supposedly buried and then rose from the dead. Christian pilgrims flocked to the country, and the Holy Land began to play host to not one but two religions.

The Jewish community, those that had returned after the last Roman expulsion, became marginalised once more. Eventually, the Sassanids overthrew the Romans in the Fertile Crescent, but even this Persian revival was not to last.

In 638 AD, an Arab army would take Jerusalem. This would be no simple war of conquest but would, again, be fought in the name of religion.

Islam, the word of Mohammed, had been born, and this was to provide an all-conquering empire throughout the entire region.

The Arab conquests were driven in part by the overpopulation and the shortage of oases in their homeland, and these hungry fighters were buoyed by the belief that death on the battlefield would lead only to Paradise.

The Fertile Crescent, as if the genealogy itself did not provide a confusing enough picture, now became home to a third religion.

So, before we attempt to cover this most momentous event in greater detail, let us take a closer look at just who exactly are the people who inhabit the Holy Land.

THE DNA EVIDENCE.

It seems that DNA can do almost anything. There are no hiding places from its immutable evidence. Can it, perhaps, shed any light on our area of concern: the ancestry of the inhabitants of Israel/Palestine.

DNA stands for Deoxyribo Nucleic Acid and contains the codes with which information is transferred between cell generations. This genetic fingerprint has proved crucial to current crime fighting techniques, but it is also a tool for looking back through time, into our origins and historical make-up.

Applied to the population of the Middle East, as certain studies have been, the results throw up a variety of hypotheses.

One study, published by Judy Siegel in the Jerusalem Post in November 2001, says that Jewish people are more closely related to non-Jewish groups in the Middle East than they are to Arabs. Therefore, though there may have been intermarriage between Jew and Gentile, for example a Phoenician during one of their historic alliances, there was little intercourse, literally, between Jews and Arabs.

This is surprising when we consider that both these parties are Semitic, from the same branch of genealogy. It has always struck me as odd that any comment deemed critical of the Jews and pro-Arab is termed anti-Semitic. This is surely a contradiction in terms. The Arabs, like the Jews, are Semites too. It is a Biblical term and applies to all the people of South West Asia, said to be the descendants of Sem, the eldest son of Noah.

In the same report in the Jerusalem Post, it was found that both parties share 18% of their genes with each other, and go their own way thereafter. They are, in effect, related by almost a fifth of their human genomes.

Within these two Semite branches, according to another report conducted by Ariella Oppenheim in 2000, Jews share a paternal ancestor with 70% of other Jews and with 50% of Arabs. Therefore, although they may share an ancient relative, of Canaanite, South West Asian stock, there has been 20% more diversification on the Arab side, with a much more insular focus amongst the Jewish population.

There is a genetic trait amongst Palestinians that indicates their occupation of the West Bank for many generations, going back three or four hundred years. According to a a report by Tamara Traubman in the Israeli newspaper Ha'aretz, 50% of Palestinians have this genetic trait and can therefore prove residency in the area prior to Zionism and the great influx of Jews returning from the Diaspora. So, at least in recent times, the answer to the important question of 'who was here first?' would seem to be the Palestinians.

The Jewish DNA points to thirteen common forefathers, who were polygamous and scattered the gene pool. In an online article by Tony Ortega, he writes that only the Cohanim amongst the Jews can claim any sort of homogeneity, not intermarrying with Gentiles and diluting the gene pool.

Remarkably, in a test conducted by Professor Michael Hammer of the University of Arizona, a particular marker known as YAP- was found in 98.5% of the Cohanim in his survey. In a second study, 97 out of 106 Cohens tested had six chromosomal markers in common, that have come to be known as CMH, the Cohanim Modal Hapoltype.

Yet the Cohanim represent only 2% of the Jewish population. The remainder have an enormous amount of genetic variation.

Despite the Diaspora, the dispersal of the Jewish community throughout the globe when exiled from the Promised Land, the Jews more closely resemble their Middle Eastern neighbours, the Palestinians and the Syrians, than they do their host communities in the wider world.

According to Robert Pollack in an article entitled 'The Fallacy of Biological Judaism' published in Forward magazine in March 2003, 'there are no DNA sequences common to all Jews that are absent from all non-Jews. There is nothing in the human genome that makes or diagnoses a person as a Jew.'

As for the Palestinians, another report stated that 'both Jews and Palestinians share a very similar HLA genetic gene pool that supports a common ancient Canaanite origin. The Jews, Egyptians, Iranians, Turks, and Armenians are probably the closest relatives to the Palestinians.'

One of the leading Jewish Zionists, Ber Borochov, in an essay written in 1905, and published in his complete works anthology, wrote: 'The local population in Palestine is closer to the Jews in racial composition than to any other people, even Semitic people. It is highly feasible to assume that the peasant farmers in Palestine are the direct descendants of the Jewish and Canaanite agricultural community, together with a very slight mixture of Arab blood. For it is known that the Arabs, as proud conquerors, mingled very little with the masses in the countries they conquered.'

As Rabbi Harold M. Shulweis says in an article published on the internet: 'The point of being a Jew is not a matter of genes and chromosomes. To the contrary, Judaism is the first religion to recognise the stranger who chooses to identify himself with Judaism. Jews are a religion, not a race or a singular ethnic group.'

His thoughts were echoed by Rabbi Rami Shapiro in the same article who said, 'Who is a Jew? A Jew is one who studies Judaism, argues with it, lives it.'

Jewishness is not defined genetically. The male chromosome can enter the gene pool through religious conversion, while Jewishness is passed down through the mother.

So, who was here first? As we have already seen, to all intents and purposes, to go back to the very beginning, they both were.

DNA cannot disprove it.

BEFORE ISLAM.

Before Islam, the story in the Fertile Crescent is a power struggle between the two dominant empires of the day: the Roman Byzantine and the Sassanid Persian.

To the south, in Arabia, the population was Bedouin, and pretty much had the place to themselves. No one else could survive there: certainly no army had been able to conquer and hold it.

The Arabs were growing in numbers. As happened with every early community, the first priority was to feed themselves and then, as a surplus was produced, it was possible to increase the size of one's own family, and eventually to trade anything left over.

This was the case for the Arabs too. Population centres popped up along the Red Sea coast, all the way to the Mediterranean junction, where goods could be exported to Italy and Greece, or sent along the Silk Road to Asia and China.

One of these emerging cities was at Mecca, deep in the Arabian peninsular, close to the Red Sea. It was there, in 570 AD, that the Prophet Mohammed was born.

At this time, in the north, the Sassanids and the Byzantines were battling themselves to a standstill, after nearly three centuries of fighting.

They would leave the door open to a new challenger, just as the Arabs began to come into their own identity. What's more, they arrived with more than just a sense of nationality, they had their own religion, scripture, and living oracle.

Mohammed belonged to a family of merchants, and Mecca was both an important trading post and also a centre of pilgrimage. A large black stone, the Kaaba, of meteorite origin had drawn Arab worshippers there for centuries.

Both Jews and Christians lived nearby, having set up camp on the trade route, while remaining within their own religious communities.

Mohammed married a wealthy widow when he was in his twenties and soon spurned the family business as he grew ever more spiritual.

Aged forty, Mohammed went up to a cave on Mount Hira to meditate, and while realising that the Jews had a scripture of their own, the Torah, and the Christians had theirs, known as the New Testament of the Bible, he wondered why his own people had nothing to guide them how to live their lives or to give them succour for the soul.

Then, the Angel Gabriel came to Mohammed in the cave and said 'Recite in the name of the Lord who created all things, who created man from a clot of blood. Recite for thy Lord is most generous, who taught by the pen, who taught man what he did not know.' And Mohammed was won.

So he began to preach the Lord's message and attracted support from members of his own tribe and family, but caused concern amongst the wider community.

Mohammed was forced to move 200 miles north, to Medina, where he found shelter amongst the Jewish and Christian enclaves, all of them believing in one God.

As Mohammed felt the word of the Lord coming through him, he named his religion Islam, meaning surrender, or submission.

The scripture was built on five pillars:

Belief in one God - Allah;

Prayer (5 times a day);

Charity (2.5 % of one's income);

Pilgrimage to Mecca once in a lifetime (known as Haj);

Fasting (from dawn till dusk for 30 days in the month of Ramadam).

Later, a sixth pillar was added, that of Jihad, or Holy War.

As with anything new, the religion was soon attacked. In 627 AD, Mohammed was forced to defend the city of Medina from members of his own tribe, the Quryshi, and from rival Arab clans. They were unhappy at Mohammed for preaching monotheism when their livelihoods largely depended on the polytheistic pilgrims visiting the meteorite shrine at Mecca.

The following year, the Angel Gabriel spoke again to Mohammed and urged him to lead 1000 men in peaceful protest to Mecca to confront the sceptics and to enter as pilgrims.

Unarmed, Mohammed led his followers to Mecca and convinced the local inhabitants to allow them entry. This became the first Meccan pilgrimage and it is today an event of ginagorous proportions.

All the while, the new religion continued to attract Arab converts. Arabia was bonding through the spiritual message of Mohammed.

Elsewhere, the Fertile Crescent was once more the subject of a battle for supremacy. In 614 AD, the Persians seized Palestine and Syria from the Byzantines in a short lived occupation that was nevertheless welcomed by their old friends the Jews. They'd had enough of occupation, and they had seen their religion sidelined by the Christian version sponsored by Rome.

It was not to last. The Byzantines wrestled back control from the Sassanids in 628 AD, ending the Jewish honeymoon period and restoring Roman supremacy in the region.

This would be the last time these two old foes would have the opportunity to share the spoils, because the Arab world was growing to maturity. The new religion was going from strength to strength and spreading like wild fire.

In June 8th, 632 AD, Mohammed took to his bed, complaining of a severe headache, and died soon after. In a short, twenty five year period, he had given the world a third major religion that is today followed by 20% of the earth's population.

Mohammed was acquainted with the Jewish and Christian ideas. He believed that Moses was the Lord's first prophet, and he even quotes him more than 100 times in the Koran, and that Jesus, rather than being the son of God, was the Lord's second prophet, although a mortal man. Muslims believe that Mohammed was the third and last, the 'seal' of the prophets. His word is the Lord's final message to mankind.

'People of the Book', is how the Jews and Christians are referred to in the Koran, for they are recognised by Muslims as adherents of Monotheism. They were known as 'Dhimmi', the protected people.

Mohammed's recitations were recorded from memory by his followers after his death, and they give social, political, and economic guidance, as well as spiritual. After the prophet's death, a Caliph, or deputy, was appointed to succeed him and carry on his work.

By 636 AD, the army of Islam was on the march, seizing control first of Palestine, and then the entire Fertile Crescent and Egypt, forcing the Byzantines into a territory that roughly corresponds to modern-day Turkey.

From the Sassanids, the Muslims took all of Persia, so that now the whole of Arabia, Egypt, Syria, Persia, and the Fertile Crescent was one united Arab state. It would stay like that for almost 500 years.

It would not, however, be without its setbacks.

The third Caliph to follow Mohammed, Uthman Ibn Abban, moved the power base from Arabia to Egypt. This was seen as a betrayal, and an uprising began in Medina and eventually reached the Caliph, who was killed by an assassin posing as an Egyptian soldier.

The argument began as to who should succeed him. The Caliph was always chosen from the ranks of the most able, but a movement began to appoint a descendant of the prophet himself, namely Ali, son-in-law of Mohammed.

This difference of opinion in 656 AD caused the split that exists to this day between the Sunni and Shia Muslims, with the supporters of Ali known as Shi'ites, and those of Mu'awiyya, the then governor of Syria, member of the powerful Umayyad tribe, the choice of the Sunni.

When a series of battles between the two sides failed to resolve the issue of succession, it was agreed to put the problem before a panel of arbiters.

This council of arbitration found in favour of Mu'awiyya, who would continue the successful system of appointing the best man for the job.

Ali and his supporters refused to accept the council's decision, and continued to agitate against the legitimate choice. For this defiance, Ali was murdered in 661 AD, and an Umayyad dynasty seized control.

For the next 100 years, the Umayyads ruled the Arab lands. With a power base in Damascus, Syria, the Umayyads were seen as largely secular, concerned more with state than religion, although concessions to the latter were made.

The Arabs were polygamous, taking numerous wives, and the Muslims presumably intermarried with the local population in the presciently-named Fertile Crescent. Although this contradicts Ber Borochov's claim regarding DNA analysis above, you do the math. Many wives requires many women.

In 692 AD, as an expression of Islam's arrival in the Holy Land, the Muslim's built the Dome of the Rock, the world-famous mosque, at the place where Mohammed rose to Heaven and the site of the former Temple of Jerusalem, which had been destroyed by the Romans in 69 AD.

Under the Umayyads, the Muslim armies crossed into Europe, entering Spain through the Straits of Gibraltar before moving into France, where their march was halted.

The French claimed a great victory, but it appears to have been more a case of the Muslims getting homesick and returning to the birthplace of their religion and its holy places. There were also great events taking place back in the Arab lands which must also have called the Muslims back home.

The undercurrent of the argument between the Sunni and Shi'te positions came to a head in 750 AD when the Umayyads were overthrown by the Abbasids, who claimed to be directly descended from the Prophet through his uncle Abbas.

They, too, proved secular, although they did rebuild the holy cities of Mecca and Medina. They moved their power base even further from the Arab heartlands, founding the city of Baghdad.

The new capital became a beacon for art and literature, and was a centre of culture. The Abbasids bedded down in their new location, and looked increasingly Eastward towards Persia, allowing Egypt, Arabia, and Syria to break away from their control and become provincial centres.

This lack of leadership and cohesion led to a fragmentation of authority, and by the mid tenth century, there were three Caliphs in Baghdad alone, while splitting the empire into numerous cantons weakened the Arab cause and allowed the first interruption in more than four centuries of rule.

It had been a golden age for Islam, from the first battle for Palestine, when the Byzantines were driven out by the desert hordes, through the Umayyad, Abbasid, and the Ikshidid dynasties. The latter ruled Egypt, but in 940 AD seized Palestine. Then the Fatimids savaged the land when fighting the Ikshidid in 970 AD. For the next sixty years, the Holy Land was almost destroyed by the warring Arab factions.

Then, in 1035, peace finally came to Palestine and the Jews and Christians who had known security and tolerance in the early centuries of Arab rule, would enjoy fifty more years of the same.

But with the dilution of Islamic hegemony, the weak, franchised structure proved tantalising for an emergent force from Asia Minor, in what would be the first of the former Hittite clans to wrest control of the Promised Land.

The new conscripts were known as the Seljuk Turks, who came sweeping into Palestine in 1079 AD. For a long time, the Turks had supplied soldiers to the Abbasids in Baghdad, until it dawned on them to create an army of their own rather than prop up someone else's.

It is not known exactly how the Seljuks treated their conquests and the religious community in the Holy Land, but it appears that they leant towards death and destruction rather than benevolent dictatorship.

Pope Urban II painted a grim picture of the plight of Christians in Palestine and at the Council of Clermont in 1095 he called for both branches of the Catholic church, that of Rome and Byzantium Greek, to unite and fight a crusade to rid Jerusalem of the barbarians and Islamists who had held sway for far too long.

78

Between 1096 and 1099, three armies, 15,000 men in total, 5000 of whom were knights, were formed in order to fight this Holy War. One was led by King Baldwin I, another was led jointly by Raymond de St Gilles, the Count of Toulouse, along with Bohemond, the Frankish governor of Antioch. The third army was led by the splendidly named Walter the Penniless.

And thus began the era of the Crusades.

THE CRUSADES.

The first Christian Crusade to head for the Middle East must have been pretty fired up. On their way there, they met and massacred 5000 Jews in the Rhineland, burying them in mass graves, even putting women and children, boys and girls, to the sword.

Walter the Penniless, possibly a distant relative of mine, never reached the Holy Land. He was stopped by a Muslim force in Asia Minor.

The other two armies arrived in the Middle East in 1098 AD. There, at the Syrian town of Ma'arra al Numan, they slaughtered the entire population, 10,000 people, Muslim and Turkish, men, women, and children. And then they ate them!

To be fair, the Crusaders were starving. They didn't know how to survive in the harsh desert surroundings, so they impaled Muslim children on spits and roasted them, and boiled the adults in cooking pots and ate their flesh.

They even bragged about it.

On the 7th of June in 1099, the Crusaders reached Jerusalem. The 40,000 strong army laid siege to the city for a month until, on the 15th of July, they breached the fortifications. Seventy thousand Jews and Muslims were killed, some burned alive, with the remainder of the population being expelled.

The Arabs as a whole remained a fractured, tribal society, and the Crusaders were able to consolidate their hold on the Holy Land for the next thirty years.

One especially negative outcome of the brutality was the eye-witness accounts of the massacre that filtered back to the Arabs. This effectively changed the concept of Jihad from an internal struggle with God to an external struggle with the infidels.

Along the coastal plain, the Christians built a number of forts to augment their presence.

In 1127, under the leadership of a Seljuk Turk named Zangi, the Arabs rallied themselves to confront the new power, and for the next twenty years, a series of running battles ensued.

The eventual outcome was the expulsion of the Crusaders from their strongholds, and this led to the Second Crusade, which began in 1147, to regain control.

This army was led by St Bernard of Clairvaux, at the behest of Pope Eugenius III and King Louis VII of France. The Crusade was a disaster, and failed to recapture any of the ground they had lost, leaving only Jerusalem and Antioch as Crusader enclaves.

In 1171, in nearby Egypt, a leader of Kurdish origin, Salah-al-Din, rose to power. He founded the great city of Cairo, eventually united Arab and Egyptian forces, and then attacked and captured Jerusalem in 1187 AD.

Saladin, as he became known in the West, was a man of his word and, unlike the Christians, he spared his captives. This kindness was not appreciated however, and in 1189, the Third Crusade began to wrest control of the Holy City once more from Muslim hands.

This Crusade also featured three armies. One was led by the emperor Frederick Barbarossa, or Red Beard as he was known, of Germany. Another was led by King Phillip Augusta of France, and the last was headed by King Richard, the Lionheart, of England.

Barbarossa was unfortunate and drowned, in full body armour, attempting to cross a river in Cilicia while on route.

After a three year campaign, the Crusaders failed to recapture Jerusalem, with the only success being to take Acre, which fell to King Richard. Despite a pledge not to harm the population, Richard's men slaughtered the entire host community, women and children included.

In 1193, Saladin passed away, and the Crusaders roused themselves for a series of invasions with ever-diminishing returns.

The Fourth Crusade, led by Pope Innocent III, consisting mainly of French soldiers, was diverted from its aim of seizing the Holy Land from Muslim or Jewish rule by a lack of funds, and concentrated instead on the plunder of Hungary and Asia Minor, eventually decimating the Catholic port of Zara on the Adriatic and then looting Constantinople between 1202 and 1204 AD. For their sins, they were excommunicated by Rome.

The next Crusade, in 1212 AD, was known as the Children's Crusade. Led by a 12 year old French shepherd boy, Steven, and a 10 year old from Germany named Nicholas, they gathered an army of 30,000 youngsters and headed for Marseille. There, according to a dream that Steven had, the sea would part and they would walk across to the Middle East. Unfortunately, the sea did not part, and most of the children turned back, while the rest were given passage by ruthless sailors and sold into slavery on the other side.

Eventually, in 1229, the Sixth Crusade returned better results, realising a treaty that allowed Christians to rule in Jerusalem for the next ten years.

As seen with earlier treaties, the Crusaders were not to be trusted, and they again failed to keep their side of the bargain. They outstayed their welcome until, in 1244, an emerging force in Egypt, the Mamelukes, expelled the Christians from Jerusalem and established a regime in the region that would dominate for the next 250 years.

The Seventh Crusade, between 1248 and 1254, failed to remove the powerful Mamelukes from the Holy Land, but did at least free Spain from the Muslim Moors who had established a foothold there.

The Jews felt safe to return to Jerusalem. They had always been offered considerably more protection under Muslim rule, while they faced death under the Christians.

In 1270, King Louis IX of France attempted an Eighth Crusade, but he died of plague in Carthage while on his way there. He had hoped that the Arabs might join him in repelling the Mongols who were then making their presence felt, but the Arabs attacked his army, and the French troops suffered from war, famine, and pestilence.

In 1291, in what would be the last in this series of Crusades, and the last for more than a hundred years, 1600 European peasants were sent by Pope Nicholas IV to the Holy Land. At Acre, the peasant army slaughtered both the Muslim and Jewish communities and, just in case they were accused of discrimination, they massacred the Christian population too!

The following year, the Mamelukes expelled these murderers from their base at Acre. Thereafter, apart from occasional Christian visits to the region, the Holy Land was back in Muslim hands.

While the Mamelukes brought some authority to the region, elsewhere the East was being terrorised by the Mongol horde under the leadership of Genghis Khan.

Originating in central Asia, Khan first moved his army eastwards, conquering Peking in 1215. In 1219, he attacked his first Muslim power, defeating Persia. He then headed north through the Caucasus mountains and into Southern Russia, before he headed south once more, having completed a circuit of the entire Caspian Sea region.

Georgia, a Christian state, then fell to the Mongols. It seemed this army conquered for its own sake, having no bias in terms of religion. Nomadic in lifestyle, it has been said that Genghis' army attacked cities for the simple reason that they couldn't understand why anyone would want to live in one!

Before his death in 1227 AD, Genghis became the greatest leveller the world had ever known, capturing China, Russia, and Asia. His son would go on to capture much of Eastern Europe, namely Poland, Hungary, Croatia, Albania, Georgia, and Moravia.

When this khan died in 1246, his successor, Hulegu, attacked the Islamic states, destroying the Assassins, a fierce warrior cult from Iran, and then pressing on to Baghdad. There, Hulegu seized the Caliph and, being superstitious and not wanting to shed his blood, he had him rolled up in a carpet and trampled to death by horses.

The Mongols were cheered on by the Christians, as they attacked the Muslim communities, but the Mamelukes would later attack the remaining Crusader forts in retribution for their support of the barbarian army.

Eight hundred thousand Muslims were slain in Baghdad alone in 1258, with the skulls of the dead piled up in mounds.

Hulegu died soon after, to be replaced at the head of the Mongol army by Kubeli Khan, the grandson of Genghis.

Kubeli was more concerned with the reconquest of China, and moved most of his troops out there, leaving a weakened presence in the Middle East, allowing the Mamelukes to inflict a crushing blow to the remaining Mongols in Syria in 1260.

Despite several attempts by Khan to retake Syria, the Mamelukes won out, with a last defeat of the Mongols in 1303.

Kubeli died in China in 1294, leaving an empire that included Persia, Central Asia, and China. He was the last of the great Khans in this period. There was, however, another force emerging to rival the Mongols: the Turkish Ottomans.

In 1336, the last of the great Mongol warlords was born. In 1369, he took the world by storm. His name was Tamburlane.

Ruling central and southwest Asia, Tamburlane agitated against the emerging Ottomans, to the extent that he prolonged the investiture of the Byzantines, keeping the threatening Ottomans at war on their southern frontier when it would rather be fighting Constantinople.

Tamburlane invaded India, then in 1401 he sacked Baghdad, killing 90,000 of the inhabitants. In 30 years, he had conquered Russia, the Indian subcontinent, the empire of the Ottomans, and most of the Middle East.

Having devoured almost as much land as Genghis Khan, Tamburlane christened himself 'Conqueror of the world' and 'Emperor of the age'.

He was also, surprisingly, a patron of the arts. At his court, he kept a certain Philosopher-Fool, named Nasruddin Hodja.

One day, Tamburlane asked him 'How much do you think I am worth?'

'About twenty gold pieces', replied Hodja.

'Why', said a disgruntled Tamburlane, 'just the belt I am wearing is worth twenty gold pieces.'

'I know', said the Philosopher-Fool, 'I included that in my estimate!'

One can only hope Nasruddin never paid too high a price for his insolence. He must have been a brave man indeed, for Tamburlane was as ruthless a leader as the world had ever known. He would ravage a city, destroying every living thing, saving only the best of everything; the workers, the artists, the women. They would be carried of to Tamburlane's capital at Samarkhand. Everyone else would be cruelly slain, their bodies piled in pyramids and set ablaze.

Tamburlane founded a dynasty, the Timurid, who ruled Mesopotamia and Asia until 1506 AD, and he also had a long reach. On his deathbed, Tamburlane threatened 'Do not disturb my grave, for if you do, a fate worse then me will befall you.'

The grave lay undisturbed until the sarcophagus was opened by a team of Soviet archaeologists on 22nd June 1941. On that day, Hitler launched the German assault that would kill 20 million Russians over the next four years.

Back in the middle ages, this flux affecting the Near East region would come to a close. Having been a magnet for every invader, conqueror, and warlord to emerge over thousands of years, to have attracted every empire and every religion, there would finally come a period of unity to provide an anchor to our story.

Having grown to maturity alongside the Mongols, and provided troops to prop up empires in Egypt and the Middle East, the Turkish people would finally seize control for themselves. The name of this emerging empire was the Ottoman, and for the next four centuries, they would rule the Middle East.

THE OTTOMAN EMPIRE.

The Turkish peoples had provided some of the finest soldiers to Middle Eastern armies for several centuries before they had a significant empire of their own.

The Seljuk Turks were amongst 24 tribes originating in Western Siberia, and they were an important branch to appear out of the region. In 1025 AD, they began to move westwards, capturing Babylon in 1055.

In 1242 AD, a Mongol invasion led to the collapse of the Seljuk Empire.

In the Turkish heartland, a ruler called Osman I founded the Ottoman dynasty in 1299 AD, and his descendants would eventually conquer Constantinople in 1453 and rule the Middle East right up until the outbreak of the First World War.

The Mongols had headed east, and were preoccupied with China, while the Ottomans ended the Byzantine era before heading south to take on the Mamelukes.

In 1326, Osman founded the Janissaries, an elite slave army, the name meaning 'new troops', from the Turkish 'Yeni Cheri', meaning the same.

In 1517, the Ottomans took control of Syria and Palestine and paired the neighbouring states, which made sense both administratively and geographically.

The Mamelukes were driven back to Egypt, overwhelmed by the Janissaries. These were originally Christian children who had been forcefully converted to Islam, and then offered the reward of land or power for performing their role well.

The Ottoman state originated within the Seljuk Empire, but when Osman I declared his independence, and when his successors finally took Constantinople, their own position of prominence was assured.

Throughout the 15th century, the Ottoman Empire stretched from North Africa to the Persian Gulf and as far north as the Caucasus Mountains to the gateway of Europe at Constantinople.

Aided by a series of brilliant leaders, the Sultans, the Ottomans came to represent a unified Muslim power at a time when the Western world was stirring, about to unleash its own potential and colonial aspirations.

Between 1520 and 1566, under the Sultanate of Suleiman the Magnificent, Jerusalem became a Holy Protectorate City, and was fortified with walls in 1542.

The city was free to enter for Muslim, Christian, and Jew alike, all under the protection of the Janissaries. For 400 years, Jerusalem was peaceful, and the Jews felt safe to return in numbers not seen since Roman times.

Eventually, after their early conquests and scrapes with the Safavids, who were another Turkish group that emerged in Persia in 1501, the Ottoman Empire began to stagnate. The new Sultans lacked the prowess of their earlier counterparts, with no further conquests, and consolidation the order of the day, the momentum ran out of the movement and left a sense that the empire was there for the taking. European powers would, over time, attempt to do just that.

Napoleon of France invaded Egypt in 1798 but, with the help of the British, the Ottomans expelled the French army in a battle at Alexandria in 1801.

This invasion of Egypt proved portentous, and the Ottomans were eventually driven out themselves by a local movement led by Muhammed Ali Pasha, who founded a dynasty that would survive until 1952 and the last king, Farouk.

The Ottomans also found themselves driven from Jerusalem during the Egyptian campaign, and into the void came numerous peoples of European descent, giving the Holy City a modern feel, and opening the area up to a new tide of religious immigration.

The waning Ottoman Empire, stung by defeat, began entering into treaties with the European powers in order to fend off attacks on its other borders. In one event, the Ottomans sided with the British and the French in order to take on Russia in what became known as the Crimean war.

Christian activity grew in the Fertile Crescent during this period of opportunity for the Western powers, but this only led to tension in the Holy Land.

The Ottomans sought to modernise and reform their empire, replacing the Janissaries with a regular, waged army rather than conscripting young boys. They sought reform within the framework of Islam and resisted Westernisation where it adversely impacted on Muslim interests.

In 1867, the Young Turks, a reformist movement, were founded in secret in order to promote democracy within the empire, and in 1876 the Ottoman Grand Vizier Midhat Pasha introduced a liberal constitution in an attempt to compete in a changing world.

The European superpowers were knocking at their door, and in 1869, the Suez Canal in Egypt was opened, linking the Mediterranean to the Red Sea, effectively rendering Africa an island. The Egyptian-French enterprise attracted a great deal of trade, and the British rushed to do business there. The new route provided a much-needed shortcut to India, without the requirement to sail around the African continent.

Eventually the British bought out the Egyptian government's stake in the venture, but when the public realised their stake had been sold to Great Britain there was uproar and the Egyptian army then seized control of the canal.

A joint British-French taskforce was dispatched to retake the canal and protect the two countries' commercial interests.

The canal was of huge significance, being strategically situated to allow a shortcut to British colonies in the Far East, but not content with retaking the waterway, the British assumed control of the whole of Egypt and remained in power there until 1922.

The Ottomans were now opposed by the British and their French allies in Egypt, and by the Russians at their northern border. The Arabs, too, threatened, as they searched for national unity in what became known as the 'Arab awakening'. All sought to tackle the 'Ailing man of the Bosphorus'.

In the early part of the 20th Century, as the world prepared for war, the Ottomans sided with the one European country lined up against the Ottoman's enemies: Germany.

The decision to join forces with Germany would later have a devastating impact on the entire Middle East, as when World War 1 was eventually decided, control of the region fell from Ottoman hands to the victorious allies, such are the rewards of conquest.

But we are getting slightly ahead of ourselves, for there was much happening in Palestine itself that requires our attention. It is possible to take a closer look at our area of interest and spotlight the wave of immigration taking place that the Jewish people called the Aliyah but the world came to know as Zionism.

THE EARLY LIFE OF THEODOR HERZL.

Theodor Herzl was the father of Zionism. A poet and playwright, it was his dream to restore the Jewish people to their historical homeland.

Born in 1860 in Pesth, Hungary, he hoped to recreate the state of Israel, originally destroyed in 722 BC, some 2600 years earlier. When Judah went the same way in 586 BC, the last Hebrew nation disappeared from the face of the earth.

Although Jewish people continued to live in the Promised Land, they were a subject people and suffered mass expulsion. The Diaspora, where they lived and formed communities across the globe, began two centuries after Jesus Christ lived in the area.

After the exile, with their sovereign state wiped off the map, the Persians, the Greeks, the Romans, Byzantines, Arabs, Mongols, and finally the Ottomans all ruled in the region the Hebrews called home.

Theodor Herzl hoped to reverse the history of the occupancy of foreign empires and restore the sacred covenant between God and His Chosen People.

To this end, Herzl began a political campaign to rally the Jews of the Diaspora in order to make this vision a reality. The movement he founded was called Zionism.

Theodor Herzl was a lawyer and journalist, who had once aimed only to be 'a member of the Prussian nobility.' He soon became the latest exponent of the dream to return the Zion, the name given to the old citadel of Jerusalem.

In the 17th Century, Sabbatai Zevi, who believed himself to be the Messiah, led a campaign to retake Palestine. He was eventually locked up in an Albanian fort where he later converted to Islam.

In 1798, a more practical exponent of the idea, Yehudah Alkelai, was born in Semlin in Hungary. This well-travelled Rabbi, when he was just 27 years of age, began to argue for a homeland for the Jewish people in the Holy Land.

Alkelai advocated the establishment of a trust fund in order to raise money to purchase land in Palestine.

Jews were scattered throughout the Ottoman Empire, but only those nations at the empire's fringes, where the indigenous people formed a majority, had managed to wrest control from their Turkish overlords. In order to exercise any power, the Hebrews would have to form a nation of their own, and where better to do that than the Promised Land?

Unfortunately for Alkelai, he was ahead of his time and his movement never took off, although he himself moved to Jerusalem, where he died in 1878.

Simon Loebl Herzl, Theodor's grandfather, also lived in Semlin, and he was a member of Alkelai's synagogue. As an exponent of the young Rabbi's ideas, he told Theo stories of the goal of a homeland for the Jewish people, planting the seed that would later come to fruition.

Theodor Herzl was the son of the beautiful Jeanette and the fastidious Jacob. He had one sister, Pauline, a year older than himself. They lived in Pesth, across the river from Buda, in a house next door to a large synagogue.

Herzl grew up admiring the 19th Century French entrepreneur and engineer Frederick De Lesseps, originator of the idea for the Suez Canal.

As the French Consul to Egypt, De Lesseps wooed the young prince, Said Pasha, and when Said became ruler of Egypt, he agreed to Frederick's ambitious plan to open up a waterway between the Mediterranean and the Red Sea.

When this feat of engineering opened in 1867, De Lesseps became an instant hero to people everywhere, including Theodor.

Scouring a map for similar opportunities, young Theo announced to a school friend, 'I am going to build a canal in Panama, but please don't tell anyone in case they steal my idea!'

Flushed with enthusiasm, Theo's parents placed him in the Realschule at the age of ten in order to follow his dream. Unfortunately, his better subjects were Geography and History, while he was weak in Maths, Geometry, and Technical

Drawing, the subjects required for engineering. His parents hadn't realised that it was the vision of De Lesseps, rather than the career, that Herzl wished to emulate.

The earnest young man turned to another of his passions and founded a literary society, of which he was president, amongst his school friends.

At the age of sixteen, after some private tuition in order to improve his poor marks, Theo moved on to the Evangelical Gymnasium, a Protestant school popular with the Jewish middle classes.

Herzl was a melancholy youth, a deep thinker, who revered poetry. He was handsome, though shy, and awkward around women.

Tragedy then struck the family, when Theo's sister Pauline died of Typhoid Fever when she was just eighteen years old.

Within a week of the funeral, in 1878, the Herzls moved to Vienna, Austria, to escape the stifling memory of their loss. The Rabbi who led the condolences cornered Theodor at the funeral and asked him what he planned to do with his life.

Having seen how fleeting life could be, Theo decided he would follow his heart.

'I want' he said 'to be a writer.'

The Rabbi approved of Theo's ambition, but he also insisted the young lad should have something to fall back on.

In Vienna, Theo was entered to the Faculty of Law, a more practical solution. Amongst his other interests, Theo joined a duelling club, the Albia, and drew blood in his only obligatory sword fight.

Between January and May 1882, Herzl withdrew no fewer than fifty books from the university library, such was his thirst for knowledge.

He began to submit short stories to the local newspapers in the hope of publication, in pursuit of his artistic goal.

Around this time, anti-Semitism was on the rise. There was a media witch-hunt against the Jews that swept through the general public.

When Wagner, the lauded German composer, died in February 1883, a ceremony of remembrance took place weeks later, with the event turning into a Right Wing rally.

Members of the Albia had taken part, and when Theo heard this, he tendered his resignation. Unsurprisingly, it was accepted.

By the end of 1883, Theo was depressed, unlucky in love, and faltering in his ambition of a literary career. The only bright light on the horizon was his graduation in the summer of 1884.

Only then, it seemed, would life truly begin.

THE FATHER OF ZIONISM.

In Theodor Herzl's graduation year, he had a short story produced in a local newspaper. In the summer, Theo left the university with moderate grades and became an articled clerk in the legal system.

Theo turned his hand to writing plays and his first, entitled Tabarin, was performed in Vienna in 1886. Over the next couple of years, further works were performed in Berlin and New York, but the Rabbi's earlier advice proved to be correct, and he did not grow rich on the results, and he needed his day job to fall back on.

Herzl grew into a confident and strong adult. 'Courage and toughness is what you have', he was told by one of his best friends, Heinrich Kana.

He began to display a wanderlust, and with money borrowed from his father, Theodor toured Italy and visited Paris, and upon his return to Austria he was appointed features editor of a Viennese newspaper.

Theo also returned to his own writing, and grew close to a woman eight years his junior, Julie Naschauer, a rich Jewish girl.

The couple were married on 25th June 1889, and their first child, a girl they named Pauline, was born a year later. Then, in 1891, Julie gave birth to a son, Hans.

All was not well in the Herzl house though. Theo, it seemed, had married for money, while Julie wanted the prestige of having a famous writer for a husband. There was material gain on both sides, but it hardly amounted to love.

When Theo was offered the position of Foreign Correspondent for the Neue Freie Presse, the most important newspaper in Vienna, he jumped at the chance.

He was based in Paris, a vibrant capital that Vienna had modelled itself on. He was soon joined by his family, and another child, Margaret, was born to them the following year.

Theo played his part well; a man about town, he never failed to forward his immaculate copy to the newspaper recording the events of the day, and he was devoted to his young family. He even agreed to have a bust of himself made by the esteemed sculptor, Samuel Beer.

Whilst sitting for the portrait, Herzl began to ponder his role in the enterprise. 'For what am I being remembered?' he wondered. 'Am I a man of letters, a playwright, a journalist, a lawyer?'

Unsure of what he had contributed, Theodor engaged Beer in philosophical debate. When the two men began to discuss The Jewish Question, Herzl became animated.

Over the next three weeks, Theodor wrote a new play, entitled 'The New Ghetto', pondering the nature of Jewishness.

The play would be performed at a much later date but, more immediately, it served to mobilise Herzl to action, and he drafted a 'Practical Programme' to address the issues affecting the Jewish people.

He claimed to have found the solution to the question of whether the Jews should assimilate with their host nations, or maintain their uniqueness and consolidate themselves within their own nation state.

Herzl approached Baron Maurice De Hirsch, a rich and philanthropic Jew, with his idea for creating a homeland for their people in Palestine. His proposal was to buy up the land and displace the 650,000 indigenous Arab inhabitants.

The Baron procrastinated right up until his death, and temporarily thwarted Theo's plan.

Returning to his first love, literature, in 1896 Theo produced a pamphlet entitled 'The Jewish State', paying for 5000 copies from his own funds. These received a great deal of attention, both at home and abroad.

In it, both Argentina, a fertile and temperate place, ripe for development and repopulation, and Palestine, the Promised Land, were suggested as possible destinations for Jewish settlement.

The pamphlet attracted a stream of admirers, and detractors, while Theo himself was growing into the role of statesman, and Messiah.

The well-acquainted Reverend William Hechler was impressed by the notion of Zionism, and he promised Theo an introduction to the Grand Duke of Baden, an uncle of the German Kaiser.

Herzl met the Grand Duke and attempted to win him over to his argument, but his performance was not persuasive enough to be passed on to leader of the German Republic.

Another useful contact was Philip Michael de Nevlinsky, an aristocrat and media magnate, who promised to lend his considerable resources to the Zionist cause.

Nevlinsky was acquainted with Abdul Hamid, the Ottoman Sultan with ultimate responsibility over Palestine, and the one man capable of ceding the territory in question.

Herzl and Nevlinsky travelled together to Constantinople, the seat of empire, but despite meeting with the Sultan's son, his chamberlain, and ambassadors from several European countries, the answer was always 'no'.

Abdul Hamid made it clear through his emissaries that he would not give up a land that his people had spilled blood for. It would be a betrayal of the Islamic faith.

Despite this disappointment, Theo was growing in political stature. At a rally in London in July 1896, a huge crowd enthusiastically backed his plans.

Certain senior Jewish figures believed that any notion of the Jews having a homeland of their own might antagonise their present host communities, but despite these reservations from some prominent financiers, such as Edmond De Rothschild, Herzl organised the first Zionist Conference for the following year.

For Theo, Zionism was not born of religion. He did not practice the faith to any great extent himself. Rather, it was a response, and a necessary one at that, to growing anti-Semitism in Europe.

One instance of this was the notorious Dreyfus Affair in France, where Alfred Dreyfus, a French staff officer, was tried on trumped-up charges of treason. Outside the courthouse, an angry mob screamed 'Death, death to the Jews.' And this was in a supposedly civilised country.

Herzl, who witnessed first-hand the hysteria and the depth of antagonism towards his people, determined that something had to be done.

Thus, at Basel, Switzerland between the 29th and 31st of August, 1897, 200 delegates attended the inaugural Zionist Congress.

Asked about the success of the conference, Theodor later wrote 'If I were to sum up the Basel summit in one sentence, it would be this. There, I founded the Jewish state.'

THE FIRST ZIONIST CONGRESS.

On Sunday, 29th of August, 1897, at the concert hall of the Basel Municipal Casino, Switzerland, 199 named delegates attended the First Zionist Congress.

The congregation were dressed in their finest clothes, with top hat and tails the order of the day. 'People should get used to seeing the Congress as a most exalted and solemn thing', explained Herzl, who had organised the convention and outlined the programme.

There was a great deal of excitement amongst those gathered amid the pomp and ceremony. One of those present, a member of the Odessa committee, summed up the atmosphere.

'When I got to the Casino', he recalled, 'I was so excited my legs were weak and I stumbled. There was tremendous anticipation. Suddenly, the hall went quiet. Old Doctor Lippe of Jassy mounted the rostrum and made a blessing. Many eyes filled with tears. Herzl then stood before us on the platform, with a deep, concentrated gaze, a splendid figure, like a man of the House of David risen from the grave in all his legendary glory.'

After speaking his opening words in Hebrew, a text that he had laboured to learn, Herzl made his opening presentation.

'On this solemn occasion, when Jews from so many countries have met at one call, we are creating with this Congress an organ for the Jewish people that it has not had before, but which it has urgently needed. You all know, that with a few exceptions, the condition of the Jews is not a happy one. We should scarcely have met here had it been otherwise. But however long it takes to complete our work, towards the ancient goal of our people, let our Congress be serious and lofty. Let it be a blessing for the unfortunate, a threat to nobody, a source of honour to all Jews, and worthy of the past, the glory of which is far off but everlasting.'

Next to speak was Max Nordau, eleven years older than Herzl, and another man of letters. He echoed many of Theodor's sentiments, but he was not reading from a prepared text and his oratory carried a great deal of passion that moved many in the congregation to tears.

'Anti-Semitism broke out from the innermost depth of the nations and revealed the real situation to the horrified Jew', Nordau explained. 'His countrymen repel him, and he feels the world hates him and he sees no place where he can find warmth. His best powers are exhausted in the suppression, for he never has the satisfaction of showing himself in all his thoughts and sentiments. He becomes an inner cripple.'

He later wrote to his wife to tell her how he had done.

'It was mad and touching', he enthused. 'Old men cried like children.'

Herzl agreed, congratulating Nordau, saying 'Your speech WAS the Congress.'

This was no idle flattery, for Theo later wrote in his diary 'He spoke wonderfully. His speech will be a monument to our age.'

A letter of welcome from Rabbi Shemu'el Mohilever to the Congress was then read out in full, followed by other opening addresses, reports on the conditions of Jews in various countries, four separate accounts of conditions within the existing Jewish settlements in Palestine, and the announcement of letters, telegrams, and petitions of support.

The delegation was then asked to debate the issue of the battle between the old and new schools of the Jewish Question of immigration to the Holy Land.

The old school espoused 'practical Zionism', whereby Jews would attempt to infiltrate Palestine by buying up land piece by piece and slowly increasing the Jewish population in the region.

That, said Herzl, at the rate of ten thousand Jews a year, would take us nine centuries to achieve!

The new school, led by Theodor, believed in 'political Zionism', creating a new state that would be recognised by other nations.

It was agreed that, rather than let this affair run and run, one member from

99

each group would be allowed to speak on behalf of their cause, and the conference would then vote on the issue.

Leo Motzkin spoke for the new radicals, saying 'We want a home of our own, a home for all the world to see. We believe it to be of the utmost importance that the Congress state its solution to the Jewish Question publicly. We do not want to be accused of concealing our aims.'

So much had been achieved in such a short space of time. The three days were almost over, and there was still the issue of the purchase of the land required to house the nation state.

Herzl had allowed only a brief reference to the financing of his great dream, but when a delegate asked for a resolution on the subject, the chairman of the proposed Jewish National Fund was given an opportunity to outline his vision for the scheme. But keep it brief, requested Theodor.

'Honoured Gentlemen, I will abuse neither your time nor your patience', began Hermann Schapira, as he used his allotted five minutes to explain that a fund would be created, that all could contribute to, that would be used for the express purpose of financing a move to the land of their forefathers.

Finally, after three days of debate, the Congress agreed to reconvene on an annual basis, and agreed four principles from this first summit.

The agreement reached was termed 'the Basel Programme', and it read: Zionism aims at the creation of a home for the Jewish people in Palestine to be secured by public law. To that end, the Congress envisages the following:

1. The purposeful advancement of the settlement in Palestine with Jewish farmers, artisans, and tradesmen.

2. The organizing and unifying of all Jewry by means of appropriate local and general arrangements subject to the laws of each country.

3. The strengthening of Jewish national feeling and consciousness.

4. Preparatory moves towards obtaining such governmental consent as will be necessary to achieve the aims of Zionism.

The delegation then voted on and approved the manifesto, and all hailed the Congress as a success. A speech of thanks was made to Herzl and Nordau by Doctor Emmanuel Mandelstamm, a leading Jewish figure, and the conference dispersed amid cheers and the waving of handkerchiefs.

Theodor later wrote in his diary, as we have seen, 'At Basel, I created the Jewish State.' He went on to say, 'If I said this out loud today, I would be answered with universal laughter. Perhaps in five years, and' he added with the utmost prescience, 'certainly in fifty, everyone will know it.'

He had worked the people into the mood for a state, and he was hailed as their king.

When asked if he was the Messiah, for it had been written that the Jewish State would only come to pass at the arrival of such a man, Herzl replied 'I cannot be sure, for I am no theologian.'

He may not have accepted that he was king of the Jews, but he did claim to have the solution to the Jewish Question. The only one.

CONGRESS CONTINUED.

The Second Zionist Congress took place in Basel in 1898, a year to the day after the inaugural meeting. It was largely taken up with the practicalities of the fund-raising required to purchase land for settlement in Palestine.

It contained little of the passion, pomp, or progress experienced in the earlier event, and was more a reiteration of the goals enshrined the previous year.

In August 1899, again in Basel, the Third Congress convened. There had been no developments in the interim. Despite introductions to the Kaiser and the Ottoman Sultan, Abdul Hamid, Herzl had not secured any undertaking from these most influential of possible sponsors.

Therefore, there was little to report to his supporters, and up on the rostrum, Theodor grew bored and allowed his mind to wander to literary endeavours.

He contemplated a new play, to be called 'The New Zion', where he could outline his vision for the Jewish State in artistic form, to give body to his political dream.

In the year 1900, the first week of August, the Fourth Zionist Congress took place in London. Herzl stayed at the Langham Hotel in Bayswater, and although he attempted to mix with the dignitaries, attending a garden party at Baron de Rothschild's residence on one occasion, he was physically in poor condition.

Theo was suffering from what he believed to be Malaria-like symptoms, maybe even Pneumonia. Later, his physician ascribed the malady to a minor heart attack, in the first symptom of a problem that would afflict Herzl for the rest of his life.

The Fifth Congress, restored to Basel, began on Boxing Day, 1901, and was largely concerned with resolving the issue of the Jewish National Fund in order to purchase land in Palestine.

The issue was being burdened with provisos. No one would commit themselves to anything definite. Herzl had to frequently absent himself from the conference to recuperate, but on the fourth day, the 29th of December, he returned to the arena and took control of the debate.

With so many caveats in the directive, he claimed, nobody would have the confidence to make a financial contribution to the cause, rendering the exercise in its current state redundant. Only by virtue of a unanimous statement of intent could they hope to attract the necessary revenue that the fund was designed to manage.

The delegates agreed with him, the issue was resolved and, despite his failing health, Theo had again led from the front and served the conference with aplomb.

In August 1903, it was the turn of the Sixth Zionist Congress, to be held once more in Basel. Herzl recorded the results in his diary on the 31st of August of the same year.

'The difficult great Sixth Congress is over. When, completely worn out, I returned from the final session, I sat with my friends Zangwill, Nordau, and Cowen in Cowen's hotel room around a bottle of mineral water. I said to them, "This is the speech I will make to the Seventh Congress. That is, if I live to see it. By then, I will have either obtained Palestine or realised the futility of my efforts. If it is the latter, I will say it was not possible. The goal has not been reached and it will not be reached for a foreseeable time. But a temporary result is at hand: we can settle our suffering masses in East Africa, and with the right of self government. I do not believe that, for the sake of a beautiful dream, we have a right to withhold this relief from the unfortunate." For the British have offered us a homeland.'

The suggestion had been made by Joseph Chamberlain, the Secretary to the Colonies for the British government, and would be subject to ratification even if the Jewish people expressed an interest.

Herzl had presented the proposal to the Great Actions Committee of the

Zionist movement on the 21st of August, 1903. The vote split the party. Some wanted Palestine or nothing at all. Theodor argued in favour of the move to Uganda, at least as an 'overnight stay', in preparation for an eventual move to the Holy land, but some feared that once established in East Africa, it would prove impolitic to move again.

The votes were cast, with 275 in favour of establishing a Jewish state in the British suzerainty of East Africa, 177 votes against, and approximately 100 abstentions. This did not, however, mean the ayes carried the day. The arguments had only just begun.

Accused of selling out their original dream, and realising that he had split the Zionists, Herzl resigned from his position as leader of the movement.

The Uganda offer was the best that Theo, his health failing, had been able to do. There were 60,000 square miles of arable land included in the deal, and that was not to be sniffed at for an emerging nation.

A good thing or not, it was still seen as a betrayal of the principles established at the First Zionist Congress.

Herzl took a back seat, due to his ill health and the adverse reaction to his proposal, and Max Nordau took charge.

While in Paris, attending a Hanukkah ball with his wife, Nordau realised the opposition to the Ugandan idea when a 24 year old Jewish student stepped from the crowd and shouted 'Death to the East African', before firing two bullets at him. Luckily, they missed Max and instead hit a bystander in the leg.

There were several reasons why Uganda had appealed to the leaders of the movement. Firstly, Arab nationalism was rampant at this time. Herzl, for one, could see the difficulty in establishing a Jewish state right in the heart of a pan-Arab empire. How right he was.

Secondly, the East Africa idea was a good one. The land was fertile, the area allotted was huge, the climate temperate, like Southern England it was said, and it was largely uninhabited.

Herzl believed his movement to be nationalistic rather than religious, and he therefore had little compunction in realising his goal somewhere other than Palestine. Obviously, for everyone apart from the secularists, this was a sacrilegious idea.

Finally, the Uganda offer was the only one on the table and, in his condition, it represented the last chance for Theo to live to see the establishment of a Jewish state.

However, the British 'offer' was more of a proposal, and was still subject to ratification.

The British had only agreed to 'lease' Uganda to the Jews, and only after a period of deliberation once a formal request had been received from the Zionists. There was no offer as such, as the British Foreign Office was quick to point out.

Even then, there were a number of conditions included.

Britain would retain the land and water rights to the territory, and would also maintain a right of veto should the experiment not be deemed a success.

Theodor Herzl, despite his failing health, continued to pursue his dream and to work on behalf of the cause.

In January 1904, in Italy, Herzl met King Victor Emmanuel III, where he again claimed that Zionism was a nationalistic, not a religious movement. The king told him he believed that the Jews would one day get Palestine, but that they had to be patient.

'But they won't let us in', bemoaned Theo.

'Bah', replied the king. 'Everything can be done with baksheesh!'

In Rome, Herzl met Pope Pius X. They talked of a homeland for the Jews, but the Pope said he could not approve of the Zionist movement.

'The Jews do not recognise Jesus', he said, 'so how can I recognise them?'

Returning to Austria, Theo visited the health spa at Franzensbad to repair to the waters. There, on the 9th of May, 1904, he suffered a heart attack. As he lay in his doctor's arms, he said, 'I didn't do too badly for my people, did I?'

Theo recovered briefly and was transferred to his home at Edlach, near Reichman where, a week later, on the 16th of May he made his last diary entry. It said simply, 'Broken down'.

He managed a few brief walks around the gardens of his home, but on the 3rd of July, at the age of forty four, suffering inflammation of the lungs, he heaved a last heavy sigh and was gone.

He was laid to rest beside his father in the beautiful hills overlooking Vienna, his graveside attended by a throng of admirers.

Forty five years later, Theo's body was moved to the newly-founded state of Israel and buried on a hillside to the west of Jerusalem that was renamed Mount Herzl.

BEFORE THE GREAT WAR.

The word Aliyah means to ascend, and this was the name given to the wave of Jewish immigration that began when persecuted Jews, mostly from Russia, would 'go up' to Palestine.

The philanthropist Baron De Rothschild supported the settlers and their goal of 'practical Zionism', reclaiming their historical homeland by the simple act of buying land and moving in.

Some 25,000 Russian Jews joined the First Aliyah and, when added to the host religious community, it brought the number of Hebrews living in the Holy Land up to the 50,000 mark, in amongst 650,000 Arabs.

The Second Aliyah began in 1904, and again consisted of a majority from Russia. The reason, as in the first instance, was a failed revolution in the eastern empire that saw a backlash in the aftermath against outsiders, amongst them the Jews. This second wave added another 40,000 immigrants to the Hebrew population of Palestine. These people now represented, to borrow a 21st Century expression, facts on the ground, but the impetus of Zionism sought to establish political orthodoxy for their presence. They did not wish to creep in by the back door.

To that end, the imperial sponsorship desired by the Zionists was focused on Britain. The new leaders of the movement were Chaim Weizmann and Nahum Sakalov, both of whom lived in England.

The two men had become friendly with half of the British Cabinet, and were constantly espousing their cause, continuing to tread the path of statesmen first pounded by Theodor Herzl.

The Ottoman Empire was crumbling under the weight of successive nationalist movements. Serbia, Montenegro, and Bulgaria had all won their independence, and Bosnia and Herzegova had been sold to Austria for 2.5 million Turkish pounds as the Ottoman's struggled to stave off the empire's debtors.

The European powers of Britain and France wrestled North Africa from Ottoman control, with the Arabs awaiting their turn to strike for independence too.

And that was only the fringe pressure. In 1908, Abdul Hamid II, the Ottoman Sultan, was overthrown in a coup by the progressive and secular Young Turk movement.

In 1930, the Palestinian leader Jamal al-Husayni would say that 1908 not only saw the end of the Ottoman era in Istanbul but in Palestine too. 'Liberty', he said 'came at that moment with the arrival of the Young Turks.'

In 1906, at the Sixth Zionist Congress, it had been decided that the Jewish homeland should be in Palestine, rejecting once and for all the suggestion of East Africa, as proposed by the late, lamented Theodor Herzl.

Using the charitable donations provided to the Jewish National Fund, settlers began buying up terrain from absentee landlords, leaving Arab farmers who had tilled the soil for generations both homeless and jobless.

Hashiloah, a Zionist newspaper, published an article by Yitzhak Epstein in 1907 where he wrote that there was no vacant land left in Palestine, and that Jewish settlement therefore meant Arab dispossession.

Purchasing land, Epstein exhorted, should not result in the expulsion of poor sharecroppers, and he campaigned for peaceful integration. He was derided for his faintheartedness.

Of course, once the Arab inhabitants tasted the reality of Jewish immigration, they took action. They began attacking the new landlords who were throwing them off their farms, only for the Jews to plead to the Ottoman governors for permission to arm and defend themselves.

With permission granted, an organisation called Ha'shomer was formed, meaning 'The Watchman', forerunner of the Israeli Defence Force.

The original brigade consisted of ninety volunteers, twenty of whom were women. They rode horses, wore Arab headgear, carried arms, and looked like gun-slingers from the old Wild West.

In 1910, the first Kibbutz was established on the southern shore of the Sea of Galilee. This was an agricultural collective settlement, and by 1914 there would be fourteen such farms across Palestine.

That same year, a secular city emerged on the Mediterranean coast north of Jaffa, consisting of 139 houses with a total of 1419 inhabitants. The named it Tel Aviv, meaning 'mound of the spring'.

Hebrew was adopted as the national Jewish language as they consolidated their presence in the region, to give unity to the various communities arriving from the Diaspora.

The native Palestinian population and the Zionist entity were at loggerheads. In 1913, in a newspaper article, Aharon Reuveni, the brother of a later Israeli president Yitzhak Ben-Zvi, wrote 'Arab nationalism vehemently opposes our entry into the country, but that will not succeed in halting what must be. Our migration to Palestine is of vital importance to us. The local population can injure or harass us, but they will be powerless to stop immigration completely.'

Then, in 1914, the Austrian Archduke Franz Ferdinand was assassinated in Sarajevo by a Bosnian terrorist. The Austrians believed Serbians were behind the attack and declared war on that province on 28th July, with the aid of their German neighbours.

Russia moved to support its protectorate Serbia. Thereafter, Germany declared war on Russia, who had an alliance with France, who in turn shared a pact with Great Britain dating back to 1904 and the North African campaign.

The Ottomans had been enemies of the British over their involvement in Egypt, and with the French for seizing control of Tunisia and Morocco. They had also long been at odds with Russia, who were threatening their northern border at Istanbul.

Therefore, the Turkish Ottoman Empire joined the Central Powers of Germany and Austria in the Great War. It was a decision that they would come to regret, and would change the face of the Middle East forever.

LAWRENCE OF ARABIA.

The Arabic people, itching to overthrow their imperial masters, the Ottomans, received much encouragement to that end from the British in the First World War.

From the ranks of the Allied army, T.E.Lawrence was chosen to lead the efforts to damage the Turkish war machine at their encampments in the Middle East.

This remarkable young man, an Oxford don, well-versed in the art of tactical warfare, had within him a desire to conjure up heroism. In the Great War, he found the perfect stage for his talents.

He was the right choice for the role. As an undergraduate, he had toured the Near East, visiting Crusader forts on foot, wandering solely in the desert wilderness, breathing the rarefied air and camping under the myriad stars.

Well acquainted with the region, with an affinity and understanding of the Semitic people, he was given the task of convincing the Arabs that the time was ripe to challenge their overlords.

In so doing, the British would be free to tackle the German army, with the Arabs left to take on the Turks.

Lawrence accepted his orders, and set about making contact with the indigenous tribes. He was able to offer, on the assurance of the British high command, the enticement of that most precious of treasure: Freedom.

This would be given to the Arabs when the Ottomans were defeated.

The prize they cherished was within their grasp. All they had to do was win the war.

Adopting Arab dress, Lawrence brilliantly set an agenda that he convinced his Moslem cohorts to accept. First on the list was the port of Aqaba on the Red Sea.

The Bedouin of the desert were attracted to the raiding party by the promise of glory and the prospect of nationhood.

Aqaba was well defended, from the sea at least. All of its guns were pointed in that direction. To its rear was a searing expanse of sand.

Even the Arab leaders questioned the sanity of Lawrence's approach. When the British officer pledged to lead them in from that direction, they could hardly refuse a mission to cross land that they knew so well, that was all too strange to the intrepid foreigner. For wounded pride, they agreed to follow.

Inspired was the move that saw an Arab army emerge from the desert to overrun the Turkish defences at Aqaba. Following their success, Lawrence crossed the Sinai in order to reach Cairo to tell British command and General Allenby, who was leading the forces, of the victory.

Allenby urged Lawrence to continue in the same vein, to frustrate the Turks and tie up their army, leaving the Brits to proceed with their own war aims.

With a programme of guerrilla warfare, Lawrence proceeded to do exactly that, blowing up trains and communication lines, and leading the Ottoman army on a wild goose chase.

All the while, the Arabs continued at Lawrence's side, convinced of the goal they had been led to believe in.

They should not have been, for dirty work was afoot. In 1916, hopeful of a positive outcome in the war, the French and British had approved a pact to divide the Near East between them in what became known as the Sykes-Picot agreement.

Then, in 1917, in one of the most electrifying statements ever issued by a British government, Lord Balfour announced that the British supported the right of the Jewish people to create a nation state for themselves within the borders of Palestine.

For the Zionists, this was Manna from Heaven. For the Arabs of Palestine, it was treachery.

Lawrence, too, felt the betrayal. Housed in Arab garb, he had fought side by side with Bedouin princes, tribal leaders, and desert warriors. He had lived, laughed, and loved with them. He almost became, in his own mind, one of them.

They had bled for him and he for them. Now, all of his promises seemed empty. Or worse, lies. As a British officer, he could have been held responsible for the betrayal. Luckily for him, he had earned their trust, and would go on earning it.

There was a war in progress, and there was still a great deal to fight for.

As Lawrence saw it, British plans for the region were short-sighted. He himself was a scholar of nomadic traditions and of the origins of the Arab peoples. Of all his compatriots, it was Lawrence who knew where the Arabs came from and in which direction they should head.

The French and British idea was self-serving and colonial. It reeked of arrogance, and would prove insufferable.

The last hope for a pan-Arab empire, to leave this unique race of people in charge of their own affairs, was to seize the important centre of Damascus before the British did the same. Then, the Arabs could claim victory over the Ottomans for themselves, and conquest and its rewards would be theirs.

Lawrence used best endeavours to drag the Arab army to the Syrian capital and arrived just ahead of the Brits.

Victory, however, proved short-lived, for as the Turkish and German forces crumbled, the Allies claimed the glory for themselves, along with the spoils of war.

Arab efforts were forgotten, their concerns were ridden roughshod over, and Lawrence was left to grieve for their cause.

Back in England, Lawrence exhorted parliament to let sense prevail in the division of Arab territories between the European powers.

To no avail. Writing letters to the Times newspaper, attempting to keep the issue on the agenda, and to gain at least some concession for their Arab allies was the best that Lawrence could do.

Some believe he betrayed the Arabs, but he truly tried his best for them. Even after the war when the future of the state was being discussed, he took his argument to the highest levels, even refusing the honours being pushed his way by the crown. In protest, he declined his just rewards, and all with the aim of highlighting the ongoing injustice.

The Arabs themselves seem to have forgiven Lawrence for any part he may have played in the deceit. They remembered his exploits, how he had fought alongside them. And, at the end of the day, he was a British officer, and his loyalty belonged to his own countrymen.

Tragically, back at home in England, while racing his favourite motorbike, one of the few pleasures to match his ache for war, he crashed and died.

He was remembered with a service at Westminster cathedral, attended by a host of dignitaries, including one of his most fervent admirers, the great Winston Churchill.

Maybe, some of his fighting spirit lived on in the little man's strength, cometh the hour of the second great war of the twentieth century. There can have been no better tribute to Lawrence than to think he provided some inspiration for the dogged refusal to submit to the force of evil that would emerge a generation later.

God knows, he foresaw the problems inherent in an ill-advised division of the lands of the Middle East.

THE BALFOUR DECLARATION.

On the 2nd of November, 1917, a sixty five word statement was written by the British Foreign Secretary, Lord Balfour, in a letter to Lord Rothschild, the head of the Zionist Federation in Britain.

It read: 'His Majesty's Government view with favour the establishment in Palestine of a National Home for the Jewish people, and will use best endeavours to facilitate the achievement of this object, it being clearly understood that nothing shall be done which may prejudice the civil and religious rights of existing non-Jewish communities in Palestine or the rights and political status enjoyed by Jews in any other country.'

As the British were in charge of the region, and would remain so for the next thirty years, it was a worthwhile endorsement of the Zionist cause.

From such a seemingly humble expression of support, the resulting arguments as to its value would run and run.

The address was not as unambiguous as the Zionists would have us believe, although it became a rallying call and was used to great effect by the leaders of the Jewish movement.

But the British would not have been moved to make such a declaration if it did not have inherent benefits for themselves.

In this instance, the reasons for so boldly stating their position were threefold.

Firstly, in 1917, there was the rise of Bolshevism and the overthrow of the Tsar in Russia. A majority of Jews in the Diaspora were resident there, and it was hoped that by declaring British support for Zionism at this stage, that if the Jews assumed significant power in the new Russian order they would keep Russia in the war on the side of the Allies.

Secondly, there was the belief in the British Government that American Jews held considerable sway in the corridors of power in the USA. If they believed an Allied victory in Europe would benefit their own aim of returning to Palestine, they would urge Woodrow Wilson, the US President, to join the war against the German and Ottoman forces.

Finally, the British army had succeeded in capturing all of Palestine in 1917, without the aid of France. They therefore had no intention of sharing the territory as agreed in the Sykes-Picot arrangement. The Balfour Declaration would serve as both an indication to the French that the situation had changed, and would also be useful in creating a groundswell of support amongst the Jewish people to ensure that there could be no possibility of the British fulfilling the earlier agenda.

In essence, Sykes-Picot, the Anglo-French arrangement prepared by Mark Sykes, an aristocrat and Member of Parliament, and his French counterpart, Georges Picot, advocated the division of the former Ottoman states between the two allies should they emerge victorious from the Great War, which looked increasingly likely.

Add a drop of Victorian Christian zeal to the mix, and we have a victorious British presence no longer prepared to share control of the Holy Land that it had conquered alone and was presently occupying.

Of course, the British weren't the only ones interested in the region. The Zionists wanted it for themselves, regardless of the indigenous Arab population.

When Lord Balfour, who was a former British Prime Minister, asked Chaim Weizmann to submit a draft proposal to be included with his declaration, the initial text called for 'the establishment of Palestine as the national home for the Jewish people.' Not just a home within Palestine. The Zionists wanted it all.

The number of Jews resident in the Promised Land by the end of the war had fallen to 60,000, due to the deprivation, starvation, and death all around them. The Arab population of Palestine was close to the 700,000 mark, and they would have something to say about their removal to make way for the new arrivals.

The Arab leaders needed convincing that the Balfour Declaration would not lead to the expulsion of the indigenous inhabitants. The statement contained some provisos concerning the status of the local people, but assurances were still due.

In January 1918, Commander D.G.Hogarth, head of the Arab Bureau of the British forces was sent to see Sharif Hussein, King of the Hejaz, in Jedda.

Arab antennae was already attuned to the possibility of treachery, after news of the Sykes-Picot agreement had been leaked to them by the Ottomans, who had seized incriminating paperwork to that effect during the war campaign.

King Hussein refused to condone any attempt to establish a Jewish state in Palestine, and Hogarth worked hard to convince him that the British, despite the Balfour Declaration, had no intention of imposing such an outcome on the region.

That said, the king was brought around to the view that limited Jewish immigration could be of some benefit to the region.

When the war finally came to an end, with victory for the Allies, the Zionist lobby wasted no time moving its headquarters to Palestine.

For Chaim Weizmann, his arrival in the region was a rude awakening. His dream of a land for the Jews was dealt a blow when he saw for himself how Arabic the area was. So much for the Zionists' rallying call: 'A land without a people for a people without a land!'

The Jews were not even ten percent of the population, they often lived in isolated settlements in the countryside, and it seemed that there was hardly a foothold in Palestine with which to begin the eventual takeover.

On the 7th of November, 1918, in the week that the armistice was signed with Germany and Turkey to end the war, the British and French made a joint statement declaring their intention to liberate all of the Arab peoples and to award them the right of self determination. They would prove to be empty words.

It seemed that the Zionist cause was an impossible task on the ground, for the Arabs were simply too entrenched, their numbers overwhelming.

Luckily, when inspiration was needed, Balfour was there to provide it once more.

In 1919, Lord Balfour wrote, 'We are committed to Zionism, for Zionism, right or wrong, good or bad, is rooted in age-long tradition. In present needs and future hopes, it is of far profounder import than the desires and prejudices of the 700,000 Arabs who now inhabit that ancient land.'

From such fractured, contradictory, and deceitful beginnings, no good could ever come.

THE PARTITION OF PALESTINE.

Sir Herbert Samuel, a British Jew, was appointed High Commissioner of Palestine in the immediate aftermath of World War 1, and he was initially welcomed by the Zionists. It was at the San Remo Conference of April 1920 where the British occupation of the region was enshrined in the idea of a Mandate, and would incorporate the Balfour Declaration. This was warmly greeted by the Jewish people, as it formalized the earlier statement of intent into policy.

The immediate effect of this development was the outbreak of violence between Jews and Arabs. The latter, already angry at the initial proposal, were reacting to a deliberate declaration that would marginalise their inherent right to remain in the land of Palestine.

There was an undercurrent to this sense of nationalism from the Arab community. US President Woodrow Wilson had canvassed opinions from the Palestinians to gather intelligence about their aspirations. The answer to the question was that the Arabs wished to become part of a Greater Syria, to include, Syria, Lebanon, and Palestine.

This would be little more than the fulfilment of the promise made by the British of a pan-Arab empire, when the Bedouins were asked to help overthrow the Ottomans in the First World War.

Prince Faisal was nominal ruler in Damascus following the armistice, but he was ousted from Syria by the French in 1920, and the British then moved to offer Faisal the throne of the new kingdom of Iraq, in order to appease their former ally.

Chaim Weizmann met the Arab prince at Aqaba in 1918 and they agreed their own entente for the region. In return for Jewish financial aid, Faisal would recognise a home for the Jews in Palestine. Unfortunately, both parties were sidelined by the French and the British, and neither would be in a position to make good on their promises.

In 1920, the British withdrew military rule from Palestine, to be replaced by a civil administration amalgamating the former provinces of Samaria, Judea, and Galilee.

This consolidation added to the awareness of Palestinian nationality, especially when added to the sense of isolation they felt when their goal of annexation to Syria and Lebanon was rebuked.

On 1st of March that year, the Jewish settlement at Tel Hai was attacked by Arab militants and eight people were killed. Amongst the dead was a prominent Zionist Leader, Joseph Trumpeldor. His last words were said to have been, 'It is good to die for our country'.

At an Easter rally in April 1920, the Zionists and the Arabs clashed again. The leaders of both factions, Amir Al-Husseini and Vladimir Jabotinsky, were arrested for their part in the disturbances.

In November, Al-Husseini gathered a Bedouin force at Aqaba in order to attack the French in Syria as revenge for overthrowing his brother, Prince Faisal.

To placate the Arabs, Haj Amin Al-Husseini was made ruler of the TransJordan region and Mufti of Jerusalem.

Winston Churchill, the Colonial Secretary, held a conference in Cairo in March 1921, counselled by T.E.Lawrence. His proposal, in what became known as the Churchill White Paper, was for the Arab empire, at least those areas of interest to the West, to be split four ways.

The British would take Palestine, the French would rule Syria and the Lebanon, Iraq would fall under King Faisal, and TransJordan would have a British Mandate, although without reference to the Balfour Declaration, and with the Amir, Al-Husseini, in charge.

The true desert lands, recently captured by Ibn Saud and renamed Saudi Arabia, were of little interest to Western powers and could be ignored in the arrangement. What little oil had been found at this point was of little concern to the industrialised nations, whose own need for such resources was still unexplored.

Two months after the White Paper was issued, Jewish immigration was at full flow, with support for the Balfour Declaration enshrined and about to go before the League of Nations for full ratification.

In Palestine, tensions continued to rise, leading to riots at the Zionists' port of entry, Jaffa, on the Mediterranean coast, which left 47 Jews and 48 Arabs dead, and hundreds more injured.

In an attempt to quell the violence, Sir Herbert Samuel called for a temporary halt to the Zionist influx, but this would be amended in July, 1921, when Churchill limited immigration to 'the economic capacity of the country'.

Even if the numbers allowed in were capped, this would not prevent the growth of the Jewish state. Alongside the National Fund that had been established in order to purchase land, a new trust was founded in order to raise money to develop and build on the land that had been acquired. The infrastructure for a new nation was being built.

This could hardly be prevented. The Zionists had proved themselves more politically astute. When the British rulers set up the civil administration, they proposed the division of the assembly between the warring parties. Rather than appear difficult, the Jews played along with it, despite the fact it was a contradiction of their own stated aims of creating their own nation in the area of Palestine.

The Zionists rightly guessed that the Arabs would reject the proposal. The latter were by far the greater in terms of population, and they had no desire to power share other than on the basis of proportional representation.

It all served to bring the British and the Zionists closer together, and to alienate the Arab majority from the political process.

In 1922, the British Mandate for Palestine was finally approved by the League of Nations, and came into effect in September 1923.

Haj Amin Al-Husseini was appointed head of the Supreme Muslim Council, and he began to agitate against the growing, Mandated, Zionist entity.

The uncomfortable situation of Jewish settlement in an overwhelmingly hostile and alien environment leant itself to continued fighting between the two groups.

It was only in 1928 that the Arabs grasped the political mantle and, by accepting the latest British proposal, forced the Israelis to show their hand and finally reject a British power-sharing programme.

For the frustrated Palestinians, newly attuned to their own nationalist cause and fighting a losing battle against Jewish immigration, the fact that the British could now see that the intransigence was not solely an Arab preserve would be small compensation in a struggle that was rapidly running away from them.

THE THIRD AND FOURTH ALIYAH.

As an exercise in the futility of predictions, the earlier British expectation that Russian Jews would have sufficient influence to keep that country in the war against the Central Powers proved more than false. Instead, the reverse was true. Not only had the Bolsheviks withdrawn the country from the Great War, but subsequently the Jews suffered a wave of anti-Semitism, which led to the Third Aliyah.

With the help of He'chalutz, a Russian Zionist Emigration organisation, the name meaning 'The Pioneer', thousands of Jews were drawn to Palestine between 1919 and 1923. There, they formed themselves into a labour battalion, known as Gdud Ha'avoda, and they went to work building roads, clearing swamps, and cleaning up the land for settlement.

Those that had fought in World War 1 would also be drafted into the new defensive league, the Haganah, which was both illegal, but necessary, to protect the growing number of Jewish encampments that were subject to harassment and attack.

The Fourth Aliyah, which took place between 1924 and 1930, consisted largely of immigrants from the Polish middle classes, who came to Palestine to escape a new series of prohibitive tax laws.

Between 1924 and 1926, 63,000 Poles came to Palestine, 35,000 of them arriving in just one year, 1925. In total, the number of Jewish people in Palestine rose from 60,000 to 180,000.

In Tel Aviv alone, the population doubled in just eighteen months. When the Polish government saw the effect their new laws were having, they made it illegal to remove capital out of the country, and this put a stop to the tide of emigrants.

In 1927, only 3000 came to Palestine, a drop from 14,000 the year before. The number entering Palestine in 1928 was only 2170 people.

The Histradut, a Zionist trade union, attempted to address the decline by improving working conditions for the immigrants, and enacted public service schemes to create employment to address a recession in the region. The numbers of those entering Palestine began to increase again, with 5250 persons entering the country in 1929.

Also in that year, the Jewish Agency, a governing body, was founded in order to represent the growing Hebrew community.

The Arabs felt the tide was turning against them. Their own efforts at sovereignty had come to nothing, and still the Zionists kept arriving. The Jewish people seemed to have their act together, and were preparing for full blown statehood.

When religious Jews sought to partition the Wailing Wall, undermining one of the most holy of Muslim sites, the Al-Aqsa Mosque in Jerusalem, full blown riots broke out.

Instead of sporadic violence or tit-for-tat actions in isolated incidents, both sides now squared up to each other in what threatened to turn into all-out war.

The British rulers would be hard-pressed to separate the two combatants in a dispute that had taken on religious as well as territorial dimensions.

A delicate situation, a heartfelt and difficult one, had just got a whole lot worse.

THE FIRST ARAB UPRISING.

Shocked by the violence of the 1929 Arab revolt, the British government established the Shaw Commission in order to find out the cause of the disturbances.

The inquiry found native Palestinians in disarray, homeless and starving, dispossessed and disadvantaged. Immigrant Jewish landlords were buying up every available acre, removing the tenant farmers, and forcing them into the hills or shanty towns at the edge of prosperous new cities springing up on the coast, such as Tel Aviv, Haifa, and Jaffa.

The Arab Palestinians were angry at their British governors for their pro-Zionist policies, and were being treated like lepers in their own land.

The Shaw Commission took heed and recommended the exclusion of the Balfour Declaration from the Mandate. They also called for a limit to Jewish immigration, and a halt to their purchase of land. This eventually became government policy, enshrined in the Passfield White Paper, named after Lord Passfield, the new Colonial Secretary, and implemented in 1930.

Lord Passfield announced that Britain was equally committed to both Jews and Arabs, and that the plight of the Eastern European Jews who wished to immigrate to Palestine, who formed the bulk of the 3rd and 4th Aliyah, was not an issue to be solved by the British, nor by Palestine.

But just when it seemed that the Arabs would receive some respite from their woes, a general election in Britain returned a Labour government in coalition with the Liberal Party.

Led by Ramsay McDonald, the Labour party was in its infancy and attempted to appease both the opposition and coalition parties. The Zionist sympathisers pressed for a retraction of the conditions outlined in both the Churchill and Passfield White Papers which limited Jewish immigration to the economic capacity of the region.

There was a global recession in the 1930's, and with calls for a reduction in foreign spending, it seemed politic to allow the Jews into Palestine and let the wealth they would bring make up the shortfall in British spending.

The White Papers were scrapped, and the number of immigrants in Palestine rose from 180,000 in 1930 to 400,000 by 1935.

In response, 500 Arab notables gathered together to voice their opposition to the British. Unfortunately, Arab unity did not last long, and in-fighting soon began between the Arab league, and their cause did not make any headway. Time for a new approach. In 1933, a Syrian preacher named Izz al-Din al-Qassam formed a guerrilla brigade of disaffected Arab farmers. They began attacking telegraph lines, police stations, oil pipelines, and any Jewish person or British soldier that they could find.

Al-Qassam was eventually killed by the British army in 1935, but he became a martyr to his people and, worse, he succeeded in allying the religious and nationalist cause. To this day, there are units of suicide bombers who serve in his name.

On the Jewish side, there was also division. The First Aliyah had brought Russian Jews, many of them Bolsheviks, who worked together, and shared the proceeds of their efforts. They established Kibbutzim, and practised collective farming.

The Second Aliyah introduced a different kind of immigrant. Monied, middle class, these later arrivals were not idealistic, they weren't even religious, and they built secular, modern cities for themselves on the coast.

This schism expressed itself in internal Zionist politics. Old-school moderates like Chaim Weizmann favoured negotiation with the British in order to have their demands met, and were prepared to compromise. The radical Revisionists, led by Vladimir Jabotinsky, were not.

In a tragic precursor of latter-day events in Israeli politics, a leading figure for the moderates, Chaim Arlosoroff, was shot at point-blank range on a Tel Aviv beach by a Jewish extremist from the Revisionist movement. Although never charged, the man responsible for the murder was said to be a disciple of Jarbotinsky named Avraham Stavsky.

But despite the differences, the immigrants kept coming. The Fifth Aliyah saw the arrival of 175,000 Jews between 1932 and 1939. Many were from Poland, but 20% came from Germany, fearing the policies of Chancellor Hitler.

By 1936, the situation had not improved for the Arabs either, so they again tried the political route, forming the Arab Higher Committee to protest at their situation under the Mandate.

In October 1936, the Arab committee called a general strike. Three weeks later, British police opened fire on a demonstration, killing several people. The violence spread in the following months, threatening to send the country into anarchy.

The British, as ever, set up a commission of enquiry to look into the events, to be led by 70 year old Lord Peel.

After visiting the region, Lord Peel delivered a mammoth 404 page report in 1937 and made some hard-hitting recommendations.

Both Arabs and Jews were in the right, he said. The Jews had both historical and religious claims to be there, while the Arabs were equally entitled by virtue of their presence in the region for the previous 1300 years.

The best thing to do, he continued, would be to partition the land, giving some 20% of the country to the Jews, with which to make their homeland, and affording the area on the West Bank of the River Jordan to the Palestinians, where they could align with TransJordan.

It sounded, in terms of demographics, an equitable split, except that all of the best land had been awarded to the Jews. For the Arabs, this was an insult too far, and the Peel Report was rejected, and the guerrilla war resumed.

The Jews were more pragmatic, even if the fanatical Zionists still proposed rejection, preferring to hold out for all of Palestine.

At the 20th Zionist Congress, in Zurich from the 3rd to the 17th of August, 1937, Chaim Weizmann urged the conference to accept the report's recommendations. 'We would be fools not to', he said, 'even if what they have offered us is only the size of a tablecloth!'

The Party accepted the motion, if only as a basis for further negotiations.

The Arabs continued to agitate, and the Jews still purported to cooperate. Finally, the British attempted to settle the matter by issuing another White Paper in 1939.

Britain removed the Balfour Declaration, limited Jewish immigration, and forbade the transfer of Arab land into Jewish hands.

This was an unexpected victory for the Arabs, and a smack in the face for the Zionist cause. The Jewish people would refer to Britain as an enemy of Zion foryears to come.

Not that the British really cared. Their patience had run out, and they'd had to do something. They were stuck between the devil and the deep blue sea. Sometimes, it seemed, literally.

Attempts to find a way out of the mess had proved elusive, and the empire had grown frustrated at the fighting taking place between the two sides.

Besides, by the end of 1939, Britain had much more on her mind than the views of a few hundred thousand immigrants in the Middle East.

THE RISE OF NAZI GERMANY.

There have been many examples in world history of powerful warlords and their destructive forces. Indeed, many have appeared in this story. From Alexander the Great to Julius Caesar, Genghis Khan, and Tamburlane. For all the devastation wrought, you have to admire their courage and indefatigability. They were men of iron. Some had a sense of nobility, and admired art, beauty, and philosophy.

Another despot now enters the picture. An evil shit named Adolf Hitler.

Hitler came to power on the back of a tide of fascism during a great economic depression, for which he blamed the Jews. The starving people of Germany needed a scapegoat, and Hitler's rhetoric won the day.

The government at that time thought to placate Adolf and his National Socialist, hence the term 'Nazi', Party by appointing Hitler to the role of Chancellor. They hoped that would be the extent of his ambition, and that they could contain him from that position. Instead, they had let the fox into the chicken coop. Hitler's supporters saw the appointment as vindication of all they had fought for. Their man was now in one of the most important seats in government, and they weren't about to stop there.

Brigades of Hitler's storm-troopers marched down the main streets in awesome displays of their strength and discipline.

The party began its inexorable rise. The people were impressed. Opposition was crushed underfoot. The Communist Party were sworn enemies of the Nazis. Both were vying for control in 1933, but not content to let the voting public decide, Hitler had plans of his own to seize power.

The Reichstag was the seat of government, much like Britain's Houses of Parliament. It was a magnificent building worthy of its responsibility. Georges Simenon, the prolific Belgian writer, creator of the Maigret detective series, was in the middle of a world tour and, in his capacity as foreign correspondent, was submitting articles to the Paris edition of Time magazine.

While in Berlin, Simenon was invited to a clandestine meeting of senior Communist Party officials. He was asked if he would do them a great service. They had information that the Nazis were about to burn down the Reichstag and blame it on the Communists, thereby ending all opposition to Hitler.

If Simenon could write an article explaining what the Nazis were proposing to do, it might prevent them carrying out the act.

So the piece was written and submitted it to the magazine. When Time was published the following week, there was no sign of it. Two days later, the Reichstag burned down, the Communists were blamed by Hitler's propaganda machine, and the Party leaders were arrested or run out of the country, if not killed.

When Georges asked his editor why the article hadn't been printed, he was told that they had declined to include it in case nothing had then happened, in which case it would have appeared an unnecessary slur on a foreign power.

With that one act of arson, all opposition crumbled, and Germany was Hitler's for the taking.

The Chancellor's anti-Jewish rhetoric continued, and those that read the signs correctly began to emigrate, either east to Poland, or to Palestine or America if they could.

Those that remained were ordered to register with their local police station, so that the Nazis would know where to find them when the time came. They were forced to wear an identification badge that marked them out as Jews.

In the streets, people shunned them. Shops put signs up barring them from entry: 'No dogs, no Jews'.

They were being dehumanised. It was time to go but, by 1939, this was no longer possible. Earlier, Hitler had been happy for the Jews to leave Germany, but just as he was trying to kick them out, the British and their latest White Paper refused them entry to Palestine, where many wished to resettle. And then it was too late. Germany annexed Austria, and then invaded Poland. A peace treaty Britain had signed with Herr Hitler was not worth the paper it was written on.

The Nazis had outgrown their national borders, and World War 2 had begun.

Forming an axis of evil with Italy, by 1941 the small state of Germany was at war with Great Britain, the United States of America, and with Russia. But while occupying mainland Europe, attempting to invade England, and fighting Russia in the east and the Allies in North Africa, Hitler still found time to implement the most despicable genocide ever witnessed.

During the course of the Second World War, as many as six million Jews perished in the Nazi death camps, either worked to the bone or gassed to death and turned into soap.

The Secret Police arrested Jews in their host countries in Europe and shipped them by train, hundreds of miles or more, to meet their excruciating end.

For example, twenty trains left Belgium for Auschwitz, with the passengers herded into cattle carts. By this point, many knew the fate that would befall them. They were going to their deaths, and therefore many tried to escape. Some succeeded.

The last train to arrive contained 1400 people. Of these, 250 were ushered into the concentration camp itself. These were the strongest, the best looking. People that the Germans may have had use for after the war. That is, if they survived the conditions in the camp itself, the starvation and the brutality of the guards.

The remainder, 1150 persons, were taken straight to the gas chambers. They were being taken 'for delousing', claimed the soldiers. This was a lie.

Meanwhile, the Allies were doing all they could to win the war. At El Alamein in North Africa, in October, 1942, one of the most decisive battles of the entire conflict took place. Indeed, it was a turning point in the whole war.

Within seven months, the Germans were removed from North Africa and the Middle East, and Palestine was at peace. It became a staging post for the British army, who operated out of Jerusalem.

From then on, the war swung in the Allies favour. The Russians began to overwhelm the Nazis in the battle for Stalingrad and, little by little, the U.S. and British forces regained a foothold in mainland Europe.

Jewish sympathisers urged the Western leaders to bomb the death camps and put them out of action before more people could be exterminated. Sadly for them, the war was a targeted campaign, and there was no room for tangential operations.

The best that could be managed was a radio address by President Roosevelt, which reached the Axis soldiers. He warned them that after the war, which was drawing to a close, they would be held accountable for their actions in the extermination programme.

Remarkably, death camp survivors claimed there was a noticeable improvement in their treatment by the Nazi guards after the announcement. If only the statement had come sooner.

Bizarrely, many Jews blamed Britain for their treatment under the Nazis. By preventing their entry to Palestine before the war, they had caused many to stay and suffer the horrors of the concentration camps. Also, the British Mandate still stood in the way of the establishment of a Jewish nation state.

There were 27,000 Palestinian Jews fighting with the Allies in the Second World War, along with 12,000 Palestinian Arabs. Chaim Weizmann for the Zionists claimed the ambiguity of the position could be explained when he stated 'We will fight the war as if there is no White Paper, and we will fight the White Paper as if there is no war.'

For many Jews though, this was not enough, and in Cairo in November of 1944, Lord Moyne, the British Minister of State for the Region, was killed by Jewish extremists.

Even Winston Churchill, no friend of the Arabs and an affirmed pro-Zionist, lost all patience with the Jews. But, by the war's end, when the world saw for itself exactly how they had suffered, there was a great outpouring of sympathy.

The new American President, Harry S. Truman, insisted Britain repeal the White Paper and allow 100,000 Jews to enter Palestine with immediate effect, and an Anglo-American commission of inquiry was set up to look into the issue.

The Zionists were almost home.

THE AFTERMATH OF WORLD WAR TWO.

Ernest Bevin, the British Foreign Secretary, announced the findings of the Anglo-American report in April 1946. He wished to continue with the Mandate and the terms of the 1939 White Paper, while agreeing to the conditions requested by the Americans of limited Jewish entry into Palestine and the reintroduction of the sale of Arab lands.

But this wasn't acceptable to either side in the disputed region, and the British were again squeezed between the wishes of both parties.

After all they had endured in the Second World War, the Zionists were in no mood for compromise, and extremist factions, namely the Irgun and the Stern Gang, began a concerted campaign of targeting British soldiers and officials.

Under the leadership of Menachem Begin, the Irgun, two of whose members had been responsible for the killing of Lord Moyne in Cairo, attacked the King David hotel in Jerusalem, the headquarters of the British army in Palestine.

Following months of planning, a band of guerrillas made their way into the basement of the hotel through the kitchens, which they had identified as a weak point in the fortified building.

After tying up the catering staff and holding them hostage, the terrorists moved their cache of bombs, hidden in milk churns, to the supporting columns of the hotel.

The detonations that followed destroyed much of the King David complex and killed dozens of people in the process, and ushered in the last days of the Mandate.

Brutalized by their treatment under the Germans in the death camps, the Jewish nationalists had more stomach for the fight than their occupiers did. After capturing and killing two British officers, the Irgun informed the army where they could be found.

The British were warned that there were booby-traps nearby.

133

Approaching with caution the two men left hanging grotesquely from a tree, no bombs could be found in the vicinity.

As they cut the men down, the explosives, which had been hidden inside the dead men's bodies, were detonated causing further casualties.

The British were left in no doubt as to the seriousness of the enemy they were fighting.

The Jewish brigades that had fought alongside the Allies in the Second World War now turned their weapons on their former comrades.

Exasperated, in February 1947, Britain turned the problem over to the United Nations, the successor to the League of Nations.

In August of that year, a special commission of the United Nations on Palestine voted by 33 to 13 in favour of partitioning Palestine into both Jewish and Arab states.

The thirteen nations to vote against the idea included the Arab lands of Egypt, Syria, Lebanon, Iraq, Saudi Arabia, and the Yemen. They were joined by four Muslim states: Pakistan, Iran, Afghanistan and Turkey.

Jerusalem was to remain under international control. The recommendation was accepted as Resolution 181 of the United Nations assembly on 29th of November, 1947.

At the time, there were 1.25 million Arabs in Palestine and half as many Jews. The partition allowed for 55% of the country to become Jewish territory, although they owned only 8% of the land at that point.

David Ben-Gurion, the head of the Jewish Agency and soon to be the first Prime Minister of Israel, called the area 'A pitifully small slice of territory.'

True, their domain included much of the Negev desert, but it also included almost the entire Mediterranean coastal region and, at 55% of the entire country, could scarcely be called pitifully small.

Britain announced that it would end its mandate for Palestine on the 15th of May 1948, at which point the partition would come into effect.

The decision led to jubilant scenes from the Jewish community, and dismay, leading to violence, from the Arabs.

On 30th November 1947, a band of settlers were attacked with seven of them killed. Over the next four months, almost 900 Jews in total met their deaths as the Arabs reacted to the imminent division of their homeland and the loss of more then half of their territory.

The Zionists themselves were no angels. In Haifa, close to Tel Aviv on the coast, deep within the new Jewish territory, Arabs were attacked in their homes with the intention, as one of the leaders of the Jewish onslaught, Amichai Paglin, proclaimed 'to break the spirit of the enemy troops and cause chaos amongst the civilian population in order to create a mass flight.'

Hostilities between the two sworn enemies were well under way. They would remain so up until partition, and a long, long way beyond.

THE JEWISH STATE.

The roads were dangerous. Jew fought Arab. Arab fought Jew. Shots were fired in both directions, into houses and cafes. Ambush was the norm.

At the end of March, 1948, Operation Nachshon became the first Jewish offensive assault manoeuvre, with the aim of opening supply lines to Jerusalem, which had been surrounded by hostile forces.

David Ben-Gurion, a tiny man who loomed large in Israeli politics, was a determined Zionist who lived and breathed the ideology and had moved to Palestine with earlier settlers.

On April 6th, Ben-Gurion, as the nominal leader, convened a meeting of the Zionist General Council to discuss proposals for the new state's constitution. They would need a central authority to organise the economy and build infrastructure. They also needed an army, but they would not restrict themselves to defence tactics. They resolved to come out fighting and attack their enemy wherever they could be found.

The Council formed a National Assembly consisting of thirteen members who would act as the inaugural, provisional government. They would begin their duties on the 15th of May, taking over from the British.

Friday, 14th of May, early morning, the group of thirteen met to discuss the terms of their Declaration of Independence, which would be delivered at four o'clock that afternoon.

They had already chosen a flag for the new country: Blue and White, with a Star of David in the centre. Now, all they needed were some words to define their nation to be delivered by the Prime Minister in a manner that would inspire their people.

At this extraordinary meeting, featuring among others Golda Meir, there was even the question of what to call this emerging nation state. 'Jewish Palestine' was one option.

Meanwhile, in New York, the General Assembly of the United Nations were having a meeting of their own, to debate a proposal to place the whole of Palestine, not just Jerusalem, under international trust. It was now or never for the Zionists.

At the Tel Aviv Museum at the appointed hour on the day that the Palestinians refer to as 'The Catastrophe', David Ben-Gurion stood on a dais, beneath a photograph of Theodor Herzl, and made a 1027 word announcement.

He declared the independence of the new country, provided for state legislation, no limit on entry for Jewish immigrants, and for self-government.

David Ben-Gurion concluded by saying, 'We members of the National Council, representing the Jewish people in Palestine and the Zionist movement of the world, by virtue of the natural and historical right of the Jewish people and the resolution of the General Assembly of the United Nations, hereby proclaim the establishment of a Jewish nation in Palestine to be called the state of Israel.'

He then held out the hand of friendship to Arab neighbours. After 2000 years in exile, the state of Israel was reborn.

AL NAKBAH.

The state of Israel was reborn on the 14th of May, 1948, and immediately attacked by all its neighbours.

Like a virus beset by anti-bodies, the Arab nations did not take kindly to the stranger in their midst.

The surrounding countries attempted to wipe Israel off the map before it could settle into permanence.

The Haganah, the Israeli defence league, was well trained, armed to the teeth, and determined. They would need to be, for their enemy was enraged by their presence in the region, and was intent on strangling the state at birth.

Israel had to repel the Arab invasion while simultaneously evicting the native non-Jewish population in order to seize the land for themselves.

The creation of Israel, and the subsequent expulsion of the Arab residents, is known to the Palestinians as 'Al Nakbah', the Catastrophe.

The Jews had suffered so much in the past, yet they set about ethnically cleansing towns and villages with a relish that is hard to understand.

As the Israelites began to spread out across the newly-created state, isolated Jewish settlements were subject to attack by Arabs, and in all some 6000 Jews were killed over the coming months in the War of Independence.

The Jewish population rose to 700,000, a figure that was increasing all the time. Immigrants were flocking to the new state to shore up its presence, and within two years there would be a million and a half Jews living in Israel.

The Arabs, meanwhile, were facing a torrid time. Those caught on the Jewish side of the divide were the victims of a targeted campaign to drive them out.

Villages would be surrounded on three sides and pounded by artillery. As the military closed in, the residents would escape through the gap left open to them, leaving the town uninhabited.

Those that remained risked death. Those that ran thought their exodus temporary, and that they would return in a short time.

Three quarters of a million Palestinians, 90% of the Arab population in the state of Israel, chose to leave at this point.

They were housed in the neighbouring countries of Lebanon, Syria, and Jordan. They lived in refugee camps, in tents provided through charitable donations and supervised by the United Nations.

Fierce fighting took place between the regular armies of the combatants. Despite what appeared to be overwhelming odds in favour of the Arabs in terms of numbers, the reality was something different.

The Haganah, an experienced military outfit, became the official army of the new state of Israel, and would soon have 60,000 well-trained soldiers in its ranks.

In opposition was a complacent and ill-ordered enemy made up of four different armies, none of whom were working closely with their allies.

As a result of this disorganisation, Israel was able to hold all of the territory awarded to it under the Mandate, 55% of Palestine, and to seize vast tracts of foreign territory. After the initial conflict, Israel held almost 80% of Palestine, and had succeeded in expelling most of the Arabs from within the borders that it had inherited.

The Israelis would call the shots, as the Jewish state smashed the opposition. In the wake of the crushing defeat, the Arab nations queued to sign armistice agreements with the new power in the region.

The Egyptians signed a peace agreement on 24th February, 1949. Lebanon signed soon afterwards on March 23rd. Jordan put pen to paper on the 3rd of April, and Syria followed suit on July 29th. Only Iraq refused to come to terms with Israel.

Following their stunning victory against the combined Arab armies, and the scare tactics that drove many civilians into neighbouring countries and the UN refugee camps, the Israelis bulldozed many of the deserted villages as soon as they became empty, removing all traces of the former inhabitants, and making sure that there was nothing left for the Arabs to return to.

A programme was instigated by the Israeli government to give Hebrew names to the places, mountains, and road of the region, to make the country appear more Jewish. By adopting biblical terms for these places, it would also create a sense of historical occupancy and cement the Israeli presence.

To control the crisis that had landed at the door of the United Nations, a new agency was created, the United Nations Welfare and Relief Agency (UNWRA) in 1949 to provide shelter through the harsh winter for the suffering refugees. Resolution 194 of the UN Council called for the right of return for those exiled.

The state of Israel was formally recognised and accepted into the UN itself on the 11th of May, 1949, and then refused to fulfil its commitments under the charter. There would be no right of return for exiled Palestinians. Not then, not ever.

Al Nakbah continues to haunt the Arabs to the present day.

Israel had survived the Arab advance and seized territory for the Jewish population. As their actions in villages like Deir Yassin, Tantura, and Haifa had shown, they would ensure their existence by any means necessary.

Despite the best efforts of their hostile neighbours, the infant state was here to stay.

THE ARAB EXODUS.

There is a museum in the town of Matchouk in Lebanon that holds a store of memorabilia from a place that no longer exists: Palestine.

The euphoria that greeted the announcement to create a home for the Jewish people to be called Israel was also the catalyst for a wave of ethnic cleansing that set neighbour against neighbour.

Protected by the passage of time, it is easy to read accounts of Barbarians massacring whole villages, or Romans throwing Christians to lions. We are immune to the suffering because it all happened so very long ago.

But when you can read testimony of survivors of massacres who, luckily, are still alive today, it makes it seem much more real, and much more horrific for it.

It would be nice to think that we have learned a thing or two since we first began to walk upright and communicate in more than a series of grunts. Civilisation, I think, is the correct word for the supposed advances mankind has made in its evolution.

It is strange then, that when reviewing the events of little more than a half century ago, civilised is not the word that springs to mind.

Early in 1948, the Haganah began to take the fight to the Arabs, employing scare tactics and, in the case of the Stern Gang, wholesale slaughter.

On the 10th of May, as an example of the fate that would befall any Arab who chose to stay in Jewish Palestine, 250 men, women, and children were butchered in the village of Deir Yassin in a merciless atrocity that would stain Israel's reputation.

Many Palestinians, who had lived in the same place for generations, fled to the safety of neighbouring Arab lands.

To maintain the momentum, the Israelis began bombing villages that were still inhabited, making it virtually impossible for anyone with any sense to remain.

Samira Daou was five years old and lived in the village of Kafr Bir'im when the planes started dropping their deadly payload. Their next door neighbour's home was destroyed. Her father decided enough was enough and moved the family to Southern Lebanon. He took a month's leave from his job, where he worked for a Jewish butcher, and borrowed his boss' van for the trip. In their haste, they left all of their belongings behind, thinking they'd be back soon.

The butcher's van came in handy. The Hebrew writing on the side prevented the Israeli planes overhead from blowing them to bits. The roads were already littered with burning cars and smouldering corpses.

The family made it safely across the border and moved in with relatives. They awaited their chance to return, but it never came.

Their village was completely destroyed from the air, the ruins of every house were then bulldozed, contents and all, and if anyone had tried to go back to Kafr Bir'im, they would not have found it.

Not that many were likely to try. Anyone attempting to cross the border back into their homeland, to check on their property, or their orchards, or to maybe retrieve some of their possessions to make life a little more comfortable, was liable to be shot and denounced as a terrorist attempting to infiltrate the state of Israel.

Thus, the people of Palestine became refugees. There would be no right of return, and their land would be shared amongst new Jewish settlements, to be given to Polish, Russian, and American immigrants.

Arab land deeds, property ownership papers, even the front door key, were all now worthless. Just like, it would seem, the expelled and their rights.

Not that the Israelis were admitting to any mandatory expulsions. Those that chose to leave had done so voluntarily. It was true that those who withstood the onslaught inherited basic rights when the dust settled and the fighting stopped, but those that had fled had done so in terror. They were in genuine fear for their lives, and with good cause. To stay was tantamount to suicide. Better to run for it, or at least that was how it seemed to most at the time, until the war was over.

142

Jaffa, on the Mediterranean coast close to Tel Aviv, was home to a large Arab community. On 25th April 1948, the Irgun began firing grenades into the city, killing and injuring scores of civilians.

One family, the Humani's, decided to leave when the mortars began landing close to their home. They told the children that they were all going on holiday to escape the bombardment, and that they would be gone for one month. They headed for Lebanon, and never went back.

But not everyone left. Although three quarters of Jaffa's population fled in terror, twenty thousand Arabs decided to sit it out.

When the city surrendered, the Irgun commanders proposed putting the remaining Arabs on buses and shipping them out of the country, but Menachem Begin ordered that they be allowed to remain.

'If they did not leave with their brothers', Begin said, 'then let them live in peace with us.'

More than 700,000 Palestinians had already run for their lives, losing everything they owned in the process. Thousands more had been killed.

The President of the infant state of Israel, David Ben-Gurion, was puzzled by the exodus. His diary entry for the 18th of May 1948 read 'I couldn't understand it. Why did everybody leave?'

Why, indeed.

THE ALTALENA AFFAIR.

Menachem Begin was head of the Irgun. His guerrilla outfit, terrorists by any other name, were a thorn in the side of the British in the last days of the Mandate.

In a campaign designed to harass and assassinate British soldiers, Begin was public enemy number one. He was described by the Chief of Police as a murderous thug.

After the bombing of the King David hotel in the struggle for the liberation of Palestine, the army raided Begin's home, hoping to capture him. The charismatic rebel leader evaded arrest. He would have faced a firing squad if caught, but he remained hidden in a special compartment he had built in his house and he avoided detection, despite being in the same room as his would-be captors.

With the establishment of the state of Israel, there was no longer the need for private militias, and Irgun members were drafted into the newly-formed Israeli Defence Force, the army of government.

But Begin continued to operate on his own terms and outside of the remit of the authorities.

When a truce was declared in the fighting between the Arabs and Israelis, both parties to the conflict took the opportunity to regroup, and to reorganise themselves for when the battle inevitably resumed.

The Altalena was a 5000 ton ship, loaded with arms destined for the Israeli army. The Irgun were tasked to do the gun-run, and 900 men took part in the operation to bring 250 machine guns and 5000 rifles and ammunition to the IDF.

Begin had other ideas though, and instructed his men to commandeer a fifth of all the weapons to the stores of his private militia.

When the Prime Minister, David Ben-Gurion, got wind of the plan, he sent his own regular forces to the ship, which lay moored off the coast in an effort to avoid detection from UN truce-enforcers.

In the ensuing gun battle, two IDF soldiers and six Irgun volunteers were killed, in a test of strength between the state and its guerrilla fighters.

The Altalena moved closer to shore, just off the coast of Tel Aviv, hoping to garner support from the Jewish public.

Ben-Gurion saw the event as a challenge to his authority and decided to come down hard on those who would turn Israel into a rogue state.

In a test of the legitimacy of his government, Ben-Gurion ordered his troops on shore to open fire on the ship.

One cannon ball scored a direct hit, and the Altalena caught fire, listed in the water, and then sank. Menachem Begin was the last to abandon ship, where he swam to shore and ordered his men, now fighting their fellow Jews on the beach, to desist.

One of those who never made it out alive was Avraham Stavsky, the man believed responsible for the murder of Chaim Arlosoroff fifteen years earlier.

Stavsky made it off the boat but he was killed in the ensuing battle. He died on the beach at Tel Aviv where, on the same date and in the exact same spot, he had assassinated the moderate leader.

Menachem Begin had promoted the Irgun as the architects of the overthrow of the British, so to many Jews the regular forces came to be viewed as traitors for tackling them. Amongst the government forces that day was Commander Yitzak Rabin. For Rabin, who would one day become Prime Minister of Israel, this taint would haunt him down the years and have tragic consequences later in life.

The Altalena affair allowed the new state of Israel to exert its authority and show the wider world that there was law and order in the land.

The government had prevented a civil war, and despite the sight of Jew fighting Jew, the country was able to regroup. They could concentrate on establishing their presence in the region. For that, and despite the uneasy truce, guns like those on board the Altalena would be required.

THE BERNADOTTE PLAN.

Within days of the end of the Mandate, with the state of Israel under attack, and atrocities being perpetrated by both Jews and Arabs, the UN appointed a mediator to find an alternative to the partition plan.

Count Folke Bernadotte, a member of the Swiss Royal family, was chosen for the difficult task.

On 28th of June, 1948, Bernadotte presented his proposal to the two sides. To reflect the situation on the ground, he suggested that the areas allotted to each region be amended.

The Israelis had made huge gains in the Galilee area, while the Arabs held a line that shut the Israelis out of the Negev desert that had been within their domain.

Bernadotte proposed to make this arrangement permanent in a land trade-off. Palestine would then be annexed to Jordan to form TransJordan. Jerusalem would fall within Arab territory, but would remain open to Jews and the international community, with the religious rights of every faith protected.

The response to the plan was outrage. For the Arabs, there was no mention of a state called Palestine. Arab nationalism had grown strong in the struggle with the Israelis, and now there would no longer be a region called Palestine. It would cease to exist, to be consumed within TransJordan.

The Israelis were also at odds with Bernadotte's recommendations, for it failed to mention that they had created a state for themselves, and did not recognise Israel as an independent nation. It also relieved the Jews of authority for Jerusalem, and this was beyond the pale.

Both parties rejected the plan, and the best Bernadotte could hope to achieve was a continuation of the truce. Even there, he would have no success.

Fighting resumed on the 9th of July. The Israelis had recruited more men into their ranks, and had been busy re-arming for the next stage in the conflict.

They continued to conquer towns and villages in the area mandated to Palestine.

When the UN introduced a resolution on the 15th of July calling for an end to the fighting, both sides finally agreed to lay down their weapons.

In the ensuing peace, Bernadotte tried again to find a way out of the mess created by the partition. This time, he made specific mention of the state of Israel, confirmed its existence as a 'living and vigorous reality', and proposed Jerusalem be placed under UN control.

With regard to the Palestinians, the Count proposed consultation between the native Arabs and the Arab League in order to identify how to assimilate them with their neighbouring Arab countries. He still favoured amalgamation with Jordan.

Bernadotte's final point called for compensation for those Arabs displaced by Israel. The UN were already calling for the right of return for the refugees, but Israel was stalling. The second plan put forward by the Count called for remuneration for those who either chose not to, or weren't allowed to, return.

On the 17th of September in Cairo, while travelling in a convoy of three clearly marked UN vehicles, a jeep pulled in front of the first car, three members of an extremist Jewish group got out and, at point blank range, in a hail of bullets, they shot Count Bernadotte dead.

The man believed to have fired the fatal shots, Yehoshua Cohen, was later appointed David Ben-Gurion's personal bodyguard.

But Bernadotte did not die in vain. His proposals were adopted by the UN as the core of their plan for the region. There would be a right of return for the refugees, international control over Jerusalem, and equitable partition of the land between the two host communities.

These tenets became the guidelines for a peace conference held in Switzerland in April of 1949. Israel agreed to discuss the recommendations, and on this understanding, the United Nations invited the new nation into its General Assembly on the 11th of May.

The next day, Israel, now a recognised nation state, refused to consider Arab repatriation. The process of destroying Arab villages continued unabated and Jewish settlements would be built on the very same spot.

Why should the Arabs be allowed to return? There was nothing left that belonged to them. Not a trace.

THE ARAB INVASION.

Within hours of Ben-Gurion's statement about the creation of Israel, the Arab League were preparing to enter Palestine in order to 're-establish peace' and, according to the Egyptian government, 'to restore security and order and put an end to the massacres perpetrated by terrorist Zionist gangs against the Arabs and against humanity.'

Thirty four villages had been attacked by the Stern Gang and the Irgun, and heinous crimes had been committed. Al-Abbasiyya, Beit Daras, Bir Al-Saba, Al-Kabri, Haifa, Qisarya, and many other places suffered similar atrocities to that carried out at Deir Yassin.

In all, 13000 Palestinians were killed and 737,166 people were forcibly evicted from their homes. The Arab populations of Acre, Jaffa, Lydda, Al-Majdal, Al Ramla, Safad, and Tiberius were ethnically cleansed.

At one minute past midnight, on the day that Israel came into existence, the Arab armies began moving into Palestine.

As agreed between the Arab governments, the joint Syrian and Lebanese forces would attack the northern flank, the eastern front would be the preserve of the Iraqi and Jordanians, while the united Egyptian, Saudi Arabian, and Yemenites would tackle the south.

Prayers were said in mosques across the region calling for success in the 'holy war for the liberation of the Holy Land'.

At dawn on the 15th of May, two Egyptian columns advanced into Palestine along the coast road and occupied Gaza. They encountered resistance at the fortified Jewish settlement of El Dangoor, which they eventually overcame before putting the town to the torch.

Egyptian forces entered the city of Gaza early in the evening, where they regrouped ready for the next phase in the operation.

Meanwhile, the Egyptian air force bombed Tel Aviv, destroying six aircraft on the ground and a runway and other airport installations belonging to the Israeli Defence Force, and the Jewish communities at Beit Hanon and Biron Ishak were also attacked from the air.

The Iraqis crossed the River Jordan at Naharayin, ten miles south of the Sea of Galilee. The Jordanians did the same further south to occupy Jericho.

In the north, the Syrians claimed to have driven the Jews out of three settlements, and to have shot down one enemy plane, while the Israelis claimed to have killed 200 Arabs in fighting at Malakir village close to the Lebanese border.

The Egyptians planned to secure a line from Majdal to Hebron before linking up with Jordanian forces and mounting a joint expeditionary force deep into Jewish territory.

Two sections of the Arab League entered the Old City of Jerusalem, a Hebrew stronghold, placing artillery at strategic positions before commencing a mortar bombardment.

At Acre, the Jews captured 4000 Arab soldiers, while they also claimed to have drowned 500 Iraqi infantrymen by opening up a dam near Daganya.

In Tel Aviv, the Egyptian air force continued its bombing raids, with civilians being shot down in the street, while a bus station suffered a direct hit which killed 41 people and left another 60 wounded.

The airfield was also targeted, with hangars and the hastily repaired runway being struck again. All of the Arab aircraft returned to Cairo unscathed.

On the 19th of May, David Ben-Gurion, Prime Minister of Israel, informed the provisional government, 'At the moment, the enemy controls the air. Everybody here knows what that means for Tel Aviv. Control of the air gives the enemy a considerable advantage, but our people are not panicking. There are grounds for considering that this situation will not go on for long.'

Fighting continued in Jerusalem, with sniper fire and ordinance from armoured cars whizzing around. The Jews were said to be 'fleeing in panic, with heavy losses in the Old City.'

The Haganah admitted that the Arabs had captured the Sheikh Jarrah area of the city, with a Jewish contingent forced to take refuge in the Hebrew university and Hadassah hospital.

The Secretary General of the Arab League stated that the purpose of the invasion was not merely to defend the Palestinians but to prevent the establishment of a Zionist state.

Egyptian troops occupied Beersheba after meeting fierce resistance, and also captured the settler town of Deir Senid after ten hours of bitter fighting.

On the road to Nablus, a single Israeli armoured car fired rounds at a convoy of seven Arab army vehicles and put them to flight.

At Neve Yaacov, five miles north of Jerusalem, Jewish settlers abandoned the town after being overrun by Arab forces. Four of the Settlers were killed and seventeen were injured.

The Egyptians captured the village of Ramat Rahel and inflicted casualties there, before going on to take the strategic objective of Majdal, thirty miles from Tel Aviv.

In Jerusalem, Israeli forces were surrounded, and artillery was falling into the Jewish enclaves.

The US Consul-General, Mr.Wasson, was in the Old City trying to broker a truce between the two sides as the situation in the Holy City deteriorated. While heading to a meeting to discuss the issue, he was caught up in the melee and shot dead.

At the United Nations, the Security Council demanded a cease-fire to begin at midday on the 27th May. The Arab League issued a statement of rejection, claiming it was the Zionists who were the aggressors for declaring their independence within Arab territory. If the Arab governments failed to react to this provocation, public opinion would oust them from power and replace them with a leadership that would engage the Jews in war, so the Arabs had no choice but to confront this alien entity.

The fighting continued. After intensive artillery bombardment, the village of Isdud, north of Majdal was captured by the Egyptians. They were now within twenty miles of Tel Aviv.

In Jerusalem, the Jews in the Old City finally surrendered, having been under siege for the past six months, and under direct attack for two weeks, they were suffering from food shortages and dehydration, they were completely surrounded, and the choice was to surrender or die.

350 Israeli prisoners were taken to Jordan, and 140 wounded were taken to hospital in the Old City.

In another part of town, the only interruption to the shelling came when the Arab fighters stopped for lunch. Once they had eaten, they resumed the pounding of the university, where Jewish mortar bombs had earlier been fired in the direction of the Legion.

The UN continued to call for a four week truce, and with both sides now entrenched in their own territories, with the Jews controlling Galilee and the coast as far as Isdud, and the Arabs in the Negev and the inland regions, the two parties indicated their willingness to stand down.

The Israeli Prime Minister had told his parliament earlier that the Arab plan to invade from the north, south, and east had been pricked like a bubble. 'We now control more territory than we did three weeks ago, but we cannot ignore the heavy losses we have suffered.'

On June 9th, the ill-fated Count Bernadotte had been able to announce that both Israel and the Arabs had unconditionally accepted the terms of a four week truce and that they would work towards 'An equitable and peaceful solution to the Palestine problem'.

After all the bloodshed of the past few weeks, things, finally, could be said to be looking up.

LOOKING UP?

One day, you're living in Palestine. The next, the land beneath you has been renamed Israel and, as an Arab, you're no longer welcome. This despite the fact your family has lived in the area for hundreds of years, the house has been yours for generations, and you have toiled the land since time immemorial.

Now, you're trespassing. If you stay here, you could be killed. If you flee, you will never be allowed back.

If you're Jewish, even if you've never set foot in the Middle East; you may be Russian, American, from any corner of the world you care to name, then come right on in and make yourself at home.

The Absentee Property Law was instigated on 14th March 1950 and allowed for the new state to confiscate all land belonging to the refugees, almost three quarters of a million of them. That's a lot of acreage.

The Law of Return, meaning a return after 2000 years in exile, allowed for unlimited Jewish entry into Israel. There were no shortage of tenants for the properties vacated in haste, and terror. There was no right of return for the Palestinians.

For the Arabs who braved the Israeli onslaught, they were granted citizenship of the new state under the Registration of Residents Act of 1949. However, they were placed under military administration and would remain so until 1966.

Following the war for independence, the Israelis occupied a total of 78% of the former state of Palestine, but the inhabitants of the remaining 22% would not give up without a fight.

In retaliation for Deir Yassin, Arabs killed fifty Jewish fighters at Gush Etzion after they had surrendered.

The Israeli Defence Force committed atrocities in the villages of Eilabun, Saliba, Safsaf, Jish, Hule, B'na, Deir el Assad, and Arab al-Mawassa.

153

The Jewish town of Tirat Yehuda was attacked with one woman and two children slain. In response, Unit 101 of the IDF, under the command of a young, committed Zionist named Ariel Sharon, tracked the assailants to the village of Qibya, where they killed 69 civilians and levelled the buildings.

Unit 101 had earlier attacked the town al-Bureig in the Gaza Strip and slaughtered twenty innocent people, and attracted criticism for its heavy-handed tactics.

Between January and May of 1953, 100 Israelis died in raids by Palestinian guerrillas. In the same period, 295 Arabs were killed, the majority of whom were civilians.

In violation of the Israel-Egypt Armistice Agreement, the IDF forced the evacuation of almost 3000 Arab villagers from the town of Faluja.

For the first time, in April 1953, Arab terrorists attempted to attack Israel along its Mediterranean coast, but one boat was captured and another escaped in the unsuccessful raid.

Eleven Jewish people died when a bus was ambushed between Eilat and Tel Aviv. Hand grenade and shooting attacks were common on the roads. Nobody was safe in their homes either. Even the synagogues were no refuge.

The Arabs were angry. No justice, no peace, could well have served as their battle cry.

But in terms of dishing out violence, of getting their retaliation in first, the Israelis were no slouches.

Led by military men; fervent and ruthless generals such as Rafael Eitan, Ariel Sharon, and Moshe Dayan, Israel was prepared and capable of looking after itself.

THE GENERALS.

Rafael Eitan was a soldier's soldier. He would one day rise to become Chief of Staff to the Israeli government, appointed by the terrorist turned politician Menachem Begin.

Eitan was born in Tel Adashim in Palestine in 1929 to Zionist settlers of Russian origin. At sixteen years of age, he joined the commando brigade of the Haganah, and from there he rose through the ranks.

He led a platoon of troops in the battle for Jerusalem in 1948 when he was a sergeant, and he soon led his own battalion of paratroopers in the campaign for Sinai. He was dropped behind enemy lines just east of the Mitla Pass, an important passageway through the mountains in the desert peninsula.

A bold field commander, Eitan was a strict disciplinarian who was not one to suffer fools. He was fiercely anti-Arab, referring to the Palestinians as cockroaches.

This attitude would later bring an end to his military career, when he was held responsible, along with Ariel Sharon, for the atrocities committed at the Sabra and Shatilla refugee camps.

Rafael Eitan lost his two sons in tragic circumstances. One died from leukaemia aged ten. Another, an airforce pilot, was killed in a training accident.

According to Eitan's own later obituary in the Independent newspaper, when a friend came to the general's house to pay his respects and offer condolences and shed a few tears for Rafael's son, the stone-faced old soldier gave his friend a hard stare and said 'No-one cries in this house.'

Ariel Sharon was born in the Jewish Settlement of Moshav Kfar Malal in Palestine in 1928 and joined the Haganah when he was fourteen years old, prior to the creation of the state in 1948. With the formation of the Israeli Defence Force,

Sharon was opted into the ranks of the regular army, where his aptitude and commitment earned him the trust of his superiors.

He was wounded at Latrun in the War of Independence when his unit were heavily mortared by a battalion of professional infantrymen from Jordan's Arab Legion in one of Israel's worst defeats of the whole war. 15 of the 35 men with Sharon were killed, and Ariel himself took two bullets.

In 1953, Sharon founded Unit 101, later renamed T'zanhamin Brigade, a cross-border raiding party exacting punishment on Arab communities suspected of housing guerrillas. They quickly earned a name for themselves for their sheer ruthlessness and zeal for their work.

At El-Bureig, a Palestinian refugee camp near Gaza, Sharon's units threw bombs through the windows of the makeshift homes and, as the people fled in terror, they were shot down with small arms fire and automatic weapons.

Then came the attack at Qibya in the West Bank. There, Unit 101 fired at the houses to force the villagers to remain indoors. Bombs were then thrown inside, bringing the roof down on top of the residents. 600 kilograms of explosive were used to raze 45 houses. 69 people died, half of them women and children.

Ariel Sharon later claimed that he believed all the houses were empty when he destroyed them. He did not say why he had blown them up in the first place, nor did he apologise for the deaths of the innocent civilians.

Sharon's men were said to be tasked with revenge attacks for any Palestinian assault committed against a Jewish person. Others claimed the unit's role was to instil terror into the Palestinian community to cause them to flee and free up the land for Jewish immigration and settlement.

Whatever it was, Sharon obviously excelled at it, and by the mid-1960's, the former Haganah volunteer was a Major-General in the Israeli army.

As Menachem Begin, former terrorist leader and the Prime Minister of Israel once said, 'Sharon is a brilliant general, but a very vicious man.'

Moshe Dayan, the ubiquitous general with the eye-patch, was the first child to be born on a Jewish kibbutz, in Deganya Alef, Palestine, close to the Sea of Galilee in 1928. His parents were Russian immigrants.

Aged just fourteen, Dayan joined the Haganah, and served with the Special Police Force to quell the Arab Uprising that took place between 1936 and 1939. When the British Governors outlawed the Haganah, Dayan was imprisoned for two years, before he was released in 1941.

Dayan fought alongside the British in World War 2 where, in Lebanon, while scrutinising operations through a pair of field glasses, the lens was shattered by a bullet, costing him an eye.

The patch Dayan came to wear gave him the appearance of a warrior, and for this, as well as his impressive war record, he became a darling of the Israeli public, and the epitome of a military hero.

In the 1948 War of Independence, Dayan led the defence of Jewish settlements and commanded attack forces on the Southern Front against Egypt. He was also in charge of the forces fighting for Jerusalem.

From 1949 to 1956, Dayan kept the Arabs at bay, taking on Palestinian terrorists as well as launching raids on Egypt and Syria.

During the Suez expedition, Dayan led Israeli operations and captured the whole of Sinai in a lightning strike that paved the way for the war of 1967. His achievements helped convince the military that Israeli forces could confront their hostile Arab neighbours and win.

Dayan, like so many men who had risen through the ranks of the military, later moved into the arena of politics, where he was to treat the Arabs far better than he ever had done on the battlefield.

With military men of such standing, fiercely-determined and committed to the cause, the future of Israel appeared to be in safe hands.

THE SUEZ CRISIS.

Israel survived its neighbours attempts to strangle it at birth and in 1949, a general election was held, and with entry to the UN, the new nation proudly took its place amongst the international community.

The military supremacy that Israel displayed in the War of Independence stood the country in good stead as it consolidated its place in the region. In fact, the new state was very militaristic in tone, and took a hard line with Arab guerrillas. Isolated attacks against individual Jews would see whole Palestinian villages punished out of all proportion.

This inordinate retribution, according to one member of the Knesset, the Jewish parliament, was fuelling the insurgency, as Arab anger rose against the cruel injustice.

This conciliatory feeling towards the Palestinians was pervasive amongst the voters, and a moderate, Moshe Sharett, replaced the intransigent Ben-Gurion as Prime Minister.

Elsewhere in the Middle East, as the Near East had become known, King Abdullah of Jordan was assassinated in 1951 while on a visit to Jerusalem. As he entered the al-Aqsa mosque, Shukri Ashu, a Palestinian youth, came up behind him and shot him in the back of the head, killing him instantly. Abdullah's crime had been to attempt to make peace with the new Jewish state. The King's grandson, Prince Hussein, who was with him at the time of the murder, succeeded him to the Jordanian throne.

In Egypt, there was a military coup when officers, led by Gamal Nasser, lost faith in their leaders after their humiliating defeat in 1948. They had been badly let down, with no strategy, aging weapons, and a lack of rations. The consensus for a coup was in place.

In this changing sea, Israel sailed strong. For David Ben-Gurion, appalled by any concession to the Arabs, this flux amongst their neighbours gave Israel an opportunity to expel the remaining Palestinians and to seize all the land from the Jordan River to the Mediterranean Sea, as the Lord God had intended. With a group of loyal supporters, Ben-Gurion set a trap for Egypt, who had recently nationalised the Suez Canal, to the disgust of the French and British shareholders.

The Straits of Tiran, which served the port of Eilat, Israel's only route by sea to southern Asia and Africa, had been blockaded by Nasser's troops. The Israelis, never backwards in coming forward, had to act. With the aid of a spy network of embedded Zionists, they planned to blow up British government property in Cairo and Alexandria and make it look like the work of the Egyptians to keep the Brits in the region.

Nasser's regime had agreed the withdrawal of British troops from the area of the canal, where they had been stationed since 1936. If the British were to leave the area, their garrisons would be taken over by Egyptian troops, and the two Middle Eastern enemies would be left without the buffer zone, increasing tension in the area.

Owing to incompetence, the incendiary devices failed to detonate and the plan failed, but it was the moderate government of Moshe Sharett that paid the price and, ironically, it was to Ben-Gurion that the Jewish people turned in their latest hour of need.

When the British and French decided to act to prevent a blockade of the Suez Canal, the Israelis, subject to the same embargo, joined forces in order to attack Egypt.

Israel swept through the Sinai Peninsula, seizing territory and inflicting casualties on the Egyptian army with the support of French and British aircraft, before the intervention of the USA and the USSR led to a humiliating climb-down from the Anglo-French-Israeli forces.

In particular, Russia threatened to 'flatten' Israel, according to one Soviet report, and was happy to provide arms to the Egyptians to be used against the infant state. Israel was simply getting too big for its boots.

At the UN, in a vote to order an Israeli retreat from the occupied territory, the consensus amongst the member states was 65 to 1, the one vote against being Israel's, for an immediate cease-fire and withdrawal.

On 16th March 1957, after four and a half months of fighting, Israel departed from Sinai, to her lasting chagrin, forced by UN consensus to forfeit her territorial gains.

Israel had lost 172 soldiers in action, with 817 wounded, but she had again humiliated Egypt. And, for her support of France and Britain in their attempt to regain control of Suez, Israel had extracted an agreement that would improve her own state security exponentially. Israel, with the aid of her allies, was about to go nuclear.

BETWEEN THE WARS.

The Superpowers, the USSR and the USA, had forced the withdrawal of Israel from the Sinai peninsular. Still, the new state, only eight years old by 1956, had again defeated one of her Arab neighbours in a war, and proved she was a force to be reckoned with in the region.

And that was before she took possession of a shipment of twenty tons of heavy water from Britain in 1958, to be used at the Top-Secret facility at Dimona in the Negev desert to build the Middle East's first nuclear weapon.

And there were other types of water making waves in the area. The Jordan River, the Dead Sea, and the Sea of Galilee were all important water sources and access to them was a necessity for the inhabitants of the sun-soaked, parched region, fringed on three sides by desert.

In 1955, Israel created the National Water Carrier to ship resources from the Jordan River to the expanding communities of Israel for both domestic and agricultural use.

In response, an Arab water-diversion project was established that threatened Israel's supply of the vital commodity. In 1964, Syria and Jordan began construction of a dam to divert the flow of the Baniyas and Yarmouk Rivers, both of which fed into the water resources required for the Jewish settlers. Israel reacted by bombing the dam before it could be completed.

Between 1951 and 1967, at least a dozen outbreaks of violence between the neighbouring states could be attributed to access to water. It was just one more element, although a vital one, to the never-ending series of conflicts. It was not as if they didn't have enough cause for contention anyway, and this showed in the continuation of war by other means.

At the First Arab summit in Cairo in January 1964, which had been called in response to Israel's River Jordan diversion scheme, it was decided that an organisation should be formally enacted to serve the Palestinian people in their continued quest for justice. This became the establishment of the PLO, the Palestine Liberation Organisation.

The stated aim of the PLO was the destruction of the state of Israel. This caused considerable concern in the latter country, and two letters of protest was duly dispatched to the United Nations with regard to the declaration.

On New Year's Day, 1965, the Fatah guerrilla wing of the PLO carried out its first attack, planting a bomb along the National Water Carrier, although it failed to detonate.

In May, Jordanian terrorists then launched an attack on a Jewish neighbourhood in Jerusalem, killing two people and seriously wounding four more. Israel retaliated by besieging the Palestinian towns of Qalqiya, Shuna, and Jenin in the West Bank.

The Second Arab summit dealt with the issue of water rights in the region, while the Third, in September of 1965, held in Casablanca, called for a military build-up in Syria, Jordan, and Egypt, with the aim of attacking Israel within two to five years, rather dispensing with the art of surprise.

On 13th November 1966, two Israeli army columns bombarded three Jordanian towns in response to a number of terrorist raids said to have originated in the area. In one of the guerrilla assaults, three IDF infantrymen had been killed by a road mine.

In the village of Samu, outside Hebron, which bore the brunt of the Israeli revenge mission, fifteen Arab soldiers were killed, along with three civilians. Having taken control of the town, the IDF planted explosive devices and blew up 125 houses, in what was becoming a familiar Israeli tactic.

United Nations Resolution 228 censured the inordinate response from Israel, accusing it, literally, of overkill.

In May 1967, Egypt expelled the UN peace-keeping force that had been stationed as a buffer in the Gaza Strip. The Straits of Tiran, despite the outcome in 1956 the last time this had happened, were closed again to Israeli shipping.

The Israeli Foreign Minister, Abba Eban, flew to the United States to seek their support in opening up the Straits, the closure of which was viewed as a Declaration of War by Israel. The US explained that they would consider the request, but that they needed time to do so.

Eban returned to Israel and informed the Cabinet of the US position. The military men in the Cabinet were enraged by the procrastination. Their army was ready, victory would be theirs, so why should they wait.

The Cabinet voted on the proposal for going to war with Egypt. Nine were in favour of a pre-emptive strike, with the same number voting to give America the time it needed to negotiate the opening of the waterway.

The hawks in the room felt the debate had moved on. It no longer mattered that the route to Eilat had been closed. More pressing were the columns of Egyptian soldiers massing in Sinai. That was the immediate danger.

Also, the IDF stood in a state of heightened readiness. They could only maintain that position for a short time, as volunteers had been drafted in from all walks of life, and the economy would soon start to suffer, while delays in mobilisation only played into Arab hands.

But not everybody shared the generals' confidence. Yitzak Rabin, who as Chief of Staff was responsible for planning the war, was so unsure of victory that he sought out David Ben-Gurion, visiting him at his home to seek advice.

Rabin was shocked when the former Prime Minister said 'It is all your fault. We must not go to war. We are isolated.'

In Jordan, King Hussein felt equally isolated. The Syrian Front was the scene of most of the skirmishes between Jews and Arabs, but now that Egypt had signed a pact with Syria, it was Jordan that feared having to tackle Israel alone.

With this in mind, Hussein flew to Cairo on the 30th of May and met President Nasser in secret. The two were not friends, but they shared a common enemy. Hussein asked Nasser to give him the same agreement that Egypt had with Syria.

A stunned Israel awoke to find its Arab neighbours in unison. An attack on any of these states would now bring a tri-partite response.

Israel installed Moshe Dayan as Minister of Defence as the Arab States flexed their muscles. Also drafted into the war cabinet was Menachem Begin.

Several battalions of Iraqi soldiers were also heading for Jordan to reinforce the eastern flank. The pressure was rising.

For President Nasser, who had hoped that his troop movements into Sinai would ensure there would be no attack on her ally Syria, his bluff was about to be called. Realising this, on the 2nd of June, Nasser called his army chief Amer and his airforce chief Sidqi Mahmoud to his office.

Nasser predicted Israel would attack in just two or three days time, but still he couldn't afford to strike first. To do so, and be seen as the aggressor, might invite a US military response.

The President asked Mahmoud how much of the air force might be lost to an Israeli strike.

Mahmoud was dismayed. It was his mistake in the Suez crisis of 1956 that had left most of the air force on the ground when the British and French planes destroyed the Egyptian air force while it was still on the runway.

Their only chance at victory was to strike first. Defence was not an option. But Nasser would not allow it.

Chastened, Mahmoud offered twenty percent as his opinion of the losses to be suffered in a pre-emptive strike by Israel. 'Well', said Nasser, 'that still leaves us eighty percent for our response.'

Meanwhile, Meir Amit, head of Mossad, the Israeli intelligence service, had flown to the US to speak with Secretary of Defence Robert McNamara.

Amit explained that war was inevitable. McNamara was cautious and favoured sending a ship into the Straits of Tiran, to draw Egyptian fire and provide the pretext for the Israeli response, but either way, Amit explained, war had to happen.

McNamara asked how long the conflict would last. A week, Amit replied. How many would die, was McNamara's next question? On the Israeli side, less than the 6000 that had died in the War of Independence in 1948, Amit explained. 'Okay', said the US official. 'Do what you've got to do.'

Meir Amit returned to Israel and immediately went into session to brief the cabinet. 'America', he explained, 'will not stand in our way.'

The votes were cast. Sixteen opted for war, with two abstentions.

The intelligence chief told Dayan, the Defence Minister, that the US still favoured drawing Egyptian fire as a pretext for the assault, but the confident former general saw no need to delay. War, now, was inevitable. It did not matter what pretexts or formalities were used to justify the engagement.

'Don't worry', Dayan told him. 'We'll start.'

The state of Israel, born in 1948, had survived a difficult birth, childhood, and teenage years. Now, at the age of nineteen, she was about to come of age.

DAY ONE.

Monday, 5th of June 1967, Israel called the bluff of the posturing Arab states at its borders when it launched its air force in the direction of Egypt.

In a co-ordinated attack of exemplary precision, sixteen enemy airfields were struck at 8.45 am local time. According to Israeli intelligence reports, the Egyptian dawn flying patrols would be back at the base and the fighter planes would be refuelling on the tarmac. The pilots would be in the mess hall enjoying breakfast, and the commanders would be in their cars travelling to work, and would therefore be incommunicado.

To make matters worse for the Egyptians, the head of the armed forces, Field Marshal Amer, and the air force, Sidqi Mahmoud, and the generals leading the troops were all on their way to a parade at Bir Tamada airfield in Sinai.

They were unable to be contacted, and a long way from their command posts.

A further calamitous decision was the order to stand down the Egyptian air defence system. Just in case, by mistake, they locked on to the plane carrying the dignitaries to the parade, the air defences were shut down for the day. With the country on the highest state of alert, given the stand-off then taking place, it was incompetence of the highest order.

Ranged against this lackadaisical enemy were almost 200 Israeli fighter planes. They would reach their targets at precisely the same time and deliver a knockout blow before the Egyptians knew what had hit them. Then, with complete control of the skies, the ground troops could go in and finish off the job.

To a man, the Israelis knew what they were doing. It is difficult to imagine a better prepared, more motivated fighting machine. Each man believed they were fighting for the very existence of his country, and wished to secure it for the coming generations.

Ranged against this well-drilled force were 350 Egyptian fighter planes, only half of them serviceable at the time. There were also 64 bombers, but less than half of these were operational on the morning of the attack.

At a quarter to nine, Egyptian time, the air assault began. Wave after wave of Israeli planes launched missiles onto the runways to put them out of use and strafed the planes on the ground with automatic fire.

Met with limited resistance, the Israelis could pick off their targets at will. In what must have appeared a shocking echo of the war of 1956, the Egyptian air force was destroyed on the ground, before it had an opportunity to scramble.

The plane carrying Amer and Mahmoud was forced to turn back. The airfield they were heading for had been targeted, and it was too dangerous to attempt to land. The other military air bases had suffered the same fate, and they were forced to head for Cairo International airport, which meant the two senior military personnel were removed from operations for a further hour and a half. Everything was going right for Israel and going completely wrong for Egypt.

The Field Commander managed to get a message to their Jordanian allies to say that Egypt was under attack and they should join the action immediately.

He added the morale-boosting report that 75% of the Israeli planes had been destroyed and that Egyptian land forces were engaging the Israelis in the Sinai Peninsula with success.

Cairo radio had begun reporting news of the Israeli attack too. Dozens of enemy planes were reported shot down. 'Israel's treacherous aggression has been repelled', the jubilant announcer cried, 'and Egypt is now advancing on all fronts and confronting the enemy.'

Across the Arab world, people rushed into the streets in celebration. Someone shouted 'It is a great day for the Arabs'. It seemed to the uninformed masses that Israel's day of reckoning had come.

Jordan possessed a modest air force consisting of 24 Hawker Hunter jets. They were slow, yet highly manoeuvrable, and they did pack a punch. Her pilots were also well-trained, and they were up for the battle.

Ihsan Shurdom, a 25 year old captain in the Jordanian air force awaited the order to attack. He could see dots on the radar heading into Israel, and his instinct said they were IAF planes returning to base. He wanted to go after them while they were low on fuel and ammunition.

Shurdom's superiors believed the planes on the radar must be Egyptian. If the radio reports were to be believed, Tel Aviv was about to feel the force of the Arab response. The young captain was refused permission to engage.

A Palestinian Brigade in Gaza had more success, shooting down an Israeli plane, forcing the pilot, Mordechai Livon, to eject over the Mediterranean, where he was picked up and taken to Cairo for questioning.

At 10.20 am, the Middle East News Agency ticker tape reported that 23 Israeli planes had been downed. This figure was revised an hour later to 42. Across the Arab world, people ran out of their houses and danced in the streets.

At ten minutes to twelve, Ihsan Shurdom finally received permission to engage. Sixteen Jordanian planes took off for airfields in Israel. They found just four planes on the ground, which they destroyed. The rest were nowhere to be seen. Shurdom and the others returned to base.

The missing Israeli planes were busy mopping up the Egyptian operation. Field Marshal Amer phoned Fayed airbase personally and asked for a damage report. He was told that all of the Mig-23's had been destroyed. A dozen bombers and three Mig-19's were all that was left.

Six Egyptian Tupolev bombers had been airborne when the attacks occurred and had therefore survived, and they were ordered to make for Luxor airport. Unfortunately, the Israelis intercepted the message and pursued the aircraft to the new location and destroyed them there.

By midday, the Egyptian air force was no more.

In the evening of the first day of fighting, Cairo Radio reported that 82 enemy planes had been shot down. The Israelis did not bother to correct the reports. They did not want the wider world to know how well they were doing.

Israel was making territorial gains, and wanted to continue doing so before a cease-fire could be agreed. Israel intended to hold onto her spoils this time, unlike in 1956 when she had been forced to withdraw to the lines held before fighting began.

With the Egyptians grounded, Israel went after Jordan and Syria. Ishan Shurdom and his men downed four enemy Mirage fighter planes, but back at base their airfield had been destroyed, along with their remaining aircraft. Then Shurdom was hit in a dogfight and just managed to escape to an alternate airport.

In just one day, Israel had destroyed the aerial forces of Egypt, Syria, and Jordan. According to Chief of Staff Yitzak Rabin, the losses amounted to 374 Arab planes: 286 Egyptian, 52 Syrian, 27 Jordanian, and 9 Iraqi aircraft. This had been achieved at a cost to themselves of 19 IAF planes and 9 pilots. Israel had lost ten percent of its air force, but it had gained supremacy of the skies and aerial cover for her ground forces.

Sixteen Egyptian airfields were put out of action in the first wave of Israeli attacks. Two more, Cairo and El Mansour, were hit in the second phase when it was found that fighter planes were being housed there. El Arish airport escaped unscathed, being deliberately left alone to be used later as a forward base for the Israelis.

It had been a stunning victory, efficient and ruthless, and a vindication of the military's confidence. It was a rout, no matter what Cairo Radio said.

Down on the ground, progress had also been made, albeit more slowly. The army were ranged in three separate positions with individual missions. One group was led by Brigadier-General Ariel Sharon, another by Brigadier-General Avraham Yoffe, and a further division was under the command of Brigadier-General Israel Tal.

Before embarking on the operation, Tal had informed his officers that 'This is a fight, if necessary, to the death. Each man will charge forward to the very end, irrespective of the cost in casualties. There will be no halt and no retreat.

The fate of your country depends on it.'

The fighting would be, at times, hand to hand. Corporal Rafael Eitan and his 202nd Paratroop Brigade were in the thick of it near Khan Younis in the Gaza Strip.

'We fought for our lives', Eitan said later. 'I fired my Uzi non-stop.'

The Israelis met stiff resistance, but the Arabs lacked leadership, and it was only the bravery of individual troops and divisions that stood in the way of the superior Jewish forces.

Artillery rained down on Egyptian positions throughout the night. Better trained and better equipped, and able to call in air support when needed, the Israelis were in pole position as they fought their way across the Sinai desert.

In the push towards Suez, by land and air, Israel made great inroads. It was one of the most comprehensive victories of any war ever fought. And that was the first day.

SECOND DAY.

Israel ruled the skies, having defeated the neighbouring Arab states' air forces the previous day. On the ground, there was still much to do. In Sinai, Egypt had strategically-placed battalions in the north, centre, and south of the peninsula, while the Syrians, Jordanians, and Iraqis were attacking Israel's northern and eastern frontiers.

In the West Bank, Palestinian resistance fighters took up weapons; small arms, rifles, and Kalashnikovs in order to defend their homes. Israel was making a bid to seize all the land between the Jordan River and the Mediterranean Sea in order to fulfil the God-given prophesy. But they would have to fight for it, inch by inch, house by house, and village by village.

For King Hussein, the situation appeared bleak. His air force had been destroyed, and his troops were facing total wipe-out. The Israelis were fighting with all the determination that their historical beliefs could instil. Hussein's only hope was for a cease-fire, and he called every foreign ambassador in the kingdom to his offices and urged them to apply pressure to their UN representatives to bring about a cessation of hostilities.

Every minute of delay in getting a UN Resolution meant more gains for the Israelis. It would be territory they would not easily relinquish, if at all.

The King of Jordan wrestled with his limited options all day. He had to withdraw his troops east of the river while there was still something left of his army. He only hoped that Israel would be content with the capture of the West Bank. If they wanted, they could invade his kingdom itself, such was the overwhelming nature of the Israeli advance.

In Gaza, the Egyptians had withdrawn leaving the Palestinians to fend for themselves. There was sporadic resistance, until the invading Israelis routed the pockets of guerrilla activity, then began systematically punishing the men of military age, whether they'd been involved in the fighting or not.

Over in Sinai, certain hardened Egyptian Brigades were punishing the Israelis. IDF tanks and soldiers were being ambushed before they were able to call in air support and direct their artillery at the entrenched Egyptians.

What they possessed in courage, they lacked in leadership. Field Marshal Amer was paralysed with fear. He knew he had lost the war the very first day, and although the best thing to do in the circumstances, according to his generals, was to organise an ordered retreat, he opted instead for all-out flight.

Covering fire was required to keep the Israelis at bay while the bulk of the men retired to the line of the Suez Canal, where they could regroup and retrain their artillery batteries, but the Egyptian army instead adopted a policy of every man for himself.

A garrison stationed in Sharm-el Sheik, enforcing the embargo on the Straits of Tiran, were ordered to abandon their posts, leaving it for the approaching Israelis to take without a fight.

Piled onto every moving vehicle, abandoning their heavy artillery, the departing soldiers became the easiest of prey for the IAF planes, which were able to pick the convoy off at will.

In Jerusalem, meanwhile, Jordanian units were well entrenched and Israeli losses were significant. There was hand to hand fighting taking place all over the Old City, as the highly-motivated Jewish brigades first surrounded, then infiltrated, the capital.

Going house to house, taking on sniper fire and tank batteries, exceptional bravery to the point of foolhardiness was required in order to seize the Arab quarter of the city.

For the Israelis, this was the greatest prize of the war. It had to happen, no matter how many men went down.

The road to Ramallah remained open to allow the Arab inhabitants to flee, but the Jordanians and Palestinians who remained were putting up one hell of a fight. With some success, too.

172

With the Israelis controlling the high ground overlooking the city, and making determined inroads through the streets of Jerusalem itself, it would only be a matter of time before this central battle went the way of those at Israel's borders.

With Sinai routed, the West Bank seized, and Syrian and Iraqi forces stuck in the Golan Heights, Israel could afford to concentrate on capturing Jerusalem, the Holy City. The ancient capital of the Jewish state was almost within their grasp.

By nightfall, the United Nations, meeting in emergency session, unanimously agreed to call for a cease-fire. Israel professed to welcome the call, but warned that implementation depended on its sincere acceptance by the other parties to the conflict. The Jewish State would, eventually, get around to it, but not before all of its objectives had been met.

The Arab ground troops, with some exceptions, had suffered in line with their air force comrades the day before. Cairo Radio was still proclaiming Egyptian successes and promising to push the Israelis into the Mediterranean Sea. By now, though, the Arabs on the ground knew the real situation. The choice they faced was stay and fight, and almost certainly die, or flee the approaching Israelis for the relative safety of the neighbouring states.

That was the second day.

THE THIRD DAY.

By the morning of the third day of fighting, most of the Jordanian troops in Jerusalem had fled. Their officers had slipped away in the night. The rank and file began to follow them. The Old City was opening up before the Jewish troops.

At 5.30 in the morning, General Uzi Narkiss was informed by the Deputy chief of Staff, 'We are already being pressed for a cease-fire. We have to go in now. We cannot let the Old City remain an enclave.'

These were words General Narkiss had been waiting to hear since 1948. He wasted no time putting them into action.

General Mordechai Gur, Commander of the Israeli Paratroop Brigade, came over the army radio at 8.30 am. 'Calling all battalion commanders', he said. 'We are about to enter the old City. All our generations have been striving and dreaming of this. We will be the first to do it.'

Colonel Gur and his driver then raced their jeep ahead of the tanks and troops making their way towards the Lion's Gate, one of seven entrances into the Palestinian quarter of Jerusalem.

Crashing through the half-open wooden door at the entrance to the gate, Gur entered the Old City.

As the Israeli soldiers swarmed through the seven portals, they were met by Jordanian sniper fire. There were losses, but they slowly began to pick off the hidden marksmen and the resistance began to ebb.

By the time Colonel Gur reached the Temple Mount, the site holy to both Muslims and Jews, he was met by the Jordanian governor and the mayor of the city and was told 'All of the soldiers have now left. There will be no more resistance.' The city belonged to Israel.

Later in the day, Moshe Dayan broadcast to the nation in a radio address.

'We have united Jerusalem', he exclaimed exuberantly. We have returned to the holiest of our holy places, never to part from it again.'

An Israeli flag was hoisted to the top of the Muslim mosque, the dome of the Rock, in a distinctly provocative act. Dayan ordered it taken down.

Shlomo Goren, Rabbi to the army, urged General Narkiss to blow up the mosque, to raze it to the ground once and for all. Wisely, for the mosque is the third holiest site in Islam, the General refused.

Having seized the old City and united Jerusalem, there was no sense risking it all with so crass a move.

Elsewhere, the Israelis were having similar success. In Sinai, it was a turkey shoot. The undisciplined retreat, with the Egyptian army literally running for their lives with no rearguard to protect them, left them easy prey for the pursuing Israeli tanks and the fighter planes that would swoop down and pick them off.

Egyptian high-command announced they had evacuated their first lines of defence and were now fighting several battles on their second front. Cairo Radio said the withdrawal was the result of 'continuous air raids in which foreign planes', meaning American and British, 'had taken part.'

Such was the fog of war, and the attempt to lay the blame for Egypt's defeat on more than Israel alone.

And who wouldn't want to deflect criticism, for it was a shambles. Commentators referred to the losses as worse than at El Alamein in World War 2. Egyptian vehicles and armour, and its soldiers, were strewn along whole stretches of the roads running from the desert to the Suez Canal.

The Arabs had one goal, to cross the canal to what they hoped would be safety. The Israelis had their own aims: to seize all of the Peninsular, and to ensure that Egyptian losses were so great that they would have difficulty mounting another offensive for years.

In the Gaza Strip, now devoid of any military personnel, men of fighting age, civilians, were being separated from their women-folk and then shot in cold blood for participating in the war. It was brutal.

175

In the West Bank, as in Sinai, IAF planes were mowing down the retreating Jordanian troops. Now helpless, Palestinian villagers, fearing another Deir Yassin, began packing up their belongings and streaming towards the River Jordan.

It was an exodus to match that of 1948. Then, Palestinians fled the new Israeli state for the West Bank. Now, they were forced to flee again. Most were veterans of that earlier flight. History had come back to haunt them.

Intent on grabbing the West Bank for themselves, the Israeli planes pursued the civilians and strafed them with automatic fire and Napalm. 125,000 Arabs fled for the safety of Jordan, if there was to be such a thing. The terror Israel inflicted as they ran for their lives ensured there would be no return.

There was supposed to be a cease-fire on, but Israel was holding out until it had secured all the territory that it coveted. By nightfall, it seemed that all of its goals had been met.

And that was the third day.

DAY FOUR.

In the hot, dusty desert, many Egyptian soldiers chose to take their chances with the heat, thirst, and the flies rather than face the fire of the Israeli artillery.

The excellently prepared IDF, with its array of highly motivated generals, was able to outflank the retreating Arab forces and ambush them as the came through the mountain passes.

The Egyptians either fought their way through, and the roads were littered with the corpses of many who had tried and failed, or scattered into the desert hoping to find another way past.

Field Marshall Amer was vacillating. He had ordered a withdrawal of all troops to the Canal, but he then sent two battalions back into the peninsular to tackle the Israelis. He had either belatedly grasped the effectiveness of a rearguard action, or he was as confused as many of his officers believed him to be.

Some brigades managed just fine without him. The Paratroopers making their way back from Sharm el-Sheik were commanded ably and arrived home more or less intact from the experience.

Major General Saad el Shazli and a force of 1500 men were positioned just across the Israeli border when they were called back. Shazli led the men, under cover of night, towards the Suez Canal and the relative safety of Egypt proper. Although they were spotted and strafed by Israeli planes the next day, their losses were minor compared to the fate of less fortunate brigades.

In Jerusalem and in the West Bank, the Occupation was starting. Arabs, who only days before were witnessing Jordanian soldiers heading into battle, now saw the vanquished disappear.

Even the Palestinian home-guard had to lay down their weapons, leaving the civilian population defenceless.

The sight of Israeli soldiers and civilians milling around former Arab neighbourhoods, wearing wide smiles, back-slapping and hugging each other, was a galling one. The memory of al-Nakbah was still fresh in the minds of many, and all were hoping the present fighting would reverse the catastrophe of 1948. Instead, it was exacerbated.

The Arabs were in danger of losing all of historic Palestine. The Israelis had won 55% of that country in the UN mandate that gave the Jewish people their independence, but war and its spoils threatened to extend Israel to its biblical horizons. The goal of a Promised Land stretching from the River Jordan to the Mediterranean had almost been achieved. It all depended on how much the world would ask Israel to give back when the dust of battle settled.

To ensure that the UN did not demand too much of her, Israel would need her friends in high places, but that seemed the last thing on her mind when she attacked the USS Liberty off the coast of Sinai.

The Liberty was a spy ship, and was operating in international waters. The United States were Israel's greatest supporter. It had supplied her with weapons up until the day that war broke out. But this did not prevent the extraordinary attack that took place on the fourth day of the Six Day War.

All day long, Israeli planes had buzzed the ship. The large American flag that flew atop her mast was clearly visible, and the off-duty personnel, sunbathing on deck, waved happily at the IAF planes. Many were reassured by their presence. They were only twenty miles from a war zone, so to have allied planes overhead was a comforting thing.

That is until their flying formation changed and the planes swooped low to attack. Bursts of gunfire and missiles poured into the ship. The attacks kept coming. Torpedo boats arrived and unleashed their deadly cargo. The USS Liberty began to list. Her personnel, those that could, abandoned ship.

In all, 34 men were killed and 174 were wounded out of 294 people on board. Israel claimed it was all a mistake. After all, the US was her ally. However, everybody from the US President to the head of the CIA failed to buy this. The documents related to the event remain classified.

Most commentators believe that Israel did not want anyone, including the USA, spying on her activities as she consolidated her gains. And, flushed with her success of the previous three days, she was prepared to take on anybody.

That was the fourth day.

THE FIFTH DAY.

All who could had fled. Those who remained were taken prisoner. In Sinai, the Israelis were mopping up after a lightning and successful campaign. Flush with victory, unrestrained by a clear policy to the contrary, vindictive soldiers were free to inflict punishment at will on the Egyptians who were at their mercy. But mercy they would not receive.

In the Peninsular, there are dozens of mass graves holding captives who were summarily executed after they had surrendered. Ordered to dig their own graves, Uzi-wielding guards would then shoot the prisoners, who would fall into the ground, to become bedrock for the next corpses that would be piled on top.

Eventually, orders were issued from the Chief of Staff outlining the official position, explaining that the killing of prisoners who had surrendered had to stop. Slowly, the message filtered through.

In the West Bank, Palestinian villagers were ordered to leave their homes, then they were herded onto buses and driven to the Jordan River and ordered to cross. As the bridges had been blown, they were forced to wade across, carrying the few belongings they had managed to salvage above their heads to keep them dry.

It was al Nakbah Mark 2. For those veterans of the first one, it was a tragedy relived. What had they done to deserve this, other than to hope for a reversal of that earlier misfortune?

The armies of Egypt, Jordan, Syria and Iraq had rallied to the cause of the Palestinian refugees. The result left them worse off than they already were, which took some doing. The injustice that had raged within these people for nineteen years suddenly seemed misplaced. Given the present situation, the years between 1948 and 1967 seemed halcyon.

It was a cruel irony. What they had thought were the bad times were really the good. The knife had been twisted. The pain increased.

180

Although many had been forced to abandon their homes after the creation of Israel, and had moved into Jordanian controlled territories, they could still consider their home to be in Palestine. They still resided in their historic homeland. Now, removed from the area known as the West Bank, lying to the west of the Jordan River, they were forced into the country of Jordan proper. More than ever, they were refugees in a foreign land.

The homes they left behind became happy hunting grounds for the jubilant Israelis. Ordered not to kill prisoners, a new sideshow emerged: looting.

Houses, shops, and civic buildings were ransacked. Clothes, jewellery, food, money, and anything else of value was taken by the troops. Everything was fair game.

They had taken the Arab's land, their country, and their homes. Why shouldn't they take their possessions too? Besides, who was going to stop them?

Egypt certainly couldn't. Neither could Jordan. Both had elected for a cease-fire to save what little they could of face, while Hussein and Nasser still had control over their own borders at least. Forget fighting for someone else.

With two enemies subdued, and with the UN pressing Israel to rein in its ambition, Moshe Dayan, Minister of Defence, decided to take the opportunity to launch an attack on Syria before the curtain came down on the war.

Of all the belligerent states on Israel's doorstep, Syria was the most annoying. In previous years, hundreds of mortar attacks had been launched into Jewish settlements close to the border between the two states.

Israel saw an opportunity to seize the high ground between them, the Golan Heights. As with Jerusalem, once captured, there would be no intention of ever returning the territory to its former owners.

So Israel attacked using all of its 200 aircraft in the last concerted effort of the war, despite Syria accepting two UN cease-fire appeals. As any gambler knows, you have to press your luck when it's in.

Egypt was finally facing up to the fact that its luck was definitely out.

181

Cairo Radio replaced the upbeat military music and the false messages of Arab conquests with sombre, solemn melodies. It was announced that President Nasser would address the nation over the radio at 7.30 that evening.

Across the Middle East, the Arabs tuned in knowing something big was about to happen. It was, and it shocked everybody, for Nasser had been so upbeat only a week before, and many still believed that the Egyptians were holding their own in the desert campaign. Nasser soon removed the wool from their eyes.

'The enemy struck a stronger blow than we had expected. Our army has fought the bravest battles, but without adequate air cover, and the enemy has been able to call upon the help of other forces who have scores to settle with the Arabs. Despite the fact that they have had help which has not been available to us, it does not mean we don't bear any responsibility for the outcome. Indeed, I am prepared to take all the responsibility. I have taken a decision to give up my official post and my political role and return to the ranks of the masses and do my duty like every other citizen.'

The Middle East was stunned, and the Arab population soon went out into the streets en masse and demanded that Nasser withdraw his resignation.

If it was a calculated gamble, somehow a bluff, it worked. It appears though that Nasser genuinely underestimated the esteem in which he was held. The grief of the people was real enough. The tears and the mass rallies were there for all to see.

Nasser had gotten them into this mess. Nasser would have to get them out. But more than that, he was loved. He, more than any other leader, represented hope for the Arab world. And hope would be required for the difficult times ahead.

And that was the fifth day.

THE SIXTH DAY.

Overwhelmed by the mass demonstrations in his favour, President Nasser of Egypt withdrew his resignation. Field Marshal Amer would not be so lucky. His incompetence in the heat of battle had played a major part in the poor performance of the Arab army, but dispensing with his services would not be easy.

The heads of the air force, navy, and land forces had all tendered their resignations in the light of the dismal performance of all concerned, and Nasser had accepted them. 15,000 Egyptian troops had been taken prisoner in Sinai. Obviously someone was to blame.

Amer was surrounded by two hundred loyal officers and troops in his palatial home, and refused to leave his fortress compound, which meant that Nasser had to resort to subterfuge to tease him out.

The President invited Amer to dinner at his home, and the Field Marshal, hopeful he had ridden the storm and might now be back in favour, gladly accepted.

Once there, Amer was informed that he had been relieved of his duties, and that he would be placed under house arrest to prevent any likelihood that he may inspire his loyalists to instigate a coup.

Later, Amer was moved to another safe house, and shortly afterwards he was pronounced dead, poisoned, either by his own hand or that of the authorities. The question remains unanswered, but the actions of Nasser's men certainly invited suspicion that they may have removed the lingering threat that Amer posed.

Egypt, with the threat of revolution removed, could go about the difficult task of rebuilding their morale and their military in preparation for a renewed attack on Israel as soon as circumstances would allow. The dust settled, Nasser survived, and the country moved on.

Over in Syria, the Israelis were busy achieving their goal of securing the Golan Heights, territory necessary to its security, before the cease-fire could be imposed.

The calls were mounting for Israel to stop the incursion, but officers on the ground deliberately made themselves unavailable and the operation continued.

It took the Russians, close allies of Damascus, to intervene. No one quite knew what Israel's intentions in the region were. As it was, it seemed they were only after a buffer zone, the high ground that overlooked and therefore threatened several Israeli outpost settlements. But after their lightning victories over Egypt and Jordan, it was feared the whole of Syria might be next on the agenda.

The USSR issued a threat to the effect that this would not be acceptable. Military action would be taken against Israel if she did not desist. For fear of sparking World War 3, Israel finally accepted, and adhered to, the UN cease-fire, but not before she had captured the vital territory that she required.

In the West Bank, Palestinians were being coerced into joining the exodus of refugees heading for Jordan.

Intimidation, bullying, threats, humiliation, and violence were all employed to encourage the Arabs to leave.

Over 400,000 Palestinians crossed the Jordan River and entered the refugee camps that were already full to bursting with those who had fled the War of Independence in 1948. Conditions in the UNWRA camps were hardly fit for human habitation, with no sanitation, inadequate accommodation, and only limited access to food and water.

It was barely an existence.

In Jerusalem, the Israelis were dancing for joy. They had captured the Old City, driven the Arabs from their homes, and united the Holy City for the first time in two millennia.

The old Moroccan Quarter, an area of 150 homes housing Palestinians, just next to the Wailing Wall, was immediately bulldozed to make a huge piazza to accommodate the Jews drawn to the Wall. Bricks and mortar, family possessions, furniture, and in several cases inhabitants, were crushed underfoot by a team of bulldozers to create an instant square.

By the 10th of June, the Six Day War was over. Israel had met all of its military objectives and then some. It had wrenched the Sinai Peninsular and the Gaza Strip from Egypt, the Golan Heights from Syria, and the West Bank from Jordan. It was a miracle, literally, as it was the fulfilment of biblical prophesy that the Jewish People should occupy this land.

Not that the joy would be short-lived, nor a Pyrrhic victory, but something was unleashed by Israel's success which would prove impossible to contain. As an occupying force, Israel would attract resistance. It has always been so. What were the Stern Gang and the Irgun if not national resistance movements?

Moshe Dayan told a colleague to expect the Arabs to turn to terrorism to continue the fight. 'In the same situation', he said, 'I would do the same.'

But as the stream of refugees headed out of the West Bank for encampments to the east of the River Jordan, these seeds of Arab resistance could be overlooked for the present. After all, Israel had fought with skill to achieve this stunning victory, and she could take a little time to enjoy the spoils of war. That was the sixth day.

And on the seventh day, Israel rested.

THE OCCUPATION.

In 1967, Israel seized the West Bank, extended her border to the River Jordan, and inherited an Arab population that would soon become a national resistance movement. Those Palestinians that would not be forced out, Israel had to learn to live with. No longer was the enemy at her gates. Now, the enemy was within.

Yigal Allon, a member of the Knesset, devised a plan for the new territory and its subversive population. By moving the Israeli defensive line to the Jordan River, they would surround the West Bank. Then, by building Jewish settlements in between the Arab population centres, a series of cantons would be created that would be easy to control.

But the stunning victory of the Six Day War would bring unforeseen problems. Israel existed by virtue of the United Nations partition of Palestine. Where was her authority for residing in Sinai or the West Bank?

To the Jewish religious community, that right had been God-given four thousand years earlier. Rabbi Zvi Yehuda Kook became the spiritual leader of the Settlement Movement, and he believed that all of Palestine belonged to Israel.

Refugees from the 1948 war of independence are known as Laji Un, while their counterparts from 1967 are referred to as the Nazihun, meaning 'the Uprooted'.

Some 400,000 West Bank Palestinians fled to the East Bank of the Jordan River in the aftermath of the Six Day War. 150,000 of these were survivors of the first exodus, being moved for a second time.

In a census of 1967, 595,000 Arabs remained in the West Bank, and 389,700 still lived in the Gaza Strip once Israel took control and began to administer, or occupy, the territory.

This threatened the demographics of the Jewish State itself. If free and fair elections were to be held for all of the inhabitants, the Arabs would comprise a significant proportion of the electorate.

Clearly, Israel would have to move carefully, and one of the ways it did this was to shut up shop. United Nations Resolutions 194, which called for the repatriation of refugees, and Resolution 242, which called for Israel's removal from the Occupied Territories, would both be ignored. It was a Jewish problem, and the outcome would have to meet Israel's own requirements.

But colonisation, which was what occupation amounted to, brought with it scrutiny from the outside world, and bred resentment in its subjects and its practitioners.

Jeremy Bowen, the BBC's Middle East correspondent, in his excellent book 'Six Days', quotes one Israeli soldier stating that being an occupier made him 'Lose respect for other people's lives.'

There must be something in the human psyche, some gene that takes advantage of the weak.

Michel Thomas, the French languages expert, has his own definition of this phenomenon.

During the Second World War, he was captured by the Vichy Government, the French regime that the occupying Germans allowed to administer the region on their behalf.

Suspected of working for the Resistance Movement, soldiers captured Thomas and subjected him to months of torture. He opened up new areas of his mind in order to escape the pain. By doing so, he discovered parts of the brain that most of us never use, and it is this extra capacity that provides the space to store and teach his language skills.

But, in all those months of torture, he never saw a German. The punishment was served up by other Frenchmen. They could have reported to their German bosses that they were working him hard while leaving him alone. Instead, they excelled at their work. Why? That oppressive gene.

Back in Israel, the legality for settlement in the West Bank came on the 24th September, 1967, when special dispensation was granted to Jews that had owned land prior to 1947 that had been awarded to the Arabs in the partition plan.

At Kfar Etzion, an area of land bought by Zionists in the 1930's, 151 settlers had died in a siege when refusing to move after the partition. Now, those that had left were going back, vowing now to leave again.

These settlers had a historic claim to the land, but their return set a precedent. The floodgates had been opened. Encouraged by the government's Allon Plan, Jewish immigrants began to pour in to the West Bank.

For the Arabs who'd resisted Israeli intimidation to leave, for whom the lure of an UNWRA refugee camp had held no attraction, life from here on in was about to get a whole lot worse. For some, life would not even be worth living. Palestinian Resistance, as we know it today, had just been born.

BLACK SEPTEMBER.

The PLO advocated legitimate resistance to Israel in the Occupied Territories. Exiled into neighbouring lands, the Palestinians launched cross border raids from Jordan, Syria, and Lebanon. In 1967, there were about 100 attacks, most of which were met by Israeli retaliation.

In March, 1968, in the West Bank village of Karameh, PLO fighters aided by Jordanian soldiers defeated an Israeli force and inspired the Palestinian people to take up arms against the occupying nation. By 1970, there were more than 2000 Arab guerrilla operations against Jewish military installations.

The freedom fighters formed themselves into several groups operating under the banner of the PLO, sharing its goals and providing a varied battle-front. Groups such as the Peoples Front for the Liberation of Palestine, the PFLP, operated independently but with the tacit approval of Yasser Arafat, the PLO chairman.

In November 1968, the PFLP hijacked an EL Al plane flying from Rome to Tel Aviv and diverted the aircraft to Algeria, where they bartered the release of the hostages for Palestinian prisoners in Israeli jails. This was the world's first civilian plane hijacking in order to achieve political aims.

The following month, spurred on by that success, a team of four terrorists attempted to take over another El Al flight at Athens airport. The plot failed when Mossad agents grew suspicious about two of the cell, Sudanese men holding passports with consecutive numbers.

With two of the team removed, it was left to the remaining pair to carry out the assault themselves. When they made their move, the pilot realised what was happening and placed the plane in a steep dive, throwing the hijackers off balance, and allowing the security personnel, which all Israeli planes have, to move in. One of the terrorists was killed. The other, a young woman named Leila Garad, was captured.

Israel responded to the growing number of attacks by bombing Beirut airport, destroying thirteen Lebanese planes as punishment for harbouring the Fedayeen.

Then, on 6th September, 1970, the PFLP commandeered three aircraft simultaneously and diverted them to Dawson's Field in the desert near Amman, Jordan.

Specially chosen for its isolated location and, as a geologist had pointed out to the group, the suitability of the terrain for landing aircraft, a runway was prepared, marked by oil drums filled with kerosene and rags for use at night. Then, ringed by PFLP fighters, the makeshift airport was cordoned off.

Two of the hijacked airplanes landed at the field within ten minutes of each other. The pilot of the third plane managed to convince the terrorists that the DC10 was too heavy for the improvised airfield and they put down at Cairo International instead where, after evacuating the passengers, the guerrillas blew up the plane.

The hijackers at Dawson's Field, renamed Revolution Airport, demanded that Leila Garad and six other terrorists held in European jails, along with 1000 Palestinian prisoners held in Israel, be released in exchange for the 310 hostages on the two planes. A three day deadline was imposed to meet their demands.

The European countries, taken by surprise, quickly acquiesced. Leila Garad and six others were set free. Israel, however, had realised that giving in to the terrorists only encouraged them. The date for the release of the 1000 prisoners came and went, and the PFLP fighters extended the deadline.

On 12th September, six days after the drama began to unfold, a third plane came to join the others at Dawson's Field. Incredibly, the two Sudanese men who had been removed from the El Al flight in Athens were allowed to board a Pan Am aircraft heading for New York. They took control of the plane after producing hand grenades and pistols and went to join the others on the runway at Revolution Airport.

Jordanian tanks and soldiers formed a security cordon around the airfield. There was a tense stand off between the terrorists and the troops. In exchange for the release of 125 women and children, the army agreed to pull back one mile.

Israel still refused to release the prisoners, so the hijackers offered to free the remaining passengers in exchange for safe passage for themselves.

The Jordanians accepted. The hostages were then released, except for the crew and a number of Jewish people on board, who the PFLP kept for further bargaining with Israel. Then, in sight of the world's media, they blew the three planes up on the runway.

The fighters and their captives went into hiding in the refugee camps of Jordan. King Hussein sent his army in after them, causing massive casualties amongst the Palestinian population as he sought to free the crew and Israeli passengers. Thousands of innocent people died before the 54 hostages were eventually released.

The month in which the Jordanians turned on their West Bank brothers became known as Black September.

FRIENDS DIVIDED.

The People's Front for the Liberation of Palestine, the PFLP, said the hijackings were a way to raise awareness of their struggle for justice. Israel had invaded her country in 1967 and no one seemed to care or even appeared to have noticed. Now, they were the talk of the world's media.

Although the hijackings had brought the plight of their people into focus, it also brought a lot of pressure on the Arab nations harbouring them.

In Jordan, King Hussein felt particularly sensitive to the accusation that he was protecting terrorists and he announced the introduction of Martial Law to crack down on the problem.

The Jordanians and the Palestinians were now at war with each other, as King Hussein attempted to rein in Arafat's men.

This caused considerable consternation amongst the other Arab nations, and a summit was convened in Cairo by Egyptian President Nasser and the heads of the Middle East countries to try to end the in-fighting.

The result of the peace conference was a handshake between Arafat and Hussein and an agreement to suspend hostilities. The meeting was a success, but it was to be President Nasser's last act.

The war of 1967 had taken its toll on the Egyptian head of state. Despite tendering his resignation in the aftermath of his countries ignominious defeat, he had continued in the role at the request of his people, and was a voice of moderation and hope in the Arab world.

A matter of hours after saying goodbye to the Middle East leaders called to the peace summit in Cairo, President Nasser suffered a heart attack and died.

Millions of people turned out on the streets of the Middle East to mourn his demise. A great leader had been lost.

Anwar Sadat succeeded Nasser in Egypt, while in Syria there was also a change of leadership, with Hafez Al Assad assuming control.

In Jordan, despite the handshake, Hussein's men continued their belligerence towards the guerrilla groups, and they actively pursued their removal from Jordanian soil.

Finally, in July, 1971, King Hussein's troops launched an all-out assault on Palestinian fighters. Chairman Arafat moved his men to Lebanon, close to the southern border, where they could continue to launch raids into Israel.

The PLO was hurt by the attack by a one time ally. Something had gone wrong with the movement if they were alienating friends and former advocates.

The organisation needed to legitimise, but there was still the need for violent resistance. At a meeting in Damascus in the autumn of 1971, Arafat insisted that the PLO must separate itself from the fighting. Another faction would have to carry out the guerrilla activities. It would consist of members of each of the terrorist branches, and would employ the skills of the PFLP. The name of the new wing was Black September.

Named after the month which saw Arab fight Arab, the Palestinian terror group would go on to strike fear into the hearts and minds of Israelis everywhere.

Starting with the murder of the Jordanian Prime Minister, Wash Tel, in Cairo, with one of the assassins drinking some of the victim's blood as it ran from his body, they instantly announced their ruthlessness.

It would not be an isolated act. With the PLO free to conduct legitimate attacks against Israel and the Occupation, the new group could concentrate on worldwide terrorism to attack their enemies and promote the cause.

The hijackings continued, including that of a Belgian plane flying to Tel Aviv in May, 1972. Then came an attack on the Israeli airport at Lod which left 24 people dead. This was followed by a bomb at a bus station in Tel Aviv that wounded eleven people, and an assault on an oil refinery in Italy, exhibiting the international range of the operations.

Finally, on the 5th of September, at the Olympic Games being held in Munich, Germany, Black September carried out its most high profile attack.

While the world watched the drama unfold, an indelible image emerged of terrorists in balaclavas holding eleven Israeli athletes hostage. The name Black September became a byword for terror.

Six months later, in March 1973, the group conducted what was to be their last major assault, when eight men shot their way into the Saudi Arabian embassy in Khartoum where a farewell party was being held for an American diplomat, Charles Moore, and others, including the American Ambassador and the Belgian Charges D'Affaires.

These three men were murdered in cold blood during the siege, and Western sensitivities finally turned against the Palestinians.

Yasser Arafat decided it was time to dispense with their deadly services, and the Black September terrorist organisation disappeared into the night.

THE MUNICH OLYMPICS.

The 20th Olympic Games were held in Munich, Germany, in 1972. For the Israelis, only 27 years after the end of World War 2 and the Holocaust, to be parading their nation's flag in the opening ceremony was an incredibly emotional affair.

To promote a relaxed atmosphere in the Olympic Village, the German authorities placed the issue of security with 2000 volunteers wearing light blue uniforms and dispensed with the services of the police.

The Israeli athletes were accommodated in five adjacent apartments in the camp. The day before the Games began, all of the athletes visited the German Death Camp at Dachau to pay their respects to the Jewish victims.

Elsewhere, at a hotel in Munich, eight Palestinian terrorists had just checked into their rooms. There were three leaders and five foot soldiers.

Jamal al Gashey was one of them. Just eighteen years old at the time, he had been born in Palestine but was forced to flee with his family to escape the Israeli onslaught and occupation. He ended up living in the shanty town of Shatila refugee camp in Lebanon.

When Jamal looked around him, and envisaged spending his life in such conditions; a tin-hut home, sewage running through the streets, a lack of food and water, and no employment, he blamed Israel for his predicament.

Jamal turned to the guerrilla groups who were at least prepared to put up a fight.

Al Gashey received training in camps in Lebanon, before moving to Libya to study advanced fighting techniques. He felt he was being prepared for a special operation. He was right.

The Palestinian terrorists left Libya for Germany. As a foot soldier, Jamal still had no idea what their objective was. With some free time on his hands, he went off to the Olympics to watch a volleyball tournament.

The next day, his mission was explained to him by the unit leaders. They were going to attack the Israeli compound the following morning.

In the evening of 4th September, the Israeli team went to the theatre to relax, where they watched a performance of Fiddler on the Roof. They returned to their rooms and went to bed, ready to perform in their Olympic events.

At 4.42 am, the Black September commandos climbed the perimeter wall to the Athlete's Village and headed for the apartments housing the Israelis. They were carrying sports bags, laden with weapons.

They entered the first apartment and found one of the coaches. When the man attempted to seize one of the guns, he was shot and badly injured.

Despite the coach being wounded, he was ordered to direct the terrorists to the other rooms where the Israeli athletes were staying.

The athletes were housed in rooms one to five. The coach had been in room one. He led the guerrillas passed room two and directed them to room three, which held the weight-lifters and wrestlers, hoping that they might be able to overpower them.

In Room 3, Joseph Romano, a big, strong athlete, attempted to grab one of the machine guns, but he was shot and fatally wounded. The coach also died from his injuries. There were now two fatalities and nine others were being held hostage.

As the world awoke, news of the crisis began to emerge. A spokesman appeared from amongst the terrorists. Dressed in a white suit, his face blacked up with shoe polish, he called himself Issa. He told the assembled media that Israel had until twelve noon to release 200 Palestinian political prisoners or the hostages would be killed.

Other guerrillas would appear at a window or step briefly on to an apartment balcony. Clad in balaclavas, the images made for eerie viewing.

In Jerusalem, Golda Meir, the Prime Minister, refused to accede to the terrorists' demands, saying to do so would imperil every Israeli in the world.

A team of German negotiators talked to Issa, offering any amount of money for the release of the hostages. Issa explained that this was not about money. It was all about the Palestinian cause.

The Germans pressed for a delay in the deadline, saying negotiations with the Israeli government had yet to be concluded.

At 11.59, Issa backed down and extended the deadline for the release of the prisoners to 5 o'clock.

All the time, the Games continued, despite the situation in the Village. It was only at four in the afternoon, amid international outcry, that the Olympic events were temporarily suspended.

It was further announced that there would be a memorial service held in the Olympic Stadium at 10 o'clock the following morning for the two athletes who had been killed.

Israel offered to send in a Special Forces unit to tackle the terrorists, but Germany refused, saying they could handle the situation. As the events were taking place on foreign soil, Israel agreed to let the Germans deal with it.

By 4.30 in the afternoon, thirty minutes before the deadline, 38 policemen wearing track suits surrounded the apartments where the hostages were being held and awaited the codeword 'Sunshine'.

All the while, television crews were beaming the pictures live to a waiting world. The images were also being watched by the terrorists on the tv set in the athletes apartment.

The guerrillas became increasingly agitated as they realised they were about to be rushed. They appeared at the windows and craned their necks to see if they could identify in person what they had seen on tv. The operation had to be aborted.

When it became obvious to the terrorists that their demands would not be met, and that the Germans were looking for an opportunity to end the siege, their position changed.

The group called for a plane to take them to an unspecified Arab country. Otherwise, they explained, the hostages would all be killed.

The Germans did not possess a special task force for dealing with such situations, so they had to go along with the instructions given.

Two helicopters arrived to fly the guerrillas and hostages to Munich airport. With the Israeli athletes bound to each other and their hands tied behind their backs, there was no possibility to escape.

No one from the task force knew how many terrorists there were until they emerged from the apartment. The Germans had stationed five snipers at the airport, three up in the control tower and two on the ground, but there were eight guerrillas to be dealt with.

The snipers were not informed of the numbers they would be facing, even when this information became known back at the Olympic village.

At the airport, the helicopters landed and the guerrillas emerged to check the surroundings before transferring the hostages. Almost immediately, the German snipers opened fire.

A fierce gun battle ensued. The terrorists had been instructed to fight to the death if ambushed.

In the panic, one of the helicopter pilots took refuge alongside a sniper on the ground. The hostages stayed on board the choppers as they were tied to each other and unable to escape.

Teams of German police, at the compound perimeter, joined the fight. One of the terrorists attempted to escape, but the sniper on the ground shot him dead. When the police officers heard the sniper fire, they mistook the shooter for one of the guerrillas and seriously wounded both him and the pilot beside him.

After two hours of intense fighting, as armoured vehicles surrounded the terrorists and the situation became hopeless, a Palestinian threw a hand grenade into one of the choppers, killing the hostages inside. His colleague unloaded a machine gun magazine into the other. All nine hostages died.

The memorial service planned in the Olympic Stadium went ahead as scheduled the following morning, but it would now commemorate eleven lives, not two.

The Games resumed that afternoon, except for the surviving Israeli athletes, who flew home with the coffins of their dead colleagues.

Five of the terrorists had been killed, and their bodies were returned to a hero's welcome in Libya. The other three, including Jamal al Gashey, were interred in a German prison.

A few months later, a Lufthansa jet was hijacked by a Palestinian group who demanded the release of the three imprisoned terrorists. Germany, to Israel's disgust, capitulated. The three surviving members of the Munich Olympic outrage were set free. Two were later hunted down and killed by Israeli Secret Agents, along with a dozen people suspected of planning the operation.

Jamal al Gashey was the only member of the Munich operation to escape his punishment and, despite several attempts on his life, he lives today in hiding with his family.

The Lufthansa plane that was hijacked had only twelve passengers on board, none of whom were women or children. There was a whiff of scandal about the entire affair, and it has since come to light that the situation had been engineered to allow Germany to rid herself of the terrorists and wash her hands of the whole affair.

Jamal al Gashey is proud of what he and his comrades achieved at the Olympic Games. Suddenly, he claimed, everyone was talking about the Palestinian cause. It was, then, mission accomplished for the Black September group. They had certainly performed their tasks with greater skill than the Germans who'd tried to stop them.

In the aftermath of the affair, a special task-force of elite German commandos was established to deal with incidents of this nature. For the eleven Israeli athletes so cruelly slain in Munich, this reform came too late.

CARLOS THE JACKAL.

One man came to symbolise Palestinian resistance. He was born in Caracas, Venezuela, on 12th October, 1949. His name was Ilich Ramirez Sanchez, but the world came to know him as Carlos the Jackal.

In his youth, Ilich trained for three years to become a priest before losing interest and deciding he was an atheist. He then became interested in the Marxist revolutionary movements that were sweeping through South America at that point. Amongst his peers, he stood out as a leader and was fiercely idealistic.

When his parents separated and later divorced, he moved to London with his mother and brothers. He attended technical training schools, and though his tutors pronounced him lazy, he managed to pass all of his subjects.

He continued to be fascinated by communism, and eventually moved to the USSR, where he soon came to the attention of the KGB.

Ilich befriended several Palestinian dissidents while in Russia and became interested in their cause. At the request of Soviet Intelligence, the young man was sent to a terrorist training camp in the hills above Amman, Jordan, where he was the star pupil.

It was in the Middle East that Ilich adopted the name of Carlos. When security forces later raided a hideout and discovered a copy of Frederick Forsyth's thriller about an assassin, the name 'The Jackal' was added to his nom-de-guerre.

Carlos fought alongside the infant Palestinian resistance forces in the conflict with Jordanian troops in 1970. Because of his knowledge of London, he was chosen to be the Palestinian Popular Front's representative in the English capital, moving there a short time later.

While the world watched in awe at the attacks being conducted against Israel, the El Al hijacking and at the Munich Olympics, Carlos was kicking his heels, frustrated at being overlooked for such high-profile terrorist activity.

Eventually, he received his orders. His campaign of terror could begin.

On Sunday, 3rd of December 1973, at a large mansion in London, the butler answered a knock at the door. He was confronted by an armed man, who went inside and found Joseph Seiff, a 68 year old businessman, in the bathroom.

Seiff was the president of the Marks and Spencers retailing group and Vice President of the British Zionist Movement.

Carlos identified his target and shot him point blank in the face. The bullet deflected off the victim's teeth and lodged in his jaw. When the would-be assassin attempted to fire again at the figure slumped on the floor, the gun jammed, and with police swiftly arriving on the scene, the gunman fled.

Seiff survived the hit, but a legend had been born. Carlos requested further operations, and now that he had shown he was up to the task, his superiors saw fit to give him fresh orders.

The most audacious of these enterprises was the assault on the OPEC conference in Vienna, 1975, where some of the most important oil people in the world were present when Carlos and a small team shot their way into the building and into the boardroom on the first floor.

With a touch of panache and an ear for drama, Carlos announced to the startled representatives, 'This is a hijack. You all know who I am.'

Three people were killed in the initial assault, and seventy hostages were taken. Statements were read to the press about the righteousness of the Palestinian cause, before Carlos issued his demands.

Given the importance of the delegates at the conference, the orders were met. A plane was placed at the terrorists' disposal and, along with the hostages, they flew to Algiers and received a hero's reception. Eventually, after receiving a ransom payment said to be fifty million dollars, Carlos set the hostages free.

The operation could be considered a great success for Carlos and the cause, but the Palestinian guerrilla movement had grown resentful of the Jackal's flair for publicity. They viewed him as self-serving, and wondered whether he had properly channelled all the funds accrued from his activities.

Disillusioned by this lack of appreciation, Carlos moved to France. In 1982, he attempted to blow up a nuclear reactor but was thwarted when his rocket-propelled grenades failed to penetrate the outer concrete walls.

Magdalena Kopp, Carlos' wife, was arrested for her part in the enterprise. The Jackal's response was to issue a threat to the French government promising reprisals unless Magdalena was released.

When this was not forthcoming, Carlos blew up a passenger train, killing five people and injuring scores more. He then bombed a French embassy in Austria and a restaurant in Paris in his campaign of intimidation.

To no avail. His wife received a six year prison sentence, eventually serving five before she was released and immediately rejoined Carlos.

Finding refuge in such countries as Lebanon, Yemen, Syria, Iraq, and Libya, as a hero of the Arab resistance movement, Carlos lived a playboy life-style. His high-profile eventually made him too hot to handle, and he was arrested in Sudan in 1994, his protectors unable or unwilling to shield him any longer.

Carlos the Jackal came to epitomise the terrorist movement. In 1997 in France, he was sentenced to life imprisonment, where he remains to this day.

THE PRICE OF OIL.

Beneath the desert wasteland lay a priceless commodity that the world would come to want. At a time when oil was being discovered in huge quantities in the Middle East, the industrialised nations were creating an unprecedented demand for it.

For more than five thousand years, oil seeping through the ground had been used for lighting, to waterproof boats, and had been used in paints.

In the temples, oil would be used to keep the eternal flame to the Gods alight, and the Bible records Moses being cast into the river in a basket of reeds and pitch to make it float.

Ancient Persian tablets illustrate the use of oil-based lighting in better-off households, while in 8th Century Baghdad the streets were paved with tar.

But these were primitive times. It would be many millennia before heavy drilling equipment would arrive to extract the raw material from the ground.

The modern history of oil began in 1853 when a Polish scientist named Ignacy Lukasiewicz produced Kerosene from crude oil by process of distillation. He named the result Rock Oil or, in Polish, Petr Oleum.

Petroleum gathers beneath the earth's surface, formed over the course of millions of years. Plant and animal matter decomposes, to be covered by layers of silt, sand, clay and other materials which crystallise as rock. The plant and animal remains liquefy for lack of oxygen to become crude oil, forming pools between the rock layers in the upper strata of the earth's crust.

The popularity of the motor vehicle, the rise of manufacturing to drive the war effort of the two major conflicts of the twentieth century, and to meet the upturn in life-style that arrived with the birth of consumerism, placed the countries of the Middle East, where oil was in abundance, in a position of importance that they had not previously held.

Between 1918 and 1934, a large pipeline was built from Iraq through Jordan and Palestine, ending up at the port of Haifa on the Mediterranean coast.

The colonial instincts of the Western powers led to a series of joint operations between British, French, and American oil companies and Arab states.

In 1933, Reza Khan, the Shah of Shahs in Persia, cancelled the concession granted to the Anglo-Persian oil company as he sought to renegotiate the deal on better terms.

The British raised the issue in protest at the League of Nations, where it was decided that the earlier terms had been unfavourable, and the contract was revised in favour of the oil-producer. In keeping with its economic independence, in 1935 Persia changed its name to Iran.

The largest discoveries of black gold in the Middle East were at the Greater Burgan field in Kuwait in 1938, believed to hold 87 billion barrels of oil. Then, in 1948, a slightly larger field, at 87.5 billion barrels, was found at Ghawar in Saudi Arabia.

In 1945, most of the world's oil had been supplied by Venezuela, but all that was about to change and the Middle East soon became the most powerful of the oil-producing regions.

With wealth came responsibility. The West had come to rely on the commodity. Recessions could be triggered by a price hike or a halt in production.

In 1953, the British and the United States overthrew the democratically-elected government of Iran in order to install a regime that would preserve supplies to the Western powers.

Elsewhere, where the industry had not been nationalized, the oil companies themselves were at liberty to raise or reduce prices. In 1959, after a serious reduction in the cost of a barrel led to a slump in revenues returned to the countries themselves, the oil producing nations formed an alliance to protect their interests.

OPEC, the Organisation of Petroleum Exporting Countries was founded by the governments of Iraq, Iran, Kuwait, Saudi Arabia, and Venezuela. The cartel accounted for 90% of global exports.

In total, by 1970, the Middle East was producing half of the world's supply. 80% of the world's oil reserves were also to be found in the Arabian Peninsula. This gave the oil-producing countries a greater say on the international stage.

For once, their arguments were listened to with interest at the United Nations. There was no longer unqualified support for Israel. The Arabs, with their oil, would have to be appeased.

The vibrant industry returned fabulous wealth to the host nations, and also provided employment across the Arab world.

Palestinian labour was much sought after. The men were skilled and dextrous, and many were drawn to work in the oil fields and refineries. They were also known for their militancy, and it was Palestinians who organised the first strike against ARAMCO, the Arabian American Oil Company.

As revenues rolled in and conditions in the industry improved, relations between the employer and workforce became amicable, and the Palestinians could go about the business of earning a living.

Many of these men had migrated after al Nakbah, and most sent money home to their refugee families. The oil industry provided an opportunity to escape the misery of the UNWRA camps and to find work amongst fellow Arabs.

The discovery in the Middle East of the precious fossil fuel placed the Arabs on the world stage. It also, through employment, rescued many of the Laji Un and Nazihun.

While the PLO derided the emigrant workers for failing their cause, there was no disputing that these men improved conditions for themselves and for their families. It is believed many donated money to the Palestinians for arms or food, too, so they made their contribution in a way they saw fit.

And, as skilled workers, they contributed to the wider Arab economy, and showed another side to the Palestinian character other than that of refugee or terrorist.

Petroleum gave the Arab nations a place on the world stage. The Middle East had an effective bargaining tool when dealing with the West, which was heavily pro-Israeli. It also set free a percentage of the oppressed people suffering occupation.

Oil, as we have seen, has many uses.

THE YOM KIPPUR WAR.

The Jewish Day of Atonement, observed with fasting and prayer, is known as Yom Kippur, and falls on the tenth day of the Hebrew calendar, the 6th of October. On that day in 1973, Egypt and Syria launched a long-mooted assault, and took the complacent Israelis completely by surprise. Egyptian President Anwar Sadat was in a stalemate situation. His peace offer to the Knesset had been rejected, and with no prospect of negotiating the return of the Sinai Peninsula, seized by Israel in the Six Day War, Egypt turned to America for advice. Secretary of State Henry Kissinger met an Egyptian envoy in Washington on the 24th and 25th of February to thrash out a deal whereby the US might persuade her ally Israel to come to the table with Egypt. Kissinger said that his hands were tied. Until the situation became a crisis, he was not in a position to act.

President Sadat viewed the response as a tacit invitation to launch an attack. Despite the fact his earlier offer of peace for land was the first such offer to be made by an Arab state to Israel, it had been turned down. Sadat had nowhere left to turn.

To correct the impasse, Egypt prepared for a 'limited' war. By provoking a crisis, the UN, and the two superpowers, the US and the USSR, would be forced to intervene and bring both parties to the negotiating table, which was Egypt's aim. A game of political cat and mouse began. Twice, President Sadat declared his intention to attack Israel. Twice, Israel was forced to mobilise its reserve forces, placing huge strains on their economy, with essential workers forced to down tools and take up arms. It was all designed to throw Israel off guard, in a campaign of misinformation.

Aided by a top double-agent, who was so highly thought of by Mossad that the intelligence reports would be read to Prime Minister Golda Meir herself, the Egyptian spy led Israel to believe that Sadat had decided to postpone his proposed war indefinitely. Israel let down her guard.

Even when King Hussein of Jordan flew in secret on the 25th September to warn Meir of imminent attack, the Israelis preferred to believe their high level mole, who was a senior aide to Sadat and a relative of former President Nasser.

Finally, Egyptian and Syrian forces were amassed near their borders with Israel, and at the agreed time, 2 o'clock in the afternoon of the 6th of October, 1973, 222 warplanes from the Egyptian air force and 60 from Syria were launched against Israeli positions in Sinai and the Golan Heights.

Some 10,500 artillery shells fell on the Bar Lev line, the Israeli frontline at the Suez Canal, in the first minute of fighting at a rate of 175 missiles every second, inflicting material and psychological damage to Israeli forces.

Eight hundred officers and 13,500 soldiers of the Egyptian army raced across the canal and broke through Israeli lines. Within ninety minutes, Egypt had captured all of the Israeli fortifications and had established their own defences five kilometres east of the canal. And there, as planned, they dug in.

The aim of limited war was to bring Israel to the negotiating table. The tactic employed, to avoid a repeat of the humiliation and outright destruction their armed forces had suffered in 1967, was to advance only as far into Sinai as air cover and their defences would allow.

The USSR were the principle supporters of the Arab governments and the suppliers of the latest weaponry. However, they had not been prepared to give Egypt armaments that would stretch into Israel itself. Therefore, Egypt could only afford to advance so far, if they wished to hold on to any gains made.

When the Israeli air force responded to the attack and launched reprisal raids, Russian-made surface to air missiles shot them out of the sky. The Israelis could not break through Egyptian lines, and all attempts to do so met with devastating losses. The Egyptians, fighting within their capabilities, were winning the limited war.

Meanwhile, faced with defeat on the Sinai front, Israel turned her attention to the Golan Heights. There were Jewish Settlements in the vicinity, something that was not the case in the Egyptian Peninsula, and these communities needed defending. Israel concentrated her forces there, and had a stroke of luck when they launched their attacks on the 9th of October, a day when the Syrians ran out of ground to air missiles. Damascus came under direct fire, and the Syrians were forced to retreat in the face of the Israeli onslaught. After days of despair, the IDF finally had something to cheer about.

Defence Minister Moshe Dayan felt the tide of war turning in his favour. Even support from brigades of Jordanian troops could not stem the losses in the Golan Heights. King Hussein would not permit attacks on Israel from Jordanian soil, but he was prepared to allow some of his forces to join the Arab cause. It was to no avail, and by the 11th of October, Syria was prepared to cut her losses. President Sadat of Egypt received word from his Soviet friends that President Assad of Syria had asked them to negotiate a cease-fire with Israel. Given that Sadat thought Egypt and Syria were partners in the conflict, the news came as a surprise.

Sadat called Assad and asked him if there was any truth in the story. Assad assured him that all he had said to the USSR was that Syria would be prepared to accept a cease-fire if Israel was prepared to return to the 1967 borders: an offer that was not at the time on the table.

President Assad further assured Sadat that Syrian forces were doing well and were inflicting heavy casualties in the Golan Heights. It was all lies, and a perfect illustration of the distrust between the supposed Arab allies.

But Sadat bought it. Urged to move deeper into Sinai to engage the Israelis and draw more of the Jewish brigades away from the Golan area, Egyptian forces moved out of the range of cover provided by the SAM missiles, and played right into Israeli hands.

All of a sudden, with the Syrian threat removed, IAF planes were free to concentrate on raiding in Sinai where, unencumbered by the threat posed by the surface to air battery, Egyptian tanks and troops were picked off at will.

Ariel Sharon, leading the forces on the ground, disobeyed orders to halt any thrust at the Suez line and broke through to the west bank of the canal, cutting off the entire Egyptian 3rd army and threatening the capital, Cairo, itself.

It was time to sue for peace. Egypt had first met then thrown away its objectives, and on the 22nd of October, all parties agreed to UN Resolution 338 calling for a cease-fire.

In less than three weeks of fighting, 2700 Israelis had been killed, along with 8500 Arabs. Israel agreed to withdraw from parts of the Sinai in accordance with the UN resolution, and in December of that year, Jordan, Egypt, and Israel, but not Syria, met for further talks in Geneva aimed at promoting a continued peace.

Once again, despite the early setback, Israel had proved her military might in the region, but despite this, there was a great deal of discontent in the nation.

For failing to prepare properly for the war, and for being caught so unaware, Golda Meir was forced to resign her position as Prime Minister. In her place came former General, Chief of Staff, and Ambassador to the United States, Yitzak Rabin.

THE INTERREGNUM.

The Arabs enjoyed early success in the Yom Kippur War. Still, despite the loss of 2687 soldiers with a further 7251 wounded, it was Israel that emerged victorious.

It was time for the Arabs to change tack. On 11th of April 1974, the PFLP took dozens of teenagers hostages in the town of Qiryat Shimona and demanded the release of Palestinian prisoners. The IDF stormed the building and 19 Israeli youths died in the fighting.

On 15th of May the same year, 100 schoolchildren were held captive in Ma'alot by three Palestinians from the Hawatma faction of the PDFLP. Again, Israel opted for a military solution and 22 children were killed in the operation.

Israel responded to the terrorist attacks by bombing Palestinian camps in Southern Lebanon. Sixty civilians were killed.

In November, PLO fighters stormed the village of Beit Shean leaving four dead and twenty wounded. Then, in December, a hand grenade was thrown into a Tel Aviv cinema injuring 51 people.

In March 1975, armed Palestinians took a number of guests hostage at the Savoy Hotel in Israel before the army was able to release them two days later.

In July, a bomb exploded in Zion Square in Jerusalem leaving 13 dead and 65 wounded.

The following year, on the 27th of June, an AirFrance jet travelling from Tel Aviv to Paris was hijacked and diverted to Entebbe, near the Ugandan capital at Kampala.

The hostage-takers demanded the release of 53 Palestinians held in Israeli jails. The government refused to deal with the terrorists, fearing this would set a precedent, and instead launched a surprise counter-attack.

Within an hour of their arrival, the IDF storm-troopers had killed the hijackers and freed the 100 hostages, losing only one officer, Lieutenant-Colonel Yoni Netanyahu, in the assault.

In Washington DC, United States President Jimmy Carter responded to the situation by calling for the creation of an independent Palestinian state and Israel's removal from the Occupied Territories.

Following criticism of his intervention from the Jewish lobby on Capitol Hill, the White House soon backed down.

In Jerusalem, Following allegations of corruption, Yitzak Rabin resigned as Prime Minister to be replaced by Menachem Begin, the former terrorist leader of the Irgun.

The Likud Party came to power for the first time, having run on a platform of no territorial concessions and no peace with the PLO.

Despite the obvious Right Wing credentials of many on Begin's platform, including the former general Dayan as his Foreign Minister and old lion Sharon as his Minister for Agriculture, Begin made a remarkable move in September when he sent his Foreign Minister to Morocco for secret talks with Egypt's Deputy Prime Minister, Hassan el-Tohami.

Dayan arrived incognito, accompanied by a bodyguard, and entered the Royal Palace through a side entrance. Inside, he ditched the disguise and joined Tohami and the King of Morocco, whom he presented with a set of ancient Canaanite weapons from his private collection. Dayan was an avid archaeologist.

The meeting began, with the king as intermediary. The aim was to lay the groundwork for an eventual meeting between Sadat and Begin.

The item most pressing for Egypt was the return of the Peninsula. The Palestinian problem could be negotiated later, but in return for peace with Egypt, Israel must return her captured lands in Sinai.

El-Tohami pressed Dayan for a commitment. If Israel were willing to return the land she had won in 1967, peace between the two countries would follow.

Foreign Minister Dayan explained that the decision was not his to make. It was for Begin and the Knesset to decide.

The secret talks ended. Although nothing had been signed, they lay the groundwork for what came next. On the 9th November, President Sadat informed a stunned Egyptian parliament that he would do anything for peace, including going to the Knesset.

Prime Minister Begin responded the next day by issuing a verbal invitation, which he followed up days later with a formal written request, that Sadat come and meet the Israeli government.

Four days later, President Sadat arrived for his historic visit to Jerusalem. His speech to the Knesset was an enormous milestone in Arab-Jewish relations, but it was not exactly what the Israelis wanted to hear.

'I have not come here for a separate agreement between Egypt and Israel', he said. 'A partial peace will only delay the lighting of the fuse. In all sincerity I tell you that I welcome you among us with full security and safety. I declare to the whole world that we accept to live with you in a permanent peace based on justice. Peace cannot be worth its name unless it is based on justice and not on the occupation of the land of others. I tell you once and for all you have to give up your dreams of conquest. Complete withdrawal from the Arab territories occupied in 1967 is a logical and undisputed fact. We cannot accept the principle of debating or bargaining over it. As for the Palestinian cause, nobody can deny that it is the crux of the entire problem. There can be no peace without the Palestinians. There is no use not recognising the Palestinians and their right of return and to sovereignty.'

It was not what the Knesset had expected. So harsh were Sadat's words that the Defence Minister Ezer Weizman handed Begin a note saying 'We should prepare for war.'

Instead, despite the content of the speech, it represented the first meaningful dialogue between Israel and an Arab state. Further talks were scheduled. Maybe peace would be possible after all.

ISRAEL AND THE UNITED NATIONS.

The United Nations was formed in 1945 as the successor body to the League of Nations. It had been hoped, after two World Wars in the first half of the 20th Century, that a forum might exist to police all countries and intercede to prevent further hostilities.

United States President Truman told the delegates at the inaugural conference that this was 'a great day in history', and that they had created 'an instrument for peace'.

When the UN approved the partition plan for Palestine, the Jewish contingent, led by David Ben Gurion, moved unilaterally to rename their portion of the land Israel.

Resolution 194 then called for the repatriation of the refugees from the War of Independence fought between Israel and the Arabs, and entry into the fold was extended on the belief that Israel would make reparations with her neighbours.

Israel feigned to comply but, not for the last time, once her own demands had been met, the terms to which they had contracted would be left to languish.

In November, 1967, UN Resolution 242 called for Israel to retire from her recently-won territorial gains in return for peace with its Arab neighbours. All parties viewed the request with suspicion.

UN Resolution 338 reiterated the earlier recommendation of 242, with an added reference to the Palestinian refugee crisis, calling for their right to return to their homes. Again, the result was intransigence.

The Security Council of the United Nations condemned Israeli retaliatory measures in Southern Lebanon in ruling 347 on 24th April 1974, while in November Yasser Arafat was invited to address the General Assembly.

The leader of the PLO, recognised by the Arab League as the 'sole legitimate representative of the Palestinian people', appeared at the convention wearing a firearm at his side.

'I have come with an olive branch in one hand and a freedom fighter's gun in the other', said Arafat. 'Do not let the olive branch fall from my hand.'

The old warrior must have impressed the gathered delegates, for he emerged with UN Resolution GAR 3236, which affirmed the Palestinians right to self determination and independence, and the right of Palestinian refugees to return to their homes and property from which they had been displaced. The General Assembly gave the PLO almost all of the attributes of statehood except a vote, and awarded them observer status in a further resolution.

The United States proclaimed that they would only deal with the PLO if they accepted UNR 242 and 338 and recognised Israel's right to exist, something that had been denied in the PLO's founding charter in 1964.

On 10th of November 1975, in an extraordinary session at the General Assembly, the member states voted by 75 to 35 to condemn Zionism as a form of racism, confirmed as resolution GAR 3379.

Then, on March 15th, 1978, when Israel moved into Southern Lebanon, at the time in the midst of a civil war, the United Nations approved Resolution 425 by a vote of 12 to 0 which called for their immediate removal from the volatile region.

An international peace-keeping force sent into the area by order of UNR 426 was forced into a tense stand-off with Israel and was not able to achieve its objectives.

Israel would maintain her presence in Southern Lebanon throughout the fifteen year civil war that would consume the country. It would be the Spring of the year 2000 before Israel would fully comply with UNR 425.

The United Nations is still waiting for Israel to meet her demands on other resolutions. It may be some time, if ever, before Israel does as the UN has asked.

THE CAMP DAVID ACCORDS.

In an historical first for the leader of an Arab state, on the 19th of November, 1977, Anwar Sadat, President of Egypt flew to Jerusalem to address Prime Minister Begin and the Knesset.

Sadat's speech was watched by millions of people across the globe. He had earlier informed a shocked Arab world that he was prepared to go anywhere to ensure peace for Egypt, including to the Holy City.

In response, leaders such as President Assad of Syria had accused Egypt of attempting to secure peace for herself at the expense of Israel's other neighbours.

Instead, when he came to address the Israeli parliament, Sadat had berated the Jewish nation for its annexation of East Jerusalem, and he spoke up for the rights of the Palestinians.

Menachem Begin stressed that the Palestinian problem was a separate issue, and one for Israel alone to resolve.

Still, a dialogue had been established, and United States President Jimmy Carter was keen that it continue.

At Leeds Castle, Kent, in England in July 1978, Foreign Minister Moshe Dayan of Israel and his Egyptian counterpart Mohammed Ibrahim Kamel met for further talks. Again, these foundered on the Palestinian question.

President Carter then sent hand written letters of invitation to Begin and Sadat to attend the retreat at Camp David in Maryland. The two leaders accepted, and on the 4th of September, 1978, both parties arrived in the United States for talks scheduled to start the next day.

There were two topics of discussion. One was to provide a framework for peace in the Middle East, ostensibly dealing with the Palestinian crisis. The other was for a separate peace agreement between Israel and Egypt.

On the second day of business, the 6th of September, Begin and Sadat had their first face to face meeting. It was disastrous.

The Egyptian President took a hostile stance and read out a twelve page document of demands that Israel had to accept in order for peace to follow. It included the removal of the Israeli military and civilian presence in Sinai, the right of return for exiled Palestinians, and the return of East Jerusalem to Arab hands.

Prime Minister Begin retired overnight to consider the proposals. It seemed he did not lose much sleep, and he returned the next day to reject the offer outright.

Frustrated, President Carter worked with his own team of advisers to try and find some middle ground. On 10th of September, he submitted an outline plan to each party that might be in some way acceptable to both. From there, he attempted to pull the two sides closer to the centre in the hope they would find something they could agree to and live with.

Although Egypt and Israel were desperate for peace, it became obvious to President Carter that negotiations were more successful when Begin and Sadat were kept apart. The two men refused to back down to each other and their personalities clashed, with each looking ready to explode when in the other's company.

This left Moshe Dayan to deal with Sadat, and when the former army general informed the Egyptian president that Israel would not be giving up the Jewish settlements in Sinai, Sadat and his entourage packed their bags and prepared to leave.

Shaken, President Carter mustered all his persuasive powers and talked Sadat into staying. He then spoke to Begin and told him that he would lay any failure in the talks at Israel's door.

It worked, and over the next 48 hours, the two sides thrashed out an agreement. Egypt agreed not to tie any deal for Sinai in with the question of Gaza and the West Bank.

For Begin, in return for a peace agreement with the Arab world's strongest nation, he was quite prepared to give up the deserted peninsula. He agreed to give

217

up two strategic airfields there, in return for American funding to build two alternative airports in the Negev inside Israel.

As for removing the settlements, Begin promised to refer the issue to the Knesset. It was not a decision he could take alone.

The issue of Jerusalem was left undecided. The status quo would remain for the time being.

The Knesset eventually voted for removing the Sinai settlements. They had little strategic or religious significance, and it freed Israel, as Begin had hoped, to concentrate on consolidating their hold on the West Bank.

As Prime Minister Begin had assured his colleagues, it was 'Judaea and Samaria' that mattered most. They were the final pieces of the jigsaw required to recreate Eretz Israel, the Biblical Promised Land.

The agreements thrashed out at Camp David were formalized into two documents. One was the Framework for Peace in the Middle East that encompassed three phases. Firstly, Egypt, Israel, and Jordan would meet to elect a self-governing body in the Occupied Territories. Secondly, after the election of a self-governing body, there would be a five-year transitional period that would allow Israel to withdraw with peace and security.

Lastly, within a year of the beginning of the transitional phase, discussions were to take place between the three parties and representatives of the Palestinians to decide on the final status of the Occupied Territories.

The other document was the Framework for Peace between Israel and Egypt. In exchange for normal relations between the two warring nations, including access to the Suez Canal, Israel would return the captured Sinai Peninsular to Egypt.

The Camp David Accords were ratified by the Treaty of Washington, signed by President Sadat and Prime Mister Begin on the White House lawn in front of 1400 guests on 26th March, 1979. The two men were jointly awarded the Nobel Peace prize later that year.

Ariel Sharon was given the job of evicting the settlers. It proved less difficult than anticipated, with most Israelis ecstatic at their first peace accord with an Arab neighbour, which represented acceptance at last.

Egypt fared less well. The rest of the Arab countries vilified Sadat for brokering a separate agreement as they had warned. The Arab League moved its headquarters from Cairo to Tunis in protest.

It was not as if Egypt could renege on the deal. Israel made it clear that termination of the peace accord would be tantamount to a declaration of war.

Shunned by the Arab world, Egypt began to turn to the West for support, which further drove a wedge between her and her former allies. Sadat also failed to support the Islamic revolution in Iran, which angered many Muslim Fundamentalists.

Under pressure and fearing a coup, the Egyptian president ordered the arrest and imprisonment of 1500 senior public figures. He had turned against his own countrymen.

Eventually, at a military rally in Cairo in October of 1981, Anwar Sadat was assassinated. His crime had been to sue for peace with Israel, turn his back on the other Arab nations, and to move increasingly westwards. He was replaced by his former Vice-President, also wounded in the Cairo attack, the moderate, Hosni Mubarak.

INTO LEBANON.

In America, a new president, Ronald Reagan, had been voted in. The former actor initially proved himself an adept diplomat, arranging a cessation of hostilities between Israel and the PLO that came into effect on 24th July, 1981.

The cease-fire was holding. Yasser Arafat had managed to rein in the terror elements in his organisation and proved that the PLO was a worthy partner to peace. This legitimacy threatened the Israeli position that claimed it could not create a peace-treaty with a non-existent partner. Now, clearly, a Palestinian body did exist with whom it was possible to negotiate.

There was nothing else for it, the cease-fire had to go, and in order to get rid of it, a pretext had to be found.

Fresh from removing the Settlements in the Sinai, Ariel Sharon, the new Minister for Defence, turned his attention to Lebanon, the stronghold of the PLO.

The Palestinian guerrillas, having outstayed their welcome in Jordan and being expelled during Black September, had been accepted into Lebanon in a deal encouraged and supported by Egypt when they were at the head of the Arab League.

From their base in Southern Lebanon, the PLO had managed to launch attacks against Israel. Yasser Arafat, however, was now prepared to accept Israel's right to exist and to renounce terrorism. He realised the best his people could hope for was a Palestinian mini-state, only he was careful when it came to announcing this to his fanatical supporters.

The political landscape in Lebanon was extremely complicated. What Israel most sought was a Lebanese partner in power who would sign a treaty. Then, Israel would have a peace agreement with two of her Arab neighbours.

Ariel Sharon favoured Bashir Gemayel, leader of the Christian militias. Having aided his path to the Presidency, Israel was on the verge of getting what it wanted, but that still left the Palestinians to be dealt with.

By February of 1982, there were 25,000 IDF soldiers amassed at the border. UN troops monitoring the situation reported provocative action including the firing of weapons close to Palestinian positions. The PLO did not respond.

On 8th of February, 700 well-armed Israeli soldiers entered Lebanon for what the government called 'a recreational trip'. Again, neither the Syrians nor the PLO took the bait.

In March, the IDF proceeded in military formation to the Lebanese town of Khaim but did not draw fire from the Palestinians and were honour-bound to retreat.

Then, in April and May, Israel launched bombing raids on PLO positions in Southern Lebanon and Beirut. On the 4th and 5th of June, in protest, the PLO launched missiles into Galilee, albeit aiming away from Jewish settlements.

Sharon called the missile attack outrageous. Prime Minister Begin called it intolerable. They quickly convened a Cabinet meeting and came up with their response: Operation Peace for Galilee.

The IDF were entrusted with freeing all of the Settlements in Galilee from the range of Palestinian fire. The operation was to last 48 hours and would establish a security line 28 miles inside the Lebanese border. That was to be the extent of the mission. Beirut, Sharon assured the Cabinet, was not in the picture.

By the 23rd of June, 9 armoured divisions consisting of a total of 90,000 men entered Lebanon, along with 1300 tanks, and a similar number of armoured personnel carriers. Israel also had complete control of the airspace and the coast.

The PLO had approximately 13,000 combatants, mostly armed with assault rifles, and just 35 tanks.

The Palestinians population lived in refugee camps and in the major Lebanese towns of Tyre and Sidon. The PLO party headquarters were located in the capital city, Beirut.

Ahead of the advance into hostile territory, Israel employed a huge air bombardment to lessen resistance rather than risk its foot soldiers in urban warfare.

Writing in the Times newspaper on the 19th of July, the redoubtable Robert Fisk said it looked as if a tornado had ripped through the town of Sidon, tearing off balconies, pulling down walls, and collapsing whole buildings. About three-quarters of the town centre was completely erased. A total of 310 buildings were destroyed and another 1550 were damaged.

In Tyre, the situation was similar. 1500 buildings were flattened and another 4500 were hit.

The refugee camps, along with the towns of Damour and Nabatieh, were also attacked. A United Nations report issued on the 23rd of June reported that at Aj Bour el-Shemali refugee camp, 35% of the houses were destroyed. At Rachidieh camp, 70% of all refugee homes had gone the same way. At Ain Hilweh refugee camp, the destruction had been total.

On 7th of July, the death toll in Lebanon stood at 10,134, with 17,337 people wounded. And this was all before Israel arrived in Beirut.

BEIRUT.

The aim of the operation, now, Ariel Sharon informed the Knesset on 30th of June, was to bring about the destruction of the PLO, its headquarters, and its infrastructure. The PLO, Sharon announced, should cease to exist.

The Defence Minister also declared that it was nine years since the Yom Kippur War, and that a whole generation of Israeli soldiers had no experience of battle and they needed some.

It reflected Rafael Eitan's view that he 'Had this vast military arsenal, therefore he had to use it.'

And what weapons they had. As well as the usual artillery shells, there were cluster bombs that dropped up to 650 grenades indiscriminately over a several hundred yard radius, and phosphorous bombs which were hugely incendiary. Both weapons were prohibited by the 1980 UN Convention in Geneva for use in civilian-populated areas.

Robert Fisk, again on hand, and eventually recorded in his book 'Pity The Nation', described the effect of a phosphorous bomb on a pair of five year old twins during the fighting in Beirut.

'A doctor took the children, even though they were already dead, and placed them in buckets of water to put out the flames. Half an hour later, when he took them out, they were still burning.'

There were four main phases to the fighting. From 4th to 24th June, the Israelis shelled Southern Lebanese villages where casualties were approximately two combatants to three civilians. Between 25th of June and 21st of July, as Israel headed north towards the Capital, the ratio became four civilians killed to every fighter.

The heaviest air and sea bombardment took place against Beirut from the 22nd to the 31st of July. In one day alone, the 27th, 120 people were killed and almost 200 were wounded. Then came the heavy stuff. From the 1st to the 12th of

August, in continuous barrages lasting up to eleven hours, the commercial and residential areas of the city were pounded. Civilian casualties accounted for 90% of the victims.

The Canadian Ambassador, Theodore Arcande, the last of the Foreign Embassy officials to leave, said Beirut at that time made Berlin in 1944 look like a tea party!

All of this despite the announcement by the PLO on the 8th of August that 'We have taken a decision to withdraw our military presence from Beirut because of the destruction taking place over the heads of half a million Muslims.'

That statement represented the fulfilment of Israel's objectives, with the removal of the PLO from Lebanon. But for Ariel Sharon it was not enough, and the shelling continued intensely for the next five days.

On the 9th of August, as the PLO were drawing up detailed plans for the evacuation of its fighters, the bombing continued for seven hours non-stop.

It was the heaviest air and artillery assault of any Arab capital in recent history, said Fisk. In Matt Jansen's book, 'The Battle for Beirut', he calculates the casualties at 12,000 dead, 40,000 wounded, 300,000 rendered homeless, and almost a million people left destitute.

The world looked on aghast. Even the Americans, normally Israel's greatest ally, ordered the bombardment to stop.

Ariel Sharon was called before an irate Knesset committee and accused of sanctioning the air strikes to deliberately sabotage the peace process. He had already destroyed a cease-fire that had lasted for a year before the Israeli provocations.

In the latest deal, Israel would pull back from Beirut once the Palestinian fighters had departed.

Yasser Arafat and his troops had not been forced out by the bombardment. Instead, they had dug in and fought hard. They claimed they had enough ammunition and supplies to last six months. They knew Israel would not commit her soldiers to a fire-fight. It was just a matter of seeing out the siege. Then, with the onslaught continuing, it was only to spare their Lebanese hosts that the guerrillas finally accepted the invitation to leave.

The PLO fighters sailed from the port at Beirut with heads held high. Many headed for Larnaca in Cyprus. Arafat headed for Tunis, via Greece. All were waved off with a military salute.

All Arafat asked was that the Palestinians he had left behind be looked after. Was it too much to ask?

SABRA AND SHATILA.

The names of these two Palestinian refugee camps, Sabra and Shatila, in Southern Lebanon, loom large in the history of the conflict. Some have called it the worst atrocity in the Middle East in the twentieth century. It conjured up memories of an earlier outrage at Deir Yassin. Times ten.

In the summer of 1982, an uneasy truce prevailed in Beirut after Arafat's fighters went into exile, removing themselves from the frontline. It also left the camps' residents undefended, with enemies railed against them on all sides.

Israel had taken many casualties in the war of attrition, attempting to impose law on a state fraught with civil war.

Patience in the region was a scarce commodity. In Beirut, where various factions were vying for power, the bullet was the preferred method of discourse when attempting to solve their differences.

There was work to be done, and much to play for. When a Palestinian terrorist cell attempted to kill the Israeli ambassador to London, Ariel Sharon wasted no time in ordering his troops back into Beirut.

Despite the removal of 13,000 PLO fighters from Lebanon, Sharon insisted that there were still 2000 terrorists resident in the camps, and he positioned his army and tank brigades outside Sabra and Shatila and set up checkpoints to control access and egress to the sites.

Arafat's men departed on the 22nd of August. They had brought so much heat to town that they would not be missed by their hosts.

The following day, a new president, Beshir Gemayel, was elected in Lebanon. Gemayel was a warlord, one of several powerful families running their own militias in the war-torn state.

Pierre Gemayel had founded the Phalangists in 1936 after a visit to Nazi Germany. Impressed, the elder Gemayel remodelled his Christian Maronite organisation along the lines of Hitler's well-ordered army.

The Maronites were a religious group exclusive to Lebanon. They had a long history, dating back to the 6th Century AD. St.Maron was a hermit monk who lived in Syria. Before the advent of Islam, and with the Hebrews sent into the Diaspora after the destruction of the second temple, Christianity managed to split itself in two.

Emperor Constantine was the first Roman ruler to adopt the religion of Christ. He held that the Middle East was the birthplace of the Messiah and of their beliefs, and based his church out of Byzantium. When the rest of Rome caught on to the new faith, and sought to bring it in house as the Roman church, the divergent forms of Greek Orthodox and Catholicism emerged.

Eventually, attempting to heal the rift, Emperor Heraclius in the 6th Century devised a third way. He proposed a new image of Jesus that would unite both sets of believers, with an embracing vision of the son of God as both deity and human being.

Unfortunately, both sides rejected the compromise, leaving only a handful of followers of the third way religion, amongst them St.Maron.

Denounced as heretical, the new religionists were expelled from Syria and forced to hide in the hills of Lebanon.

When another group of religious outsiders, the Crusaders, came to the area in the 12th and 13th Century, the Maronites aligned themselves with their Christian comrades and fought against the Muslim armies.

Having formed an alliance with the Franks in these wars, the Maronites enjoyed a long-lasting relationship that survived to the 20th Century. In 1920, after the Great War, when France took possession of Syria, they awarded Lebanon to the Christian Maronites, then a majority in that country, with supreme control over the nation.

By the 1970's, the Maronites no longer held numerical advantage, with Shia and Sunni Muslims being the predominant communities. Still the Christian rulers would not let go the reins and prepared to fight to hold on to what they had.

Christian politics in the region were dominated by two rival families, the Franjiehs and the Gemayels. In 1970, Suleiman Franjieh seized control of the presidency in a coup when he stormed the parliament building while it was in session voting for the top position. At the point of a gun, Suleiman emerged victorious from the democratic process.

The new president was no shrinking violet. He boasted that he had personally killed more than 700 men over the years in various conflicts and feuds. The regime he instigated was no less discerning. His son, Tony, head of the house militia, oversaw the massacre of 300 Muslims in one day in 1975, slitting the throats of each as they passed a checkpoint while returning from a mosque.

Despite their bloodlust, the family were not immune to takeover themselves. A bitter contest had existed for generations between the town of Bsharre, home of the Gemayels, and Zghorta, stronghold of the Franjiehs. Both were vying for control.

The two groups were Christian Maronite, but essentially private armies with self-serving interests. In the civil war racking Lebanon, it was possible for Muslim to fight Muslim, Christian to tackle Christian, and any combination thereof.

It was certainly possible for a Gemayel to fight a Franjieh, and this was the case when an assault on the private mansion of Tony Franjieh saw his bodyguards drawn into open battle and killed before Tony and members of his immediate family were slaughtered in their home. The reins of power were changing hands.

The Phalangist Maronites were pro-Israeli, for the historical reason that Syria had always wished to annex the Fertile Crescent, which threatened their independence, and the Israelis were nothing if not anti-Syrian. Also, the presence of the PLO had stoked the fires and added to the suffering of the war-torn region.

The day before Bashir Gemayel was to take power, on the 14th of September, the president-elect was killed by a massive car-bomb in Beirut.

Having endured the reign of their rivals, the Franjiehs, and on the eve of assuming control, the Gemayel militia, the Phalange, suffered the loss of their leader and were bent on revenge.

In this heady climate, Israel was responsible for policing the peace. Either convinced that there were still fighters enrolled in the camps, or negligent as to the consequences of their actions, on the night of the 16th of September, just two days after Bashir was murdered, the Israelis opened the doors and allowed 500 of the blood-thirsty Christian militia into Sabra and Shatila.

INTO THE CAMPS.

On 15th September 1982, Israeli Defence Minister Ariel Sharon tied the killing of Bashir Gemayel to the Palestinians, saying 'It symbolises the terrorist murderousness of the PLO terrorist organisations and their supporters.'

Some said it was the work of the Syrians, who feared their expulsion from Lebanon if the new President allied himself with Israel. Others felt it was Israel who had done the deed, when Gemayel refused to commit Lebanon to the peace deal that Israel so wanted. He had already told Begin that the matter would be one for the Lebanese parliament to decide, and that he wanted his country to remain part of the Arab family. These were not words Sharon wanted to hear.

Just two days after the murder of the President-elect of Lebanon, with Sharon announcing the presence of as many as 2000 PLO fighters left in the refugee camps, the Phalange entered Sabra and Shatila.

Journalist Robert Suro had visited the area only days before and reported that there were no Palestinian militiamen in the camps.

Sabra and Shatila are situated in a narrow strip of land less than half a mile wide and one and a half miles long. Shatila was built by the UN to house refugees fleeing Palestine in 1948 during Israel's War of Independence. Gradually, the camp spread north to meet the poor district of Sabra.

Initially home to 5000 Palestinians, Shatila eventually became home to 20,000 people, many of them migrants from Syria, Iraq, and Southern Lebanon drawn to Beirut looking for work.

Israeli troops moved to surround the camps, positioning themselves less than one hundred metres from the perimeter, and placing check-points at every access point. Sabra and Shatila were, according to Rafael Eitan, the Chief of Staff, 'hermetically sealed'.

Therefore, no one could enter or leave without permission from the Israelis.

The gates guarding the entrance were opened to allow 500 men from the Christian militia in to search for the men said to be hiding amongst the civilian population.

But, as agreed, Arafat's army had already left, leaving the residents unprotected and at the mercy of a blood-thirsty group bent on revenge for their leader's assassination.

The IDF, under the command of Rafael Eitan, stood by as the well-armed militiamen strode into the camp. For the next 40 hours, Israel ignored the massacres taking place on their watch, as the Phalange wrought havoc and brought death and destruction in an orgy of rape and murder.

Whole families were slaughtered. Children were shot in the head. Young girls and old women were not spared the sexual violence that occurred. It was collective punishment of an entire community, while a modern, sophisticated army sat nearby and did nothing.

People were shot, either individually or in groups, bodies lay intertwined in the streets. Some had their throats cut or were strangled. The bodies were mutilated, either before or after death. Genitalia was sliced off in a grim ritual of humiliation.

Some exponents of the massacre proposed beheading their victims with axes, as the sound of gunfire might induce the Israelis to put a halt to the action. But with widespread panic and the screams of the unfortunate casualties rising above the camps, the assault was loud enough to be heard anyway and could have been stopped at any time. Instead, it was allowed to continue unchecked for two nights.

At night time, the IDF fired flares into the sky to illuminate the Phalange' deadly work.

Corpses lay in the streets, in groups, bodies entwined in a macabre dance of death. Charred remains, deformed figures, hands outstretched in protest at the onslaught, dotted the dirty streets of the tumbledown camps.

If there were 2000 Palestinian fighters in the camps, why did they not defend their wives and children? The PLO guerrillas who had held the might of the IDF at bay for almost two months in Beirut would surely have been more than a match for a few hundred militiamen. Maybe they had all departed, along with Arafat, after all.

When the Christian militia eventually retreated, having worked out their particularly cruel brand of aggression, news of the massacre, and photographs of the event, began to emerge.

In Tel Aviv, on 25th September, 300,000 people marched in protest at the government for allowing such criminal behaviour. Even after seven years of civil war in Lebanon, with an estimated 100,000 casualties in total, the Israeli public were shocked into action.

A commission of enquiry, under the guidance of Yitzak Kahan, was established to look into Israel's part in the slaughter.

The Kahan Commission report, published in February 1983, found the Phalangists directly responsible for the massacre, and Ariel Sharon, the Defence Minister, and Rafael Eitan, the Chief of Staff, indirectly responsible.

Eitan resigned, and Sharon was ordered to do the same or be removed from office. Sharon refused, and his hand was eventually forced.

Israel's response to their army's dereliction of duty was honourable. The public voted with their feet, the government conducted their enquiries, and heads were made to roll. For once, at least, not literally.

By contrast, when 600 Palestinians were slaughtered in 1986 by a Muslim militia, again in Shatila and in the camp at Burj-el Barajuch, there was barely a murmur of protest in the Middle East.

Back in 1982, it had been Elie Hobieka who led the Christian militia into Sabra and Shatila where the massacres took place. In 2002, a group of Palestinian survivors of the carnage launched a prosecution against Ariel Sharon in the International Criminal Court in Belgium.

Elie Hobieka, still a prominent figure in Lebanese politics, agreed to testify against the former Defence Chief, promising to reveal what orders and guarantees he'd received before he was allowed into the camp with his murderous thugs.

On 24th January, a day after agreeing to testify, Hobieka was killed by a massive car bomb in East Beirut.

The operation at Sabra and Shatila, supposedly to root out 2000 Palestinian terrorists, instead left 2000 civilians dead. None were terrorists and, such was the nature of these camps, many of them weren't even Palestinian.

NO MORE WAR.

Israel had fought five wars against the Arabs. In 1948, it was the War of Independence. Then came two conflicts fought at her insistence, of aggression rather than a response to an attack. In 1956 she had joined Britain and France in Suez against Egypt and in 1967 there was the Six Day War.

In 1973 came the surprise Arab offensive on Yom Kippur. In 1982 came Israel's obliteration of Beirut.

Even for a battle-hardened nation, the carpet-bombing of the Lebanese capital, and the horrific massacres at Sabra and Shatila, shocked the public and ended the notion of 'loyal opposition' in Israel. Now, there was outright discontent.

The President of Israel, Yitzak Navon, 27 former ambassadors, 100 prominent poets and writers, 200 scientists, and the entire Bar Association rose up in protest. 350,000 people marched in the streets of Tel Aviv to announce the arrival of the 'Peace Now' movement.

One hundred IDF officers stood up in a meeting with Ariel Sharon and demanded his resignation. This, surely, had been a war too far.

When Israel invaded Lebanon, Ariel Sharon hoped it would force the PLO into neighbouring Syria. The Syrians, no friends of the Palestinians since they appeared on opposite sides in the Lebanese civil war, would presumably then expel them. The Palestinians would inevitably move on to Jordan, where many of them already lived.

By virtue of this exodus, Israel would have created a Palestinian state in Jordan, which would then allow her to annex the West Bank and send the remaining Arabs across the river to their new home.

Instead, in the eyes of the world, Israel had lost face. There was sympathy for the battered Palestinians. The Jewish state had enjoyed the story of David and Goliath, but now it was Israel that was seen as the aggressor. It was not how it was supposed to be.

Sharon was eventually ousted after it was recommended that he resign in the Kahan report into Sabra and Shatila. Begin left office citing exhaustion, to be replaced by Yitzak Shamir.

Born in Poland in 1915, Shamir came to Palestine in 1935, at that time under the British Mandate.

In 1939 Shamir joined the Haganah, and when this was disbanded a year later, he joined the outlawed Stern Gang. When Avraham Stern, the arch terrorist, was gunned down by the British in 1942, Shamir moved up in the organisation and was on the British army's most-wanted list, along with Menachem Begin.

If the British had caught up with Begin, they would have hung him. When they eventually captured Shamir in 1946, they merely expelled him, deporting him to Africa, from where he escaped to Paris. Six days after the creation of Israel in 1948, Shamir came home.

In the early 1980's, Israel's economy was in dire straits. Inflation was running in excess of 130 percent. Shamir was unable to turn things around, and with public opinion at the time one of reconciliation with the Arabs, a Prime Minister who had opposed the Camp David Accords and who believed in Eretz Israel soon faced calls for his resignation.

Instead, the general election that followed ended in a dead heat, and a coalition government emerged between Shimon Peres of the left wing Labour Party and Shamir's right wing Likud.

The deal was that the likeable Peres would assume the Premiership, with Shamir his deputy for the first two years, then they would swap over.

In less than a year, inflation was brought down to 20%, and Israel had withdrawn from much of Lebanon, maintaining only a buffer zone to protect herself from attacks by the militant Shi'ite Hizbollah.

Peres managed security as well as the economy, and he was also a man of his word. When his two years in power were up, Shamir became Prime Minister as agreed, while Peres became Foreign Minister as well as Deputy PM.

Shimon Peres continued in his enthusiastic manner and turned his attention to acquiring peace treaties with their neighbouring Arab states.

With Israel withdrawing her troops from Sinai by 1982, peace with Egypt was assured. The Lebanese border area was fairly quiet, and normal relations between the two sides were possible. Next up was Jordan.

Peres arranged a meeting with King Hussein at the home of a mutual friend, Lord Maschon, in his London home. There, the Foreign Minister outlined an idea for an international peace conference between Israel and a joint Jordanian and Palestinian delegation to produce a peace agreement.

King Hussein liked what he heard and was keen to sign up, but Peres still needed to run it by the Israeli Prime Minister first to get his approval.

When Yitzak Shamir came to view the peace plan, he rejected it outright, partly out of jealousy that Peres had gone it alone, but also out of concern at the conditions an international conference might place on Israel. Shamir was disinclined to make concessions.

It was a decision that Israel would come to regret, for an opportunity had been missed to quell the rising tide of Arab anger.

Having grown up without a voice, and sceptical that they would ever have one, a popular uprising began amongst the Palestinians living under occupation.

The First Intifada was about to be born.

INTIFADA.

The Palestinian Uprising, known as the Intifada, the word meaning 'to shake off', began with an incident that appeared unremarkable when compared to the larger events of the day.

On the 6th of December, 1987, an Israeli plastics salesman named Shlomo Sakal was stabbed to death in the town of Jabaliya in Gaza. Two days later, a tank transporter rammed two vans taking Palestinians to work, killing four and injuring several others.

At first, it appeared to be a traffic accident, but the tragedy took a sinister turn when it appeared that the driver of the military vehicle was a relative of Sakal's.

There had been countless incidents of greater loss and consequence. There had been wars, massacres, aerial bombardments, mass expulsions from home or village. Neither side could claim they had done no wrong in word or deed to the other. So why should it boil over into civil disobedience for which Israel had no immediate answer?

The deep-seated reasons have to do with the nature of occupation. It had been twenty years since Israel emerged victorious from the Six Day War. Even then, in the heady days when their Might seemed confirmed, there were worries about the whirlwind co-opting another territory might reap.

It has always been thus. The North Americans fought for their independence against British rule. Mahatma Gandhi freed India from the yoke of empire with his non-violent resistance movement, while in South Africa it required an abhorrent apartheid regime to maintain colonial advantage that was eventually overthrown.

In the Second World War, under German occupation, a resistance movement rose up in France. The men and women who sabotaged trains carrying Jews to the death camps were terrorists?

In 1987, the Palestinians had suffered a generation of living under occupation. For everyone under the age of twenty, they had known nothing else.

Unemployment was prevalent. Those who managed to get work did so largely for the benefit of the Israeli economy. Travelling from the Occupied Territories into the Jewish state everyday, to earn wages half what an Israeli would earn and to witness the relative opulence that had been monopolized, was enough to breed resentment.

Then, at the end of the day, the Arabs would pass through the ubiquitous Israeli check-points and return to the shanty towns they had built following al-Nakbah or when they had become Nazihun.

Yitzak Shamir then rejected all talk of a peace deal with Jordan and refused any concessions to the Palestinians. With the PLO in Tunis, the Arabs of Gaza and the West Bank were left without a voice. Finally, at the annual Arab League summit, the item topping the agenda was the Iran-Iraq War. The Palestinian problem didn't even appear in the final dispatches.

With no one to speak up for them, no leadership to deal on their behalf, and with an occupying force that brooked no compromise and made daily living harsh, even intolerable, only a spark was needed before the people would react.

In December 1987, that spark arrived and lit the touch paper. The flames of unrest caught Israel, the PLO, and the Palestinians themselves by surprise.

No one really knew how it started. For sure, no one knew either how to put it out.

A SIMPLE PLAN.

Often, the best ideas are the simple ones. Complication leads to errors. Simplicity is the key. There appears to have been no planning for a Palestinian uprising, on either side. For the Arabs, it was organic. For the Israelis, it was merely unforeseen.

Complacent might sum up the attitude of Israel's leaders. The IDF had always emerged triumphant from battle, despite the odd bloody nose. The United Nations had proved incapable of bending Israel to the will of several resolutions, and the Arab population in the Occupied Territories were a commodity to be bandied about, as and when the conquering state found more pressing needs for their land.

There was no impetus to push for a peace deal with her neighbours. Israel had lain waste all opposition. There was no reward in concession.

But even Achilles had his heel. Israel, for all her armoury, state of the art weapons, and control of the airspace, could not cope with a grassroots uprising of youths armed with little more than stone and slingshot.

From Gaza, the Intifada spread to towns in the West Bank. Soon, all of the Occupied Territories were united in opposition. There were spontaneous demonstrations. Palestinian flags were raised, despite this being illegal.

Tyres were burnt in the roads, barricades were erected to keep the IDF soldiers at bay. The Arabs were repossessing their towns.

Workers went on strike, denying Israel the cheap labour that her industries depended on. There was a boycott of Israeli goods and services, giving back a further taste of economic hardship.

Most of all, there was the 'War of Stones'. Images appeared on televisions all across the world of groups of stone-throwing children facing heavily armed soldiers. For the Israeli's, still sensitive to criticism following the destruction of Beirut, it was another Public Relations disaster.

How could Israel play the put-upon state surrounded by hostile nations when all the pictures pointed to soldiers fighting children?

A generation is a long sentence under occupation. There is only so much pressure that the human heart can endure. And then it erupts.

Israel's sophisticated army had trained for war, not insurgency. Her commanders were capable of outmanoeuvring her enemies in the skies or out on the desert plain, but they had not prepared for civil disobedience.

The Israelis tried to figure out who was fuelling the uprising. Assassination would have swiftly followed. But they did not know who was behind it, or understand how it got started, or how it would end. They were not the only ones.

In Tunis, Yasser Arafat was as taken aback as anyone else. He was pleased that his people were trying to end the occupation in the West Bank and Gaza, he willed their success, but the impetus had not come from him or his organisation. Instead, it began in the refugee camps themselves, and the momentum came from the disaffected Palestinian communities.

Since 1967, encouraged by several Israeli Prime Ministers, most notably Menachem Begin and Yitzak Shamir, Jewish folk had moved into Arab Palestine.

There were two reasons the government promoted this annexation. Firstly, establishing Jewish communities there would help bring about the ideal of Eretz Israel. Secondly, encroaching into Arab territory and changing the place-names into Hebrew disenfranchised the Arabs and encouraged their departure to neighbouring Jordan.

The effect of dropping settlements into open countryside was to cut off Arab villages from each other, leaving a hateful rat-run to be negotiated when travelling through what was once a contiguous state.

The result was a series of isolated Palestinian Bantustans, open prisons that impacted negatively on an already meagre quality of life.

The response was the first Intifada.

THE OFFSPRING OF INTIFADA.

Within a week of the children launching the first stones, the Muslim religious organisation HAMAS was formed, with the stated aim of reuniting Palestine, and destroying Israel.

Another group to be inspired by the rebellious youth were the Arabs of Israel. Back in 1948, when most had fled the Jewish half of Palestine in the War of Independence, some people chose to remain in their homes.

Although these die-hards were awarded only second-class citizenship in the Jewish state, they still fared better that those who fled to the refugee camps. The latter had left everything behind and were denied the right to ever return.

Israeli Arabs represented almost a fifth of the population, and their expression of solidarity with the Palestinians in the Occupied Territories frightened the Jewish state, who now believed they had an enemy within.

The final source of support for the Palestinian uprising came from the 'Peace Now' movement, established to protest the siege of Lebanon, and organisers of the 350,000 march in Tel Aviv.

Then, the PLO finally announced their acceptance of UN Resolutions 242 and 338, accepting the original two-state solution and recognising Israel's right to exist. This lay the groundwork for peace. The US, for one, saw the possibilities this represented and, compared to HAMAS, the PLO were preferred negotiating partners.

But Israel was still caught like a rabbit in the headlights of the Intifada. The rebellion was still going strong, with no sign of abating. To prevent youths launching stones, Defence Minister Yitzak Rabin ordered that they be beaten and their bones broken.

Curfews were introduced, sometimes for days at a time, to impose order on the recalcitrant Arabs. Olive groves were destroyed, depriving people of food and livelihood.

Homes were demolished in acts of collective punishment. Beforehand, a ministerial order was required to raze a house to the ground. That responsibility was devolved to area commanders.

In the first year of the Intifada, 311 Palestinians were killed, over fifty of them children under the age of sixteen. Thousands were wounded. Tens of thousand were arrested. More than 500 homes were demolished.

With an uncompromising Israeli government in power, the uprising was set to continue with varying intensity until 1993, a six year war. The Intifada only abated when there came a hope of peace.

THE MADRID CONFERENCE.

After almost a decade of fighting, the war between Iran and Iraq came to an end. The continuing Intifada threatened to return the Palestinian cause to the international stage, but then came Saddam Hussein's invasion of Kuwait in 1990. It seemed the Occupied Territories might be pushed down the agenda once again.

Instead, Saddam offered to comply with United Nations Resolutions and withdraw from Kuwait if only Israel would do the same. Of course, that was not about to happen and instead Israel joined Syria and Saudi Arabia and the allied forces to oust Iraq from its southern province.

With the defeat of Saddam, America was keen to reward the Arab countries that had supported the war effort. It was time to put some pressure on Israel.

Syria, the Lebanese, the Jordanians, and a Palestinian delegation all agreed to appear at an international peace conference to be held in Madrid in October, 1991. Israel responded to the invitation by promoting hard-liners such as Rehavam Zeevi to the government and announced a plan to double the number of Jewish Settlements in the West Bank.

Their plan was to scupper the deal before the parties even got to the table, but the USA were not about to let down their new allies, and threatened to withhold a series of loans to the Israeli government if she did not comply.

The Knesset backed down, and Yitzak Shamir agreed to appear in person, even though the conference was only aimed at Foreign Ministers.

President George Bush Senior opened the talks. He outlined the agenda. The ultimate goal was for 'total withdrawal from the Occupied Territories in exchange for peaceful relations'.

The enormity of the task became apparent when the Syrian Foreign Minister, Farouq al Shara, denounced the Israeli Prime Minister. He held up a photograph showing Shamir as a 32 year old man in an old British 'Wanted' poster.

Al Shara called Shamir a terrorist accused of the murder of Count Bernadotte, the UN official in charge of the partition talks in 1948. 'This man kills peace negotiators', said the Syrian minister.

Shamir responded by calling the Palestinian delegates terrorists, this despite the fact the PLO had been excluded from talks and in their place were a group of moderates and intellectuals.

It didn't matter. The discussions weren't very diplomatic and descended into farce, and there was never any prospect of peace emerging.

As the Israeli Prime Minister later confirmed, 'I was happy to keep talking for another ten years. By that time, there would be half a million Jews in the West Bank and it would be too late for the Arabs to do anything about it.'

The Madrid conference came to a close, but a modicum of communication had been established, some of which would later prove fruitful.

For Yitzak Shamir, despite his truculence, the fact he'd appeared at all at the talks angered the extremist groups keeping his coalition government in power.

A vote of no confidence in his leadership was returned in the Knesset, early elections were held in June 1992, and Shamir was defeated. In his wake came the Labour candidate who offered both the Israelis and the Palestinians their best chance of peace. His name was Yitzak Rabin.

YITZAK RABIN.

Yitzak Rabin was the first Prime Minister of Israel to have been born in the land of Palestine. The son of American immigrants, Rabin was born in March 1922 in Jerusalem. His father had fought with the Jewish Legion alongside the British in World War 1. His mother was a founding member of the Haganah fighting force.

Upon leaving school at the age of fourteen, Yitzak immediately joined the Palmach, the commandos of the Jewish defence league.

By 1948, in the War of Independence, Rabin was commander of the Har'el Brigade, operating in and around Jerusalem. He ultimately led the assault that captured Mount Zion amid fierce fighting.

Despite these Jewish gains, with support from the Jordanians, the Palestinians were able to hold onto the Old City of Jerusalem. This failure to unite the Capital under Israeli rule would haunt Rabin until 1967 when, as Chief of Staff of the army, he would have the opportunity to put that right.

Married with a son and a daughter, Rabin was the most reserved of men. He was not given to emotional displays, to humour, or to any evidence of sentiment. Instead, he chain-smoked cigarettes and displayed a dour demeanour.

Rabin's greatest military triumph, the Six Day War, also showed up a weakness, when he supposedly had a nervous breakdown prior to giving the order to engage.

This was later denied, with his medical condition put down to nicotine-poisoning instead.

Yitzak Rabin's first stint as Prime Minister ended in ignominy when he was found to hold $2000 US dollars in an American bank account, contrary to Israel's fiscal rules.

After resigning from the top job, Rabin returned to the Cabinet where, as Defence Minister at the time of the First Intifada, he urged the army to 'break the bones' of the protesters.

He then resumed the position of Premier in 1992. It was as Prime Minister, faced with evidence that there would be no end to the Intifada for as long as the occupation continued that Rabin finally decided to sue for peace.

THE OSLO ACCORDS.

The world was in flux. The Soviet Union had collapsed, and so had the Berlin Wall. The old order was changing, and there were new opportunities for peace, and for fresh partnerships.

The Gulf War had seen the first Arab-Israeli joint enterprise and, flush with the support they had received in the Allied effort, the United States of America, and President George Bush senior, wished to repay that goodwill by ushering new rounds of talks between Israel and her neighbours.

Talks began in Washington in 1992, but these soon ran into trouble. Attempting to resolve major differences under the media spotlight proved impossible.

There was too much braggadocio on display, and having made public pronouncements to their supporters, neither side could then be seen to back down.

What was required was a back channel, where negotiations could take place in secret without the incumbent pressures of a peace summit. Also, in private, between two small teams, they would be free from much of the attendant protocol and ceremony that usually ate up much of the timetable of such events. And with the USA Israel's greatest supporter, American-led talks could not be viewed by Arab delegates as impartial.

The small Scandinavian country of Norway however was perfectly placed to host such a private conference.

Having maintained a position of equality and support to both Israelis and Palestinians, being a generous donor and a friend to both, Norway had earned their trust. This would prove invaluable, and contributed greatly to the ambience in which a series of talks could survive.

The Labour government of Yitzak Rabin had run on a platform of peace with the Palestinians. The consensus now existed to resolve the differences that had kept them apart.

Terje Roed Larsen was the head of a research unit conducting a social science project amongst Palestinians to determine how the occupation was affecting their lives. He was also married to the assistant Norwegian Deputy Foreign Minister.

Through his Middle Eastern contacts, Larsen was introduced to Yossi Beilin, the Deputy Israeli Foreign Minister. The two men hit it off, and they shared the belief that the time was right for a peace deal, and that it would have to involve the PLO.

At that time, Beilin had proposed a bill in the Knesset to revoke the law against communicating with the outlawed Palestinian group. Knowing this would soon be passed, the Deputy FM agreed to allow talks to begin, although these would, to begin with, be on an academic rather than a political level.

Larsen was introduced to Abu Ala, a senior PLO official and one of Arafat's most trusted aides. Ala had recently written an economic paper that accepted and included Israel in its calculations for easing the Palestinian burden. The report had been circulated in the Israeli government, and Yossi Beilin viewed it as progressive and believed he might at last have a partner for peace.

The Norwegian government let the parties know that they were happy to arrange and host the secret talks, and under the guise of Larsen's research outfit, delegates were invited to Oslo for the first tentative seminar of a process that had potential but not promises.

On 19th of January, 1993, the restriction on dealing with the PLO was revoked by the government of Israel, and the next day the first meeting between the two teams took place in Norway.

Led by Larsen, who was there to facilitate, not mediate, an isolated location was chosen to allow the talks to take place in a relaxed environment.

For the Palestinians, there was Abu Ala in charge, supported by two aides. For the Israelis, there were two academics, Yair Hirschfeld and Ron Pundak, who were members of a Beilin-led think-tank.

248

The talks were convivial, but Ala was disappointed that the two Israelis were not government officials, and therefore appeared to carry no authority. It might all be just an academic exercise, but Larsen assured Ala that these were Beilin's men, and all of the other stuff would follow.

The discussions got off to a good start, with the Palestinians conceding that they were ready to consider the option of Gaza First, with an Israeli withdrawal from the Occupied Territories beginning in the Strip. Previously, there had been reluctance to consider this event for fear that Gaza First meant Gaza Last, and that having awarded this concession, Israel would refuse to give any more.

When the news filtered back to Beilin, he recognised the conciliatory approach of the PLO and eagerly approved a return visit to Oslo for his two academics.

From the second meeting came the Sarpsborg Document, where both parties attempted to agree a Declaration of Principles (DOP). This included the Palestinian willingness to accept the Gaza option, and an Israeli commitment to gradually release the remainder of the West Bank to Palestinian control.

When the Sarpsborg Document was shown to Shimon Peres, the Israeli Foreign Minister who had ultimately approved the talks, he said of the rough copy, 'It's an awful paper, but I can tell that something serious is going on.'

By the time of the third meeting, in March, there was talk of including the town of Jericho with the Gaza transfer, to confirm that the West Bank would follow in a phased withdrawal.

The Palestinians were greatly encouraged by this, and suggested that an agreement could soon be signed, but they still had doubts as to the official status of Hirschfeld and Pundak, and insisted that an Israeli government representative attend the next meeting.

Uri Savir was the Director General of the Foreign Ministry and the highest ranking diplomat in Israel. Along with a lawyer and trusted aide of Prime Minister Rabin, Joel Singer, the two men headed for Oslo in May.

Such was the secrecy surrounding the talks, Savir flew first to Paris, checked into a hotel, placed a 'Do not disturb' sign on the door, and slipped out and caught a plane to Norway.

Abu Ala made a great impression on Savir. After Singer had drilled the Palestinian with more than 200 questions related to the Sarpsborg Document, Savir turned to Larsen and said he believed that Abu Ala 'Knows it all. I can do business with him.'

When the Palestinian balked at the amount of information he was being asked to give, answering questions on the PLO's position on finite details, Singer assured Ala that the list of questions came straight from Rabin himself.

Back in Tunis, home of the PLO leadership, this news was greatly received. Now, both sides, at the highest level, were attempting to break the deadlock through the Oslo channel.

At the next meeting, things did not go so well. Joel Singer had prepared a document of his own, which included all the points that the Palestinians had indicated that might be prepared to move on. There was no inclusion of any compromise on Israel's behalf.

The Palestinian delegates were furious. They felt cheated. What about the Sarpsborg Agreement, they wanted to know? You have changed everything, they exclaimed.

Eventually, the Israeli team agreed to go through the document word by word, noting any Palestinian objections. These would then be included in a revised draft.

At the next meeting, Singer presented a revised DOP. The Israelis had been given the authority by Prime Minister Rabin to sign the agreement, if the terms were acceptable to the PLO.

Unfortunately, despite greater parity between the two positions, the Palestinians saw this only as a basis for further negotiations and returned to Tunis to discuss it.

A week later, both parties were back in Oslo. This time however, it was the Palestinians who had altered the document, including 25 new points for consideration. It was the Israelis turn to be furious.

Nevertheless, the two sides managed to find agreement on nine of the points, and each took eight of the remaining principles home for further discussion to try and bring them closer to a deal.

This was done at another secret meeting held 13th August, with the outstanding issues later negotiated in a three-way phone call between Peres, Arafat, and the Norwegian Foreign Minister.

The United States had some knowledge of the Oslo channel but little conviction that it would achieve anything. With talks in Washington at an impasse, the good news was welcomed by the Clinton administration.

In Oslo at an official state visit by Foreign Minister Peres, a 23 page document entitled 'Declaration of Principles on Interim Self-Government arrangements' was signed by Abu Ala and Uri Savir.

The waiting world could now be told of the breakthrough. The secrecy had worked, no news had leaked about the events, and as a result the negotiations had gone ahead unhindered and unscrutinised.

In the Gaza Strip and the West Bank, Hamas and other militants protested the peace deal. Jewish settlers similarly raged against the peace.

Despite the angry scenes back home, all parties met on the White House lawn on the 13th of September, 1993, where a beaming Bill Clinton stood between Yitzak Rabin and Yasser Arafat and ushered them together for an historic handshake.

Washington could take none of the credit for arranging the accord, but was perfectly positioned to hold the parties to their commitments.

The hard work had been done by the Norwegians, Larsen chief amongst them, as well as the willing Israeli and Palestinian negotiators. The credit belonged though to the city the peace agreement was named after: Oslo.

Asked about the Accord, and how he felt about taking the credit for it, Bill Clinton said generously, if truthfully, 'It's a gift.'

AFTER OSLO.

The problem with an interim agreement is that it gives the opposition time to derail the process. The Oslo Accords had merely set an agenda and a timetable for proposed actions. Events on either side of the Middle East divide ensured the treaty would never come to fruition.

On the 25th of February 1994 in the troubled town of Hebron, a Jewish settler named Baruch Goldstein massacred 29 Muslims praying at the mosque of the Tomb of the Patriarchs.

At the funeral of Goldstein, who was killed at the scene by surviving members of the congregation, the Rabbi told the mourners that the fingernail of a Jew was worth a hundred Palestinians. Baruch's widow kept the machine gun he used to commit the murders on a mantle-piece at home as a souvenir.

The response was the first ever Palestinian suicide bombing, carried out by a Hamas activist on the 16th of April 1993. It was a tactic that had been employed by Hizbollah against the Israelis, and with the war of stones achieving little, a more effective weapon was required.

Yitzak Rabin and Yasser Arafat were at first unmoved by this development, and headed to Egypt where, on the 4th of May, the two signed the Cairo Agreement instigating a three-phase handover of power from the Israelis to the newly-inaugurated Palestinian Authority. Yasser Arafat, as Chairman of the authority, returned in triumph to Gaza.

Rabin signed a further peace agreement with Jordan in July and normal relations between the two countries were established by the end of the year.

Then came Oslo II, signed in Washington on the 28th September 1995, a 410 page document outlining the handover of territory to Palestinian control. The Knesset had only voted to accept the deal by the narrowest of margins, with 61 votes in favour and 59 against. It expressed the division felt in Israel about the nature of peace with their arch enemy.

Despite the suicide bombing campaign damaging the peace campaign, Arafat could at least point to the Accord and the instalment of a Palestinian security apparatus as achievements. On the Israeli side, Rabin was under a lot more pressure.

The arguments seemed to settle on the old divide of the secular and religious movements. The former, usually Western emigrants, were in the peace camp. The latter would not accept anything less than Eretz Israel.

Rabin had entered dangerous waters. The old general, who had served in every one of Israel's five wars against the Arabs, had to contend with militant Jews burning effigies of him, complete with Nazi uniform, in the streets.

A huge peace rally took place in Tel Aviv on the 4th of November in support of Rabin and the Oslo Accords. Despite threats to his personal safety and a hostile atmosphere, Rabin shunned advice to boycott the event.

As the Prime Minister prepared to leave the rally, he was gunned down by a 25 year old student from the Bar-Ilan religious university, Yigal Amir, a Jewish extremist of the Settler movement.

This was the price to be paid by anyone willing to cede land to the Palestinians. It seemed the war would never end.

AFTER RABIN.

The Foreign Minister, Shimon Peres, replaced Rabin. An old political hand, Peres lacked the material for top office, and although he had held that position previously, his grip on the Premiership was always tenuous.

Peres called an early election, hoping to cash in on the wave of sympathy for his party that followed Rabin's untimely demise. Unfortunately for him, the Labour party's early lead in the polls disappeared in the wake of two calamitous decisions he made, both of which backfired to great effect.

The first was his decision to assassinate Yahya Ayyash, the Hamas engineer who had masterminded the recent bombing campaign.

Following the successful operation to eliminate Ayyash, Hamas responded with four suicide attacks on Israeli buses the next week, causing mass casualties and panic, and providing a stark visual image of the failure of Peres' policy.

In a further attempt to show the political Right that he could be hard on the terrorists, Peres ordered Operation Grapes of Wrath, a 25,000 shell onslaught of Southern Lebanon aimed at preventing Hizbollah guerrilla activity in the area.

Instead, 200,000 Lebanese civilians were forced to flee the assault, and when one missile landed in a United Nations compound killing more than 100 innocent people sheltering from attack, Peres had again got it badly wrong.

In the election called for April 1996, Labour lost to Likud, the hardliner Benjamin Netanyahu replaced Shimon Peres, and the Palestinians, who had hoped for some concessions after Oslo, now had a more difficult opponent to contend with.

The Oslo Accords had postponed the negotiations related to the important issues such as Jerusalem and the right of return for Palestinian refugees. That turned out to be a mistake, for their Israeli partners were now of the intransigent set.

There was no incentive for the Israelis to compromise, and certainly not while the terror campaign against them continued. Rabin's assassin had achieved his aim. The peace movement in the Middle East was all but finished.

MR.PALESTINE.

Yasser Arafat was born in Cairo to Palestinian parents on 24th August 1929, the fifth son of a businessman. Arafat is the place of a holy shrine near Mecca, and was the name given to the boy to show his Islamic piety. The name Yasser was his family nickname and, ironically, it means calm, easy-going.

This element of Arafat's nature would allow him to endure the endless negotiations and in-fighting which beset the Palestinian national cause, and is indicative of his ability to stay at the head of the movement as chairman.

After the death of his mother when he was just five years old, Yasser was sent to live with his uncle's family in the Palestinian quarter of Jerusalem.

Four years later, Arafat returned to Egypt and as a young man enrolled as an engineering student at Cairo University. It was there that he began to display his militant tendency, aligning himself with the body of student politics, whilst waging low-key guerrilla warfare on the weekends, crossing the Suez to join attacks on the infant Israeli state in 1948.

Continuing with his studies, Yasser chaired the student union and joined the radical Muslim Brotherhood organisation, who later figured strongly in the 1956 war against the allied Israeli, British, and French forces.

In 1958, encouraged to leave Egypt because of his guerrilla activity, Arafat and a group of friends moved to Kuwait to put their degrees to good use, while forming themselves into a group they named FATAH, meaning conquest.

President Nasser supported the establishment of the Palestine Liberation Organisation (PLO) in 1964, hoping to unite the Arabs in a cause to aid their displaced and put-upon brethren.

Following the debacle of the Six Day War, when the regular armies of the Middle East were humiliated by Israel, Yasser chose to change tack. Having witnessed the inability of an outright military defeat of the Jewish state, Arafat turned instead to irregular forces.

Arafat installed himself as the Chairman of the PLO and led the fighting at Karamesh where, aided by the Jordanians, the guerrillas inflicted heavy losses on the Israelis, killing twenty four soldiers, and giving their own cause a massive boost in the process.

Young disaffected men flocked to join the movement on the back of that success and, in the hills of Jordan, they were trained to fight the Zionist entity.

The Palestinians, flush with new recruits and protected by their Jordanian allies, became a state within a state, and threatened the reign of King Hussein himself.

When Arafat later approved the actions of terrorist groups such as the PFLP and brought trouble to the door of the host nation, the PLO were expelled, finding sanctuary in Lebanon instead.

All the while, Arafat raised his profile. When the world media was drawn to the cause by the plane hijackings and other headline-grabbing, if notorious, acts, Arafat was there as the public face of the legitimate side of the struggle.

As a figurehead, Yasser was a great asset for the Palestinian people. Arafat was one of the most recognisable people on the planet. He portrayed himself as an Arabic Fidel Castro, appearing in army fatigues and always sporting his Keffieh headgear.

Whether he was speaking to the United Nations General Assembly, the Pope, a King, or a world leader, Arafat was always the humble spokesman for a disparate group of refugees.

It was this humility, and his generosity, that allowed him to spearhead the campaign for a Palestinian homeland for more than four decades. Another reason for the unchallenged duration was his dictatorial style. He held tightly onto the reins of power, and he discouraged anyone from promoting alternative leaders.

Even when he was exiled to Tunis, and his loyal aides were picked off in the Israeli backlash to the continued campaign for independence, Arafat still remained the focal point for his people.

The first Gulf War in 1990 appeared to dent his public aura, when Yasser made the mistake of siding with Iraq in the war with the Western Allies. Even Syria knew better than to support the brutal Saddam Hussein, the gas-master.

Paradoxically, this weakened the PLO to the extent that Israel viewed this the ideal time to negotiate. Also, with the emergence of Hamas, originally supported by Israel as a counter-weight to the PLO, but now in danger of overtaking them, the PLO were considered the more moderate of the two groups.

Yasser Arafat revelled in the glare of the world's media and the attention of the United States President as he shook the hand of Israeli premier Yitzak Rabin.

Together with the Nobel Peace Prize that followed for both men in 1994, it was to be his finest hour. And, yet, it achieved nothing.

The Intifada had emerged from grass-roots Palestinians and had taken the PLO by surprise. The people were capable of acting independently, but they still recognised the need for a leader with worldwide leverage.

When Arafat returned to Gaza as part of the Oslo Accords, he was greeted like a triumphant hero, which in a way he was.

Sadly, despite real attempts at diplomacy throughout the 1990's, by the decade's end, with the failure of the most recent US efforts to establish peace in the Middle East, Arafat gave the green light for the Second Intifada, five years to the day from the signing of the Oslo II agreement.

The time for negotiation was over. Israel had failed to meet the schedule it had signed to turn over the West Bank to Palestinian rule. With the former much the stronger, there was no political will to give the Palestinians anything. Arafat, in his time-honoured tradition, turned the problem over to the guerrillas to see if they would have more success.

By 2001, with Arafat's old nemesis Ariel Sharon in charge of the Israelis, Yasser was confined to his compound in Ramallah and held under siege. He would never be allowed to leave, except to die.

In 2004, struck down by a mysterious illness, Arafat was flown to France, and awarded a statesman's welcome on arrival, before being treated in a Paris hospital.

Arafat's condition deteriorated, and on Thursday, 11th of November, he died. The cause of death could not be established. Some suspected he had been poisoned.

With Sharon announcing that Israel could not pursue peace without an effective negotiating partner, and refusing to deal with Arafat, it was true that the hostage of Ramallah was holding up the deal.

Had the Israelis finally run out of patience and ushered Arafat out of the way, permanently?

It was a sad end to the life of a man who had achieved little for his people, either on the battlefield or through diplomacy, with few notable successes to his name. When his body was returned to Ramallah for internment, he was mobbed by hundreds of thousands of hysterical mourners.

Like his people, he was long-suffering, and he was the greatest symbol ever of the Palestinian cause.

SUICIDE BOMBERS.

The first Palestinian suicide bombing in Israel took place in April 1994 in response to the massacre at the Tomb of Abraham mosque in Hebron in February that year.

Hamas claimed responsibility for the two bus attacks that followed in the towns of Afula and Hadera and murdered 13 innocent civilians and wounded eighty.

Another bus was bombed in Tel Aviv in July, and in a further attack in the same city in October, 22 people died and forty were injured.

And there was Yitzak Rabin, in the midst of all this violence, attempting to make peace with the perpetrators. His 25 year old assassin, Yigal Amir, said he was happy that he had killed his Prime Minister.

Shimon Peres then called for early elections and tried to convince the hardliners that he could get tough on the terrorists. He took out Yahya Ayyash, the 'Engineer' of Hamas. In the wake of his killing, a huge backlash occurred against the Israeli public.

On February 26th, 1996, a bomb exploded in Jerusalem killing 26 and wounding twice that. An hour later, a suicide bomber blew himself up at a bus stop in Ashkelon used by soldiers for hitchhiking that left one dead and thirty wounded.

A week later, to the hour and day, again in Jerusalem, a bus exploded and destroyed 19 lives. The next day, in Tel Aviv, another suicide bomber killed 13 and wounded more than 130 people. By June, Israel had a new Prime Minister, Benjamin Netanyahu.

The Likud leader refused to countenance peace talks and instead chose to fight fire with fire. In March, 1997, three Israelis had been killed in an explosion at a Tel Aviv cafe with almost fifty wounded. In July, two bombers simultaneously blew themselves up at an open-air market in Jerusalem in a joint operation between Hamas and Islamic Jihad.

Netanyahu's response was to order the assassination of the leader of the terrorist wing of Hamas, Khaled Mashaal, at that time a resident of Jordan, but the operation was bungled and left King Hussein fuming.

In an attempt to placate their Arab ally, Israel agreed to release Sheikh Ahmed Yassin from jail.

The wheelchair-bound Yassin was the overall leader of Hamas. His return to Gaza prompted a welcome that surpassed even that given to Yasser Arafat when he'd arrived back from Tunis.

Sheikh Yassin was the founder of the Islamic organisation that had come to mean so much to the Palestinian people. Hamas was founded in 1987 during the First Intifada, and was built on a platform of social welfare as well as military resistance to Israel. The stated aim of the organisation was to create an Islamic state in the land of historical Palestine. This therefore meant the destruction of Israel.

The social welfare aspect saw Hamas building schools, hospitals, and infrastructure, but its success in targeting the Israelis, and the assassination of their own leadership by IDF reprisal raids had contributed much to the ongoing cycle of violence in the area.

Another group contributing to the carnage was Islamic Jihad. A loose connection of terrorist cells, they announced their determination to upset the Oslo Accords with two suicide bombings in Israel in 1995 and 1996, one of which killed 19 soldiers and another a gruesome nail bomb in Tel Aviv. They remain one of the most potent of the Jihadis.

In June of 2002, the group exploded a car bomb beside an Israeli bus, murdering 17 people. On 15th November that year, an attack on Settlers and soldiers in Hebron left 14 Israelis dead.

With no respite, Israel again targeted the leaders of the uprising and those directly behind the terror campaign. In March 2004, Sheikh Ahmed Yassin, being taken for a walk in his wheelchair, was struck by an IDF missile fired from the air.

The direct hit left only the mangled wreckage of the disabled man's transport and a pool of blood on the floor. It caused outrage, but was it any more shocking than the sight of an Israeli bus torn apart, where even more lives were lost?

Back with the government, the right-winger Netanyahu had lost the 1999 election to Ehud Barak of Labour, a former army general who promised to push for a settlement with the Palestinians to finally bring peace.

This commitment led directly to the talks at Camp David, where President Bill Clinton, in his last act of government, hoped to tie up the deal that had eluded him in the Oslo Accords of '93.

Even as the two combatants, Arafat and Barak, made to follow Clinton indoors after another historic photo-shoot, neither could agree who should go first. It looked for all the world that they did not trust each other even to turn one's back for a moment.

As could be derived from the body language, the talks would ultimately founder. The five year anniversary of Oslo II would come and go, and the commitment given there for an autonomous Palestinian state produced nothing.

In this climate, Israeli Prime Ministerial candidate Ariel Sharon caused outrage when he visited the Temple Mount, home of the Al-Aqsa mosque, Islam's third holiest site.

The result of this provocative act, on the back of the failed peace talks, was the Second Intifada. Unlike the first, it would be a war not only of stones but also of bombs.

THE ROAD TO PARADISE.

Palestine has always loved her martyrs. When the female terrorist Dala Mughrabi led a team onto the beach at Tel Aviv in 1978 and detonated explosives that killed 36 Israelis, Arab schools and summer camps were named in her honour.

According to Abdul Rahman Makdad, who organised two bus bombings in Jerusalem, 'Finding a martyr is always the easiest part of the operation. We have thousands who are waiting.'

There are four Palestinian Islamist organisations that carry out suicide attacks, although they prefer to call them martyrdom operations. They are the military wing of Hamas, known as the Al-Qassam Brigade; Islamic Jihad; the still-functioning PFLP; and a terrorist group allied to Yasser Arafat's Fatah party, the Al-Aqsa Martyrs Brigade.

Together, they sponsor suicide bombers, providing financial relief to the families of those prepared to die for the Palestinian cause. The price of this support varies from $1500 to $3000 for the immediate family.

Usually, the groups reject applicants who are under eighteen years old, or who are the sole wage earners in the family, or if they are married and have responsibilities.

Most who choose to end their life in this most destructive of ways are not suicidal, they are not simple-minded, not uneducated, nor even depressed.

Instead, they have simply had enough of living under occupation. Asked if they are happy to kill innocent women and children, in a survey conducted by the novelist Nasra Hussan of 250 people connected with this activity, those who's bombs had failed to detonate, the families of the bombers, and those that sent them to their deaths, many replied, 'The Israelis are happy to kill our women and children, so why not?'

The Palestinians are always quick to name their suicide bombers. One who completed his deadly mission was Mohammed al-Ghoul.

Al-Ghoul was studying for a Master's Degree, and came from a well-off family. He claimed his martyrdom operation was a response to the separation wall, which he hoped to 'set aflame' by his action.

Mohammed's father was interviewed by Hussan and offered this reason for his son's attack.

'Every day we wake in a small prison. For most people here there is no work, no normal life. Every day the Israelis enter our cities, kill, and then they leave and no one says anything. As long as the Occupation continues, so will the Intifada.'

One way in which Israel has sought to deter the bombers is by bulldozing the family homes of those who have taken part. This collective punishment on the bomber's family has had little impact, if any, on the waves of attacks.

Many are willing, for life has not improved, and conditions continue to be exacting, making the prospect of a release to a better place an attractive one.

Once a prospective suicide bomber has been accepted by the sponsoring group, he is assigned to a terrorist unit known as Al-Khaliyya al-istishadiyya, meaning 'martyrdom-cell'. The bomber, he or she, is called al-Shaheed al-hayy, 'the living martyr'.

The sponsors select the target, provide transport to the place, and set the explosives. A mentor might be chosen to bolster their resolve.

There are no shortage of takers and the streets of Palestine are littered with their portraits.

Three weeks after Sheikh Yassin was blown apart in his wheel chair, his successor as leader of Hamas, Abdel Aziz al-Rantissi was also assassinated by an Israeli missile. Interviewed by the BBC in 2002, Mr.Rantissi had this to say about the ongoing crisis.

'The main aim of the Intifada is to liberate the West Bank, Gaza, and Jerusalem. Nothing more.' This basically meant a return to the positions the two sides held prior to the Six Day War of 1967.

Rantissi continued, 'We haven't the force to free all our land. It is forbidden in our religion to give up part of it, so we cannot recognise Israel, but we can accept a truce with them and we can live side by side and refer all the issues to the coming generations.'

No wonder he had to go.

HEBRON.

The Lonely Planet travel guide calls the Palestinian town of Hebron 'The place of greatest unrest in the West Bank today'. They're not wrong.

The resting place of the Jewish Patriarch Abraham and his wife who, in the Bible, purchased a double cave in hills above the town for 400 sickles of silver, Hebron is no longer a place at peace.

In the early 1970's, a group of Jewish settlers, led by an extremist Rabbi, Moshe Levinger, entered the town posing as Swedish tourists. They then refused to leave.

Hebron is the second largest Palestinian city, and also the oldest. It lies deep inside the West Bank, within the region awarded to the Arabs in the UN partition plan of 1948. Since the Six Day War, the entire area has been occupied by the Israelis.

Those committed to establishing the religious state of Eretz Israel headed straight for the towns of Biblical reference. Hebron is mentioned in that ancient text eighty times or more. Also, as the burial place of Abraham and Sarah, Isaac and Rebecca, and Jacob and Leah, it is of sacred significance.

Abraham is also revered as a prophet of the Lord in the religion of Islam, and the Tomb of the Patriarch mosque was built to commemorate this fact close to the believed burial spot.

Following Israel's defeat of the Arabs in 1967, the government encouraged Jewish settlement in order to consolidate their gains. However, Hebron is the only Palestinian city were the settlers live amongst the Arab community, rather than outside the borders as is the case elsewhere.

The tension produced by this close proximity between hostile peoples has produced many shameful episodes. The worst of these occurred in February 1994 when Baruch Goldstein, a doctor, entered the Hebron mosque and machine-gunned 29 worshippers to death before being overpowered and torn limb from limb.

267

The Rabbi at his funeral made his despicable statement that 100 Arabs were worth less than the fingernail of a Jew. Goldstein's widow kept the murder weapon, a Galil assault rifle, on a mantlepiece above the fireplace as a souvenir.

Appalled, Yitzak Rabin proposed shipping the Settlers out of Hebron, but his Chief of Staff at the time, Ehud Barak, warned this could lead to civil war. It was to be of great regret to Rabin that he never followed his gut feeling in this instance.

When Rabin himself succumbed to an assassin's bullet, that of Yigal Amir, the police later searched Amir's home in the wake of the killing and found a book applauding Baruch Goldstein.

Today, 600 Jews live in four settlements in the centre of Hebron. 1500 IDF soldiers protect them, while the Palestinians are barred from the town centre and forced to live in the outer boundaries.

The Association of Civil Rights in Israel has said of the arrangement, 'The protection of a few hundred settlers and the repression of the majority Palestinian population is reminiscent of an apartheid regime.'

In 2004, a group of former soldiers who had served in Hebron staged an exhibition in the city entitled 'Breaking the silence.'

One of the officers described how the settlers had 'kicked the shit out of my soldiers.' Another described what happened when he found a settler breaking into a Palestinian store.

'I tried to prevent him from destroying the property but he attacked me, punched me straight in the face, and accused me of being a supporter of terrorists', said the confused ex-soldier. 'I don't know if we were there to protect the Settlers from the Palestinians or the Palestinians from the Settlers.'

THE END OF PEACE.

Ehud Barak was elected Prime Minister of Israel in 1999 on a platform of finding peace with their hostile Arab neighbours, namely Syria, Lebanon, and the Palestinians. It was an ambitious proposal.

Barak was no stranger to conflict. He was part of the commando unit ordered to take out the terrorists and planners behind the murder of Israeli athletes at the Munich Olympics in 1972. He had gone undercover, personally donning female attire, including false breasts, to get close to the perpetrators and perform assassinations.

After retiring from the military in 1975, Barak moved into the theatre of politics.

The Israeli public eventually tired of Benjamin Netanyahu's leadership. His hard-line attitude and indifference towards the Palestinians had not brought security to the country, and in 1999 Ehud Barak was chosen to deliver the calm the people so desperately desired.

Naively, Barak believed he could deliver peace with the same military precision that he had conducted his clandestine operations. He announced a fifteen month timetable for settling disputes that had raged for generations.

Turning first to Syria, Barak attempted to conclude a deal where Israel would return the Golan Heights in exchange for a peace treaty.

To President Bashir Assad, the recently-installed son of the former leader, the offer was attractive. Unfortunately, the deal fell, literally, yards short of coming into effect.

The Sea of Galilee, lying between the two nations, had previously formed the border. Now, when Syria wished to return to that line, they found that overuse of the water by Israel had reduced the lake, and Barak now claimed the body of water fell within Israel's borders. He would not permit the Syrians to dip their toes in the Sea of Galilee, and Israel would control the entire perimeter of the lake.

Syria could return to the geographical mark it had once held but, unfortunately, that was no longer at the shore of the sea.

Exasperated, the Syrians refused to negotiate.

The knock on effect of this failure was felt in Lebanon. There were some 30,000 Syrian troops in that country capable of reining in the Hizbollah militants who were agitating against the Israelis stationed in the South Lebanon security zone. Having failed to reach an agreement over Syria, Israel could no longer expect their support on the northern border.

Instead, in 2000, Israel opted for unilateral withdrawal from the buffer zone in Lebanon, and in a fragmented retreat, Hizbollah claimed to have defeated the Israeli forces and to have liberated Southern Lebanon. This gave succour to other armed militant groups prepared to take on the Israelis.

Having already made a mess on two of the three fronts he had pledged to resolve, Barak then turned his attention to the most difficult conflict of all, the Palestinian.

The outgoing United States President Bill Clinton was keen to mark his departure with the peace deal that had escaped him in the Oslo Accords of 1993, so when he received a call from Ehud Barak, asking him to convene another Middle East summit, Clinton was willing to oblige.

Yasser Arafat was reluctant to answer to the summons. He preferred that talks begin at a lower level, in the way that they had done in Oslo, to facilitate an agreement the leaders could then sign up to. He felt the parties were too far apart at this juncture to conclude anything of note, and he was concerned that failure to achieve anything might further frustrate the Palestinian people and that they might then resort to violence.

However, with Clinton insistent, Barak willing, and not wanting to be seen as the obstacle to peace, Arafat eventually agreed.

At Camp David in 2000, the Israelis offered concessions to the Palestinians greater than any ever tabled before. The Gaza Strip and most of the

West Bank would be handed over to a Palestinian state. An area equal to any Israeli territory maintained in the West Bank would be ceded to the Palestinians to make good any losses. East Jerusalem could remain in Arab hands and, perhaps most importantly of all, the refugee situation would finally be addressed.

Ever since al-Nakbah and the Arab exodus of 1948, and the second wave of expulsions in 1967, there were up to four million refugees in neighbouring lands.

Barak offered financial reparation to the tune of $20 billion dollars, as well as support for the legitimisation of the Arabs in their new host countries and limited return to Israel, capped at 10,000 persons a year, in order to reunite families. All Israel asked in return was that Arafat end the conflict and agree to make no further claims on her.

The Israeli public had not even been consulted on this generous offer. There had been no referendum and Barak had not achieved a consensus. Instead, he set out alone to achieve the peace that he had promised to deliver in his election pledge.

President Clinton supervised proceedings, but with the clock running out on his term in office, and to his dismay, he could not convince Arafat to accept Barak's offer.

For the Palestinian leader, anything less than the full right of return for all displaced refugees was tantamount to defeat, and he could not bring himself to agree to these terms.

It was a blow to Bill Clinton, who was soon to leave the Oval office. When Yasser Arafat telephoned the US President, days before his departure from office, to wish him well, Arafat said 'You are a great man'.

'No', replied Clinton, 'I am a great failure, and it is you who has made me one!'

Although Arafat was blamed for the failure to reach an agreement on a peace deal, it was Barak who would suffer most from the fallout. The Israeli Prime

Minister had campaigned on the promise of normalising relations with the neighbouring Arab countries. He had failed to deliver, and now the hawks were circling back home.

Benjamin Netanyahu hovered in the wings as Barak's Knesset majority crumbled, making the prospect of an early election possible.

But even Netanyahu met with opposition, as Ariel Sharon made his own bid for the Likud leadership and, ultimately, for that of Prime Minister.

Yasser Arafat, for all his perceived intransigence, was right about one thing. The failure of the Camp David conference served to instil in the Palestinians a sense of hopelessness. The path to peace had proved to be a dead end.

Tensions in the region were simmering. All that was needed was a spark to set it alight.

In September 2000, accompanied by 1000 armed security men, looking like something off the set of Reservoir Dogs, dressed in a suit and dark glasses, Ariel Sharon made a provocative appearance at the Al-Aqsa mosque on the Temple Mount, ostensibly to show Netanyahu who was in control.

By stoking a situation that unsettled the last vestiges of calm in the area, it was obvious that any subsequent revolt would require a tough Israeli hand to deal with it. Security was traditionally the preserve of the right wing in Israeli politics. Labour, and Barak, would be the ones to pay the price for any unrest. And, as an added bonus, it would be Sharon, who had caused the uproar, who would be called upon to halt it.

Insensitive and Machiavellian maybe, nevertheless Sharon's visit to the Temple Mount went almost exactly as planned.

The tinderbox was lit, but even the battle-hardened Sharon could not have predicted how fierce would be the Palestinian response.

In the centre of Jerusalem, in one of the holiest places on earth and a place of pilgrimage for three religions, the Second Intifada, with a vengeance, was about to erupt.

THE PASSOVER MASSACRE.

The Park Hotel is a modern seven storey affair, with balconied apartments, overlooking the Mediterranean Sea in the Israeli city of Netanya. There, a shore of white sand stretches in either direction and draws tourists from miles around.

On 27th March 2002, the hotel was hosting a Passover Seder, a meal to mark one of the most important holidays in the Jewish calendar, celebrating the Exodus from Egypt.

The Seder is meant to recreate the conditions of that early journey: unleavened bread that had not had time to rise as the Israelites fled from Pharaoh's soldiers; the parsley dipped in salt water to represent their tears; the bitter herbs the taste that slavery left in their forefathers' mouths; and the lamb, whose blood had been smeared on every household doorstep to ward off the Angel of Death.

This was also a notoriously tricky meal to prepare for, requiring special crockery and cutlery as well as the carefully ordered food, and the option of leaving all the hard work to others was an attractive one.

By seven o'clock that evening, the hotel lobby had filled with more than two hundred guests, many elderly, dressed in their finest clothes, with the ladies in evening gowns and the gents in dress shirts. The meal was scheduled for half past, and people began to make their way into the restaurant area on the ground floor.

Standing in the lobby, waiting for her family to arrive, one female guest went to speak to the receptionist.

'The security guard', she asked. 'Is that it? Only one of them?'

'Yes, ma'am', came the desk clerk's reply.

'Is he armed?'

'He is', she was assured.

The enquiry was a valid one. The past month had seen the bloodiest fighting thus far of the second Intifada, or uprising, of the Palestinian people against the Israeli Occupation.

Only a fortnight earlier, two people were killed and dozens more injured when terrorists threw grenades and shot at cars and pedestrians on the boardwalk of this seaside resort, and now everyone was on a state of high alert.

Everyone, it seemed, except the lone security guard sitting close to the entrance doors, dressed casually in a white sweater, looking relaxed and blending in to the surroundings.

At a quarter past seven, the guard left his post in order to carry out a security check of the hotel grounds. While he was gone, a 25 year old Palestinian, Abdul Basset-Odeh, dressed in either the black garb of an Hasidic Jew or a ladies dress, reports were sketchy, entered the hotel lobby carrying a heavy suitcase.

Hailing from the town of Tulkarem, just inside the Arab West Bank, only ten miles from Netanya, Odeh knew the area well. He had been employed as a waiter nearby, and he had enjoyed mixing with foreigners and practising his English. He was now a member of the militant wing of Hamas, an organisation with the destruction of Israel as its stated aim.

Unchallenged, Odeh proceeded to the restaurant, glanced around momentarily at the clientele, then detonated ten pounds of explosives, wrapped in ball-bearings, nails, and assorted pieces of metal, ending the lives of 29 men and women and injuring another 140 people.

The blast shattered the windows and brought down the ceiling. The survivors, such that there were, sought shelter beneath the tables from the falling debris. Thick black smoke filled the eyes and the lungs of the distraught, and shrieks, screams, and sorrowful moans filled the air.

Scores of ambulances raced to the scene and the injured were ferried to several hospitals.

The Mayor of Netanya, Miriam Feyerberg, witnessed the carnage and later gave a statement.

'I saw the bodies of women and children' she said 'and I want to say something to the Arab leaders. This is not resistance, this is murder.'

The remark was well aimed. On that very day, the leaders of the Arab nations were at a summit meeting in Beirut to discuss a cessation of hostilities with Israel, if only the latter would retreat to the borders it held prior to the 1967 war in the Middle East.

Asked about their position towards the Arab summit in the light of the Netanya bombing, an Israeli Foreign Ministry official had this to say.

'We want a cease-fire but we have a right to self defence and we will not sit and wait for the next suicide bomber.'

This view was echoed by the hard-line Israeli Prime Minister, Ariel Sharon, and by members of his cabinet, who called for a comprehensive response.

United States President George Bush urged Yasser Arafat, the Palestinian leader, to do everything in his power to stop the terrorists, but Arafat was not at the Arab summit, having been refused permission to travel by the Israelis, and he remained captive in his headquarters in the town of Ramallah.

Israel had ideas of its own for improving security, and one proposed solution had lain on Ariel Sharon's desk for some time. The Prime Minister had resisted for as long as he could, as the response would draw a lot of ink, but the Passover Massacre, as the Netanya hotel bombing became known, was the sixtieth suicide bombing in the previous eighteen months. It was also, from the Israeli point of view, the last straw.

Operation Defensive Shield was the name for the largest Israeli military offensive since the Six Day War of 1967, with the aim that all of the towns under the aegis of the Palestinian Authority would be seized, and the terrorists within them squeezed.

After much deliberation, in a session that lasted throughout the night, the cabinet and Ariel Sharon approved a plan that was not without its own risks.

Within hours, twenty thousand Israeli reserve soldiers had been called up, and operations were beginning in Ramallah, Bethlehem, and in Jenin refugee camp, the so-called suicide bombers' capital.

ISRAELI INCURSION.

As-simat-al-istashidin, the snake's head, otherwise known as Jenin refugee camp, sits on a hillside of cypress trees, overlooking a fertile plain. It is also one of the most crowded places on earth, with some fifteen thousand Palestinians living in the one square kilometre camp situated at the edge of Jenin town.

The inhabitants originally hail from Haifa on the Mediterranean coast, but fled their homes during the fighting that greeted the creation of Israel in 1948.

The camp is a warren of cinderblock houses, fed through with narrow, sloping alleyways that are plastered with posters of their martyrs. It is a hotbed of resistance.

By midnight, 3rd April 2002, the Israelis were ready. Backed by enormous Caterpillar D-9 bulldozers, tanks, and armoured personnel carriers, the Israeli Defence Force (IDF) prepared to enter Jenin from three sides. The Namal Brigade and commandos would enter from the west, Battalion 51 of the Golani Brigades would take the southern entrance, and the Fifth Infantry Brigade, a unit of reserves under the command of Corporal Rafi Lederman, would come from the east. Counting special units, such as the Navy Seals, there were 1000 troops.

The plan to take the camp had been dreamt up by Major General Yitzak Eitan, Israel's Chief of Central Command. He believed that they could take the camp in two or three days.

Helicopter gun-ships were on standby to lend additional support, should it be needed, but this was primarily a ground assault. In order to protect the civilian residents while fighting in such a densely populated camp, it was necessary to get in close or risk hurting the innocent and handing the Palestinians a publicity coup.

The Israeli army is largely made up of young people performing National Service. All able-bodied men join the ranks of the reserves. Modern Israel was forged in the fire, and it must fight for survival, unloved by its Arab neighbours, and prepared for the worst.

Many of these IDF reservists, as well as willingly defending their country, are also the lifeblood of its public services: its teachers, doctors, or other professionals, like Corporal Lederman, a marketing consultant. This is why Israel takes extra care of them. With soldiers in head to toe body armour, and usually ensconced in some impenetrable vehicle; for many Palestinians, the face of the occupation is a metal one.

Ranged against this army was a bunch of resistance fighters and a couple of dozen policemen, in total, between one and two hundred people. They would be no match for the IDF, and many of the guerrillas thought of escaping, along with the civilian population, to other nearby towns. Once it became clear that the troops massing at the edge of the camp would be coming in on foot, however, many militants chose to stay on.

The sight of dozens of foot soldiers, preparing to enter the camp minus their usual protection was both an affront to the resistance and an opportunity many had long relished: a chance to fight one to one, on almost equal terms, without Israeli armour to separate them, and on their home turf.

As one militant put it, when it became clear Israel would use infantry and not air power, 'I've been waiting for a moment like this for years'.

The resistance set about booby-trapping houses and laying crude bombs, known as Kuwa, along the roads into the camp, with an estimated 1000 to 2000 bombs and booby traps spread throughout the buildings and alleyways. Big ones were laid for the tanks, some weighing 250 pounds, ten times greater than those used by a typical suicide bomber. Others were only the size of a water bottle.

Variants on these bombs included boilers: small cans containing explosives. These had a bark far worse than their bite. Mostly, the resistance were armed with little more than Kalashnikovs and courage.

The IDF, using loudhailers, began calling for the civilians to leave the camp. They could capture any known militants who tried to flee, and would isolate those that chose to stay and fight.

The response came from the speaker of a local mosque: 'Calling all Palestinians, Hamas, Fatah, Islamic Jihad. Resist the army. We are on alert.'

One of the men to answer the call to arms, and one of Israel's chief targets in the operation, was Mahmoud Tawalbe, a 23 year old father of two who worked at a local record shop. He was also the leader of a branch of Islamic Jihad, and was believed to be responsible for numerous deadly assaults.

As the Merkava tanks prepared to roll in, Israel sent the huge bulldozers in advance to clear a path, and one engineering corps officer logged 124 separate explosions in a single stretch of road.

Not everyone who decided to stay in the camp was a fighter. Many civilians did not hear the call to evacuate, while other chose to stay to lend support to the resistance factions.

Others stayed in order to protect their homes. One old man exclaimed 'Fifty years ago you removed me from Haifa. Now I have nowhere to go.'

About half of the camp's residents were still in situ when the army appeared. Many of these would flee over the following days as the battle raged.

For now, the IDF were expecting a tough fight in Jenin, where the resistance was expected to be the fiercest of all the towns to be visited, but the Israeli reservists were still expected to cope.

Operation Defensive Shield began with the memory of the Passover Massacre still fresh in everyone's mind. Motivating the soldiers would not be a problem. Seizing control of the camp most certainly would be.

THE BATTLE RAGES.

The Israeli government pursued a course that reduced the danger to Palestinian civilians and placed much greater risk on their own soldiers. Instead of bombing the camp from the air or using tanks and heavy artillery, the soldiers were sent on a harrowing mission. So claimed Natan Sharansky, a former Deputy Prime Minister of Israel in his book 'The Case for Democracy.'

Around fifty tanks rolled into Jenin, part of the wider operation that saw Israel take over the towns of Nablus, Hebron, and Tulkarem, not to mention the gripping scenes in Bethlehem and Ramallah (of which more later). In total, more than eighty percent of the population of the West Bank were now under siege.

In Jenin, helicopter gun-ships laid down machine-gunfire and destroyed water tanks that lay on the rooftops. Electricity cables and telephone wires were torn down or shredded, cutting off communications, making conditions even harder than they already were.

The IDF soldiers on foot began to move cautiously through the refugee camp, moving from place to place, avoiding the streets where possible by knocking holes in the dividing walls in the homes.

One reserve soldier described the operation.

'At the first stage we went from house to house. There was a security team outside and a team that went in. You take the ID's from the men and phone them in to the General Security Service. You put all the women and children in another room, and you take one man and search for weapons throughout the house. The man touches what you ask him to for fear of booby traps. It makes the search easier and you don't have to turn the house upside down. For catching specific wanted men, you go to a neighbour and get him to go in first. If there is something planned, the neighbour will get it.'

A Palestinian teenager, Reem Saleh, told the Times newspaper about the soldiers who came to her family home.

'Troops broke into our house. They seemed very angry and smashed furniture. Some were nervous. They took my father into another room to use him as a shield while they shot from holes they made in the walls.'

Many families moved houses, trying to find the most secure. Sometimes hundreds of people crammed into tiny spaces, as the sounds of Kalashnikovs, M16 rifles, and rocket propelled grenades exploded outside. All the while, a bank of helicopters hovered menacingly overhead, sporadically firing into the camp.

One resident, Samer al Ahmad, said 'The Israelis have been shelling us all morning. The Apache helicopters keep shooting and shelling, and there is fire and smoke coming from the camp, and resistance from the Palestinians.'

The militias, small units and snipers, were positioned throughout, and they returned gunfire and made whatever stand they could before retreating towards the centre of their domain.

Brigadier General Eyal Shlein told Israel Radio 'The Palestinian fighters have their backs to the wall. We trapped them in there and attacked them with the intention that they should surrender. Those that don't surrender, we kill. It is determined fighting.'

Very little news was reaching the outside world. Journalists, as well as relief agencies and United Nations personnel, were not permitted access. It was just too dangerous, but it led to accusations that Israel had something to hide.

As Lior Yavme from the Israeli human rights organisation B'tselem put it: 'Something very bad is happening and we have no way of knowing what it is.'

Abu George of the Palestinian Red Cross said 'I am 200 yards away and I don't know what is happening. We don't know how many dead are lying there or how many injured. We only hear the sounds of gunfire and war.'

The disquiet reached the White House, and President George Bush ordered the immediate withdrawal of Israeli troops. He later emphasised this, as the onslaught continued, telling reporters 'I meant what I said to the Prime Minister of Israel. I expect there to be a withdrawal without delay.'

Ariel Sharon responded by saying that their mission was not yet complete.

Many civilians decided it was time to leave. They abandoned their homes and waved white flags to declare their peaceful intentions. Many of their houses were smouldering ruins by this time, and children were screaming from fear and for water, choking in the dust and the heat.

The women were ushered to nearby towns, while the men and boys were stripped to their underwear, before eventually being led into Israel, to an army barracks where many claimed to have been beaten. Some were offered money if they would return to the camp and act as spies.

After being interrogated, the innocent were left without shoes and told to make their own way back to the West Bank.

Meanwhile, the resistance were hitting their stride. They had survived the initial onslaught and had inflicted casualties of their own. Two IDF soldiers were dead, and five injured, according to Israel Radio. One of them was shot in Reem Saleh's home. He was seriously injured, and screamed for his mother.

An Israeli general referred to Jenin as the Palestinian 'Masada', recalling days of lore when 1000 Jews had held the Romans at bay in a hilltop fortress before taking their own lives rather than surrender.

Jenin's modern day resistance fighters were threatening to make history themselves, or facing similar extinction.

THE AMBUSH.

On Tuesday 9th April 2002 the Israeli Defence Force suffered its greatest single military loss in more than twenty years in the most devastating attack of the Second Intifada.

The army believed some twenty Palestinians were involved, and the resistance fighters claimed they had targeted twenty soldiers, having watched them enter a house before detonating explosives inside.

Reports were sketchy, the scene was confused, but terror reigned and thirteen lives were lost. A bomb was said to have been detonated, causing a number of breezeblock homes to collapse on a group of soldiers.

Others spoke of a possible suicide bomber, a booby trapped building, or a sophisticated device setting off a chain of explosions.

The truth, it seems, was a little of all of this, and then some.

Brigadier-General Ron Kitrey, the chief army spokesman, said six or seven reservist soldiers had been killed when a booby-trapped device exploded and then a terrorist blew himself up. Remains of the man were found on a wall nearby.

At the same time, a second group of soldiers in an enclosed courtyard came under fire from gunmen on surrounding roofs. Thirteen infantrymen were killed and nine others were seriously injured.

'It was', said Ariel Sharon, 'a difficult day.'

Indeed it was. The IDF met fierce resistance every step of the way. Nine soldiers had been killed in Jenin during the operation so far, even before this double ambush.

The reservists were expected to sniff out wanted terrorists while wading through an elaborate system of tripwires. It was, literally, a minefield.

Added to this, suicide bombers were busy strapping on the deadly belts, and five of them were reported to have blown themselves up whilst pretending to turn themselves in.

The names of some of the thirteen victims were released. Captain Ya'akov Azulai, aged 30; First Lieutenants Dror Bar and Yoel Eyal, both aged 28; First Sergeant Majors Yoram Levy, Tiran Arazi, and Avner Yaskov; and Sergeant Majors Menashe Hava, Eyal Zimmerman, Ronen Alsochat, Shmuel Danny Meizlish, and Amit Poseidon.

These soldiers were on a search mission, away from the most intense fighting. At first light, residents in the nearby village of Burkin reported hearing a huge explosion. According to Ron Drori, one of the IDF party, the men had met with little resistance as they approached three houses they wished to take over.

The commander decided it was too dangerous to enter the buildings, so the soldiers moved into a narrow alleyway where a device, possibly thrown by a militant, suddenly tore between them and all hell broke loose.

A group of naval commandos sent in to rescue them came under a barrage of gunfire and additional bombs.

Tiran Arazi, 34 years of age and hailing from the town of Hadera, was one of the thirteen killed. A self-employed contractor and a father of two, he had been mobilised through the emergency call up eleven days before. He had reported for duty willingly, but his wife had then been involved in a serious road accident and was recovering in hospital. She had asked Arazi's commander if he could be released, and it was agreed. He was due to go home on the day that he died.

The ambush came just as Israel pulled out from two West Bank towns that it had occupied the previous week, in an effort to complete the mission before the arrival of Colin Powell, the United States envoy, who had demanded their withdrawal from all Palestinian territory.

Following the massacre, Ariel Sharon vowed to press on with the destruction of the terror infrastructure, claiming 'This is a battle for the survival of the Jewish people, for the survival of the state of Israel itself.'

In the camp, as news of the ambush spread, soldiers began crying, before their thoughts turned to revenge.

'When the soldiers were killed, the Israelis became more aggressive', said Ali Damaj, a Jenin resident. 'In one night I counted 71 missiles from a helicopter.'

Aishe Saleh, whose home was occupied by the army, claimed to have seen an aerial map on which the IDF had outlined, in a blue marker pen, homes for demolition in order to create a path through the camp for their tanks. It was a detailed map. Aishe could even recognise her own home on it.

'After the 13 soldiers were killed', she said, 'there were a lot more squares on the map.'

At this point, Israel appeared to have abandoned foot patrols. A crossroads for the tanks was created in the centre of the camp. The Guardian newspaper described it as a 'vast plaza' of bulldozed homes.

Hania al-Kubia, a mother of six, said 'They just started demolishing houses with the people inside. I used to hear them on the loudspeaker shouting "come out, come out". Then they stopped doing that, but they carried on bulldozing.'

The fighting was now confined to a 70 square metre section of concentrated houses where the militants were holed up. It doesn't sound la lot, but one Israeli soldier, Dori Scheuer, claimed that in one metre you could find 20 small booby traps. Every single step was dangerous.

The IDF called on the militants to surrender, but even those that appeared to do so were likely to attempt to blow themselves up, shouting 'Allah hu-Akhbar', God is Great, as they went.

The resistance had decided to fight to the last man, preferring death to surrender, and to make the battle as bloody as possible. But in response to the 13 soldiers killed, Major General Yitzak Eitan said 'We will continue to fight despite this loss. We will continue until we make this camp submit.'

ISRAELI RESPONSE.

The Israeli army claimed that 180 fighters surrendered on 8th April 2002. The Palestinians said that they were civilians who had given themselves up. The militants had vowed they would fight to the end.

The resistance fighters were well prepared, having learned how the soldiers operated during three recent IDF incursions. They also feared being captured and spending the rest of their young lives in prison.

Mahmoud Tawalbe decided to take a break from the fighting in order to visit his mother, Tuffahah, who lived in the camp. He looked pleased with his work thus far. He and his crew of about fifty fighters had been hitting the Israelis hard.

'Don't worry about me', Mahmoud told his mum. 'I feel strong'. The next day, he was killed.

Tawalbe and two of his team had entered a house to try and creep up close enough to a Caterpillar D9 bulldozer, twenty feet tall and weighing fifty tons, to plant explosives on it. These would be useless unless placed directly on the vehicle's armour.

The bulldozer driver spotted the men and rammed the wall of the house down on top of them, the falling masonry mangling the three so that, a week later, when the bodies were retrieved, they could not be distinguished from one another and were buried together.

Not all of the Palestinians who came to grief in the camp were fighters. Fathi Shalabi, 63 years old, was at home with his family when their neighbours came running from the Israeli soldiers who had decided to set up operations in theirs. Thirty soldiers followed, ordered the women and children out, then took the men, Fathi, his son Wadh, who was a school caretaker, and his neighbour's son Abdul Karim Al-Sadi into a narrow alley and ordered them to strip. This was common practice. They were looking for explosive belts or devices.

Abdul was wearing an elasticated bandage, support for a bad back. When the soldiers saw it, they thought it was a suicide belt. One of them, a man called Gaby who appeared to be in charge, shouted 'Kill them. Kill them'. Two of the soldiers immediately opened fire on the men, and the three of them fell to the ground.

Miraculously, Fathi was not hit, but he lay there for an hour while the blood of his son ran between his legs and soaked his body, until the soldiers left. Later, Abdul's father came to Mr.Shallabi's house and said 'They have killed my son and yours.'

'I know', replied Mr.Shallabi, 'I was there.'

Elsewhere, Yusra Ahmad, a mentally disabled woman, was killed in her home by a helicopter rocket.

Munir Washashi was hit by a round from a helicopter and he bled to death over several hours. When an ambulance came for him, Israeli soldiers shot at it. When Munir's mother, Maryam, ran into the street crying for help for her son, she was shot in the head and died.

Another civilian, Hani Rumeleh, was shot as he tried to look out of his front door. He lay in the street, crying for help. Rufaida Damaj came running to his aid, but she was shot in the leg. There were a lot of resistance fighters in the area at the time, and the Israelis were shooting in that direction. When Rufaida's sister, Fadwa Jamma, a nurse in full uniform, came to tend to her, she was shot in the abdomen.

'I'm wounded', said Rufaida.

'I'm wounded too', said Fadwa, before she was again shot, this time through the heart. Rufaida asked her where she was wounded, but this time there would be no reply.

The stepmother of Hani Rumelleh saw her husband die. He had gone to check on two rockets that had landed in another part of the house. He called to his wife, crying 'I'm wounded'. When she appeared, he fell down, shot in the head.

The ambulance that was called was sent back by the Israelis.

Doctor Ali Jabareen was unable to reach a wounded man lying in the street about 50 metres from the Al Razi hospital, and the victim bled to death over several hours.

Kemil Zughayer was shot in his wheelchair while trying to get up the road. His white flag clung to the mud in the ground, crushed under foot by a tank, just like Kemil.

A pregnant lady named Hyam knocked at the Salem household, looking for shelter. The soldiers told her to turn back, and shot at her. When she returned to her home with her daughter, she found out her husband had been arrested.

Another home that of 15 year old Ashraf Abu al Haija, was occupied by soldiers for a week. The family were huddled in the kitchen. They tried negotiating to move somewhere safer. 'Whoever leaves the house will die', was the response. Ashraf's dead body lay in another room of the house, killed days earlier by a helicopter rocket. Yet another reason to leave.

Jamal Sabagh stayed in the camp, while his wife and children fled, because he was a diabetic and too ill to run. He was also fearful he'd be mistaken for a fighter.

He only left his home when the Israelis threatened to blow it up, joining other men in the street, being told to strip. He clung to his bag of medicine as he attempted to undress, and this slowed him down. He was shot by soldiers who thought he was being evasive.

Ali Mustapha Abu Sani had the dubious honour of being a human shield, placed ahead of the IDF soldiers, and was wounded by a second Israeli patrol for his efforts.

In a house overlooking the Hawamish district of the camp, the soldiers came and blew open the door. There had been no answer to their knock. How were they to know Afaf Dusuqi was slow on her feet? The shrapnel killed her instantly.

Mohammed Abu Sba'a, 65 years old, left his home in Hawamish, scene of the ambush, to warn an approaching bulldozer that the house was packed with families. The bulldozer turned back, but Mohammed was hit in the chest almost immediately by an Israeli sniper.

Ismael Khatib also lived in Hawamish. He was forced to act as a human shield and knock on his neighbours' front door with an army rifle balancing on his shoulder.

Two fighters up the alley started firing and the soldier fired back wildly. Bombs were hurled at them. Khatib threw himself to the ground and crawled home, climbing in through the back window.

'I felt like I died and was born again', he said.

The whole scene was a quagmire. The world was demanding Israel's withdrawal, but this was not forthcoming while there was still a job to do. In order to deal with the terrorists, the remaining civilians would have to be extricated.

Told they could retrieve water, their own supplies having run out, the battered civilians emerged from their homes, and were arrested.

The IDF then began calling to the resistance men to surrender or see their women and children die.

A week earlier, Peter Hain, a European minister, had called it the most dangerous conflict in the world.

What was it now?

By Thursday, April 11, two days after the massacre of the thirteen infantrymen, Hawamish district had gone.

THE AFTERMATH.

In Jenin, the Palestinian death toll was placed at more than fifty, almost half of whom were civilians, women, children, and the elderly. Twenty three Israeli soldiers were killed. Many more, on both sides, were wounded.

Israel also said that it had detained 4185 Palestinians, 60 of whom were known fugitives, with 30 more wanted for murder.

Operation Defensive Shield, in its entirety, is said to have resulted in a total of 497 Palestinians being killed, with 2800 refugee housing units being damaged, 878 homes destroyed, leaving more than 17000 people homeless or in need of shelter.

Saeb Erekat, a negotiator for the Palestinian Authority, told CNN news channel on the 12th of April that a massacre had been committed in Jenin. The word proved to be an emotive one, and was like a red rag to a bull to the Israeli public relations machine.

Reporters Sans Frontiers, an international pressure group for journalists, accused Israel in a statement of wounding 7 journalists, arresting 15, detaining a further 4, with a further 60 being targeted by gunfire and another 20 being roughed-up or threatened.

No pictures or information had been given of the incursion while the operation was ongoing, and this led to conflicting testimonies from residents fleeing the camp accusing the IDF of committing atrocities, followed by outright denials of this from the Israeli side.

The world's media reported events according to their own particular bias. Whereas the British Independent newspaper was happy to use words like 'atrocity' in its reporting and referred to the camp as a 'slaughterhouse', the New York Times felt able to say 'as Israeli forces pursued militants, civilians kept getting in the way and died as a result.'

All depends on your point of view.

Michael Ben-Yair, a former Attorney general of Israel has described the Palestinian Intifada as a 'war of national liberation'. He accused Israel of ignoring international treaties, stealing lands, transferring settlers to the occupied lands, and creating an apartheid state.

Uri Avnery, a co-founder of Israel's peace coalition said 'no good will come of this adventure. The concept was stupid, the implementation cruel, and it will not bring peace and security.'

In a Commons debate on the issue, Gerald Kaufman, Britain's most prominent Jewish politician, called Ariel Sharon 'a war criminal'. United States President George Bush called Sharon 'a man of peace'. P.O.V. again.

Tony Blair, the British Prime Minister commented 'what is happening in Jenin is appalling and tragic, but so is large numbers of Israelis being blown up in cafes.'

The preliminary findings of an Amnesty International delegates visit to Jenin did not find there had been a massacre of innocents, but did call on the United Nations Security Council to establish an inquiry into war crimes.

The crimes listed by Amnesty International included a failure to warn civilians to flee before launching air strikes, failure to allow humanitarian aid into the camp, denial of medical assistance to the wounded, deliberate targeting of ambulances, using civilians as human shields, and extensive damage to property without military necessity. All are contrary to the Geneva Convention, most notably Article 147, concerning the use of hostages as human shields and the wanton destruction of property. Not that it matters. Israel does not recognise the applicability of the Convention to the Occupied Territories.

In the resulting United Nations report to the Secretary General, the intimidation, sometimes assassination, of medical and relief agency personnel got a mention. The head of the Palestinian Medical Service had been killed by an Israeli rocket whilst travelling in a clearly marked ambulance, and a staff member of UNRWA, the relief arm of the UN, was also shot dead by Israeli troops.

The military incursion had continued in spite of United Nations resolutions 1402 and 1403, calling for the cessation of hostilities and withdrawal from Palestinian Territory.

Some of the aid workers allowed into Jenin were veterans of previous conflicts. They said that in Afghanistan, they had been prevented from bringing medical services and humanitarian aid to the refugee camps there for an entire day. In Jenin, they were refused access for ten.

What also wasn't disputed was that the wounded were left to die in the streets. Anyone who came to their aid risked drawing the snipers' fire, and ambulances that attempted to reach the injured were shot at or turned back by the IDF. The Israelis claimed the ambulances were being used to transport combatants and weapons.

In sum, said the UN report, Israeli forces had committed war crimes and serious violations of international humanitarian law, including inhuman treatment, wilful killing, and other grave breaches.

A Chinese journalist, Shu Suzki, wiped away tears in Jenin to say 'I have covered a great many events and tragedies around the world, but the scenes I have witnessed in Jenin are the most violent and the ones that touched me the most. The bodies that were found under the rubble were those of children, women, and teenagers, all civilians. Some of them had been fatally injured and their deaths were attributable to the fact they were unable to receive aid. Any person who has a conscience anywhere in this world should work to bring an end to this war.'

Zvi Rav-Ner, later an Israeli ambassador to London, told the BBC news website, 'Let us not exaggerate. The bulldozing of a couple of houses has been described almost on the scale of Rwanda. It is a gross, gross, exaggeration.'

It all depends on your point of view.

THE BETHLEHEM SIEGE.

The Church of the Nativity is one of the holiest sites in Christianity, built at the supposed birthplace of the man who gave the religion its name: Jesus Christ.

On 2nd April 2002, as part of Operation Defensive Shield and the wider incursion into West Bank towns, helicopter gunships, tanks, and infantrymen pursued wanted militants who fled to the safety of the Church in Manger Square, Bethlehem, and barricaded themselves inside.

The Basilica of the Nativity is surrounded by a Franciscan friary, a parish church for Roman Catholics, a pilgrim's hospice, and monasteries for monks from both the Greek and Armenian Orthodoxies. Together, they cater for the many thousands of visitors from around the world drawn to this sacred place.

Gunfire announced the arrival of the visitors, 208 Palestinians in total. There were uniformed policemen and security men; members of Hamas, the Tamzin militia, and the Al Aqsa Martyrs brigade; and a number of civilians and families; each constituting about a third of the number.

The gunmen reasoned that Israel would not dare storm the church; not the birthplace of Jesus. The policemen had joined the militants rather than engage the Israelis. The rest were just scared.

The Israelis were prepared to wait. The church was surrounded, snipers were positioned, and the siege began.

There were 31 friars, 4 Catholic nuns, and 9 Greek Orthodox and 5 Armenian monks in the church when the Palestinian entourage came running in, chased by the clamour of gunfire.

Some of the militiamen were on Israel's Most Wanted list, and there was no way the army was going to back off and let them escape. Seven of the men were injured in the fighting prior to breaking into the church.

The Palestinians were in no rush to go outside. There were already 4 dead men lying in Manger Square, killed in the fighting that led them here.

Talks began between the Israelis and the militants, in an effort to end the deadlock. The men refused to be drawn out, and gunfire continued to echo around the church. Both sides denied they had discharged weapons so close to a holy shrine, and the impasse became one of words as well as actions.

On April 4th, Samir Ibrahim Salman, 45 years of age and a Palestinian Christian, left the church, where he was the bell ringer, and began crossing Manger Square. He was struck down by a single bullet to the chest and died immediately. The Israelis claimed he had ignored warnings to stop, and they had therefore concluded that he was a suicide bomber.

Later that same day, an explosion blew the southern door off the church, and led to fears the army were about to overwhelm those inside.

Issa Abu Sror, one of the men holed up in the church described one attempted infiltration by the Israelis.

'I was woken up at 2.30 am by the sound of soldiers climbing into the church from the hotel next door. They started shooting. Suddenly, the office and the library, which was full of very old books, caught fire. We tried to put out the flames. A policeman called Khaled was in the front. He got shot and died at once, then the soldiers ran away. I don't know why.'

The electricity was cut off, but luckily there was a backup generator. When this failed, two days later, they used candles, of which there were plenty.

Many of the Palestinians had run into the basilica wearing only T-shirts, and the nights could be cold.

The food had run out, and on April 10th, the water was shut off too. Luckily, there was a well within the compound.

Two days later, the phone lines were cut. Journalists had earlier been banned from Manger Square, the IDF shooting at the cars of those who got too close. Taking pot-shots at the birthplace of Jesus would not make for the kind of coverage Israel was looking for. Not when the rest of the West Bank offensive was also being widely criticised as too broad-ranging and heavy-handed.

Four Franciscan monks walked out of the church. Their colleagues inside were 'voluntary hostages', they said, and were staying put to act as protection against the Israelis and to help avoid further bloodshed.

Firebombs were aimed at the church and caused extensive damage. Pictures of the fires caused upset around the world, including in the Vatican, where Pope John Paul II called for Israel to respect the holy site. A gunfight that erupted saw one Palestinian killed and two Israeli soldiers injured. The next day, an Armenian monk was shot dead, and another was seriously wounded. The Israelis claimed to have mistaken them for militiamen.

In response to calls from George Bush, Ariel Sharon decided on April 14th to attempt to talk again to the militants and to cut a deal. His offer was for the wanted militia men to face an Israeli court or to go into permanent exile. The deal was rejected.

For the most part, throughout the siege, the friars, monks, and nuns carried on with their normal routines whilst within the confines of the building, but anyone venturing into one of the courtyards in the grounds risked falling prey to one of the sniper positions surrounding the church.

For their part, the militants acceded to the clergymen's request that they not raise their weapons within the sanctity of the church.

This was confirmed by Father Amjad Sabarah, one of the priests, who told The Guardian newspaper that the men were armed but had not used their guns. The Israelis said that the Palestinians had shot at observation posts and had thrown grenades.

By April 20th, the rationed food had run out. Those inside were forced to eat the plants growing in the courtyard.

Face to face negotiations began to bring an end to the affair, but the Palestinians preferred to see the wanted men tried in their own courts, and refused to hand them over.

Stalemate, and the siege dragged on.

Two men were shot in the compound, one of whom later died. A group of teenagers were allowed to surrender, and they emerged with the decomposing remains of two of the militants who had come to grief earlier in the campaign.

Four men gave themselves up, and a further two were shot by sniper fire and were evacuated for emergency treatment on April 26th.

Three days later, Nidal Abayat, a militia leader, and one of the men in the church that Israel had most interest in, was killed by a sniper shot in the courtyard.

Fires broke out in a building adjoining the church after an exchange of gunfire. The Palestinians blamed the Israelis, saying that their patience must have run out and they were now trying to smoke them out.

The world's press, camped out nearby, captured images of the fire next to the holy church, and in an attempt to quell the public relations disaster, Israel warmed to the press and allowed them the access they wanted.

With Manger Square opened up, albeit still swarming with IDF troops and the siege still in progress, a group of international peace activists risked their lives to deliver food to the incumbents of the church. A photographer from the Los Angeles Times joined them. They later described the appalling conditions inside: people starving, shot up, petrified, surviving on grass and leaves, and all the while being surrounded and risking death for stepping into the sunlight.

The gun battles continued, as did the negotiations. Two more Palestinians were killed, another two injured, before a settlement to end the siege was finally reached on 10th May.

After almost six weeks, a deal was brokered between the warring parties, via agents of the United States. Thirteen of those who finally emerged from the Church of the Nativity were sent into permanent exile; the rest were sent home.

The outcome mirrored the offer made three weeks earlier. Why then had the siege dragged on so long? Maybe because one of the leaders essential to negotiations was a virtual prisoner himself, holed up in the compound of his headquarters in Ramallah.

THE RAMALLAH COMPOUND.

The headquarters of the Palestinian leader, Yasser Arafat, were in the city of Ramallah in the West Bank. As Israel began its massive clampdown on the terrorist infrastructure, it moved to place the erstwhile warrior under a form of house arrest.

At the risk of being shot for venturing outside, Arafat hunkered in the bunker of his official compound. The Israelis blocked the roads leading to it with piles of rubble, of which there was no shortage. Cars were turned over and used as barricades, and the leader of a people became a prisoner in his home.

Suspected of arming and directing the militias defying the Israeli occupation, Ariel Sharon was taking the fight to his old enemy. If Arafat should attempt to escape his isolation, one of the troops surrounding the camp would surely take his life.

Colin Powell had evidently received assurances that this would not be the case. 'Whatever action Israel takes', he said, 'it will not include killing or harming Chairman Arafat.'

Asked how his leader had survived one of the nights where the shooting and shelling was particularly bad, Palestinian Authority intelligence chief Tawfik Tarawi, who had been beside him said, 'Just like the rest of his people. Without water or electricity.'

The compound was surrounded by tanks and armoured personnel carriers, and soldiers took aim from every side.

There were between 50 and 100 people trapped with Arafat inside the group of offices and barracks that constituted the headquarters of the Palestinian Authority. They were without food, water, electricity, and telephone communications.

The road to the compound climbs from the centre of this, the most attractive of all the Palestinian cities, past wealthy hillside suburbs and comes to a halt at the top of the rise. There, behind a huge wall and gate, were the Chairman and his administrative and security people. The Israelis didn't bother knocking, sent tanks crashing through the entrance gate, and were soon holed up in seven of the buildings inside the headquarters, with only a door separating the IDF troops from Arafat and his security men and other loyalists. A tank barrel was aimed directly at this single layer of separation.

The Deputy Prime Minister of Israel, Natan Sharansky told the Observer newspaper that the aim of Defensive Shield was to dismantle the Palestinian security apparatus. It was a plan for a war that would strip Arafat of his power and leave him isolated. If they couldn't kill him, they would decapitate him operationally.

In a televised address, Ariel Sharon branded Yasser Arafat 'an enemy of Israel. An enemy of the entire free world'.

The Palestinian's chief negotiator, Saeb Erekat, dismissed Sharon's speech saying it was 'void of substance, void of hope, void of realism.'

Colin Powell, still negotiating his way to Israel, via Spain, Jordan, and Morocco, urged an end to Arafat's isolation, asking that he be allowed to communicate with the outside world.

Yasser Arafat himself was livid. 'I have to ask the whole world', he said, 'I have to ask President Bush, I have to ask the United Nations, is this acceptable that I can't go outside the door?'

The siege finally ended in May 2002, but Arafat remained confined, on pain of death, in his compound for another two years, and was only finally released when frail and dying.

Airlifted to France, suffering from a mystery ailment, the tired old man acquiesced to martyrdom in 2004, poisoned, many believe, by the state of Israel.

With the thorn of Arafat removed, Ariel Sharon was now free to seek a new partner for peace from the Palestinian side.

Soon, the words ceasefire and disengagement were being uttered, and it seemed a new dawn might have sprung from the dark night of the Second Intifada.

The furore in the press and the world's media subsided; the word 'massacre' to describe the depths of the Israeli operation of April 2002 slipped into the annals of history.

The army withdrew from most of the towns and villages it had occupied in response to the Passover Massacre, and life would return to the kind of grotesque that most Palestinians had only ever known.

FROM 2000 TO THE PRESENT.

In recent times, this part of the Middle East has captured the headlines for all the wrong reasons. The Intifada, the accompanying suicide bombing campaign, targeted assassinations of Palestinian militants, Operation Defensive Shield and collective punishment, and all taking place as the world was changing around it.

September 11th, 2001, four planes were hijacked in the USA. Two were flown into the twin towers of the World Trade Centre. Another hit the Pentagon. The last was aimed at the White House before the passengers heroically brought down the plane.

Republican President George Bush responded to the attacks by dividing the world into good guys and bad. 'You're either with us or against us', he said. Israel was very much with him.

Ariel Sharon labelled Yasser Arafat a terrorist and claimed to be fighting the War on Terror, as the United States-led invasions of Afghanistan and Iraq were called.

In the West Bank and Gaza the situation was deteriorating. The world witnessed the death of twelve year old Mohammed al-Dura on live television as he crouched in fear beside his father in the midst of a fire-fight.

The Palestinian response to the strong hand of Sharon was to instil terror into the Israeli public with a procession of suicide bombs. The images of shattered buses, blood pooled on the floor at the roadside, made life in Israel precarious.

The response came in the form of Operation Defensive Shield, with the aim of rooting out the terrorists in their homes. The result was a PR disaster. There was so much destruction wrought that the watching world accused Israel of overkill.

Meanwhile, the Palestinians have waited for almost sixty years for justice. They have twice been displaced and have won no concession from their occupiers and carry so much anger towards them.

The ritual humiliation suffered at the checkpoints serves to alienate the two sides further. If a child sees his father being pushed around by a young soldier, he isn't going to look up to his old man in the same way again. So when a child sees a guerrilla in the camp, armed, attitudinal, and a symbol of resistance, he has found someone to look up to. No one aspires to a life of subservience.

And Israel has showed no inclination to deal with the Palestinians, to find a moderate leadership who can be a partner for peace. Despite hopes that this might happen with Palestinian President Mahmoud Abbas, first Yasser Arafat and then Hamas have sidelined the amiable Abbas, giving him no real authority to negotiate. Instead, Israel has decided to impose a unilateral solution.

The withdrawal from the Gaza Strip is a prime example. Although claimed by jubilant militants as a victory for the resistance movement, the truth is that Israel wanted out.

Six thousand Settlers surrounded by more than a million Palestinians require a lot of looking after. The huge army presence taxed not only Israel's military resource but her economy in general. Also, the negative impact on Palestinian lives was exorbitant even by the usual standards, creating fertile ground for radical fundamentalism.

Despite the Settler protests, and the teary scenes when the IDF came to remove them from their homes, the withdrawal had to happen.

Ariel Sharon took a brave step in pushing through the decision to disengage, and there were fears he might go the way of Rabin, falling to an Israeli extremist's bullet.

The Settlers and the religious Right accused the government of pandering to terrorists and abandoning Eretz Israel. Ariel Sharon's deputy, Dov Weisglass, addressed a meeting in the Knesset when he attempted to assuage these fears.

'Don't worry about what we are doing in Gaza', he said. 'We are not giving in to the Palestinians. By coming out of the Strip, we are placing the rest of the peace process in formaldehyde.'

With such resolute words from the deputy Prime Minister, the future for the Israelis, if not the Palestinians, looks assured.

NEW BEGINNINGS.

The death of Yasser Arafat removed the impasse that the Israelis claimed stood in the way of peace. Then, in the Spring of 2006, the Palestinians voted in democratic elections for the party of Hamas. Despite their social agenda, the organisation is still considered terrorist by much of the Western world.

Impasse resumed.

Ariel Sharon went into a coma following complications after a heart operation. Kadima, the political party Sharon founded in order to push forward his disengagement agenda, won the 2006 Israeli election, with Ehud Olmert the new Prime Minister. He has vowed to continue with unilateral withdrawal from the Occupied Territories, leaving the Palestinians behind a separation wall built on lines of Israel's choosing.

This wall, twenty five feet high, detours from the old green line border of 1967 and cuts deep into Palestinian territory to encircle and protect Jewish Settlements. It separates many Arab farmers from their arable lands, and imposes unnecessary hardship on the local residents. It is in effect a land grab and its construction has been declared unlawful by the International Court of Justice.

Nevertheless, it is going ahead and, once completed, it will allow Israel to turn its back on its truculent neighbour and hopefully deliver the security craved.

However, there can be no guarantee of Israel's safety while it is possible to launch a mortar over the barrier. There will still be tension and hostility on both sides of the separation wall.

In the Second Intifada, between September 2000 and the suicide bombing in Tel Aviv in April 2006, 3241 Palestinians were killed by Israeli forces in the West Bank and the Gaza Strip, more than half of them civilians. At the same time, 976 Israelis were murdered in terrorist acts, 305 of them soldiers, policemen, border guards and checkpoint personnel, according to the human rights group B'Tselem.

There is no doubt that these two combatants need separating, but whether a wall imposed by one side on the other will really bring peace and security is open to question.

If injustice is continued or even exaggerated by the presence of the wall, then this tragedy will run and run.

A majority of the Israeli and Palestinian general public now support a negotiated two state solution, according to a recent survey conducted in the United States by the Institute for Peace.

The situation at the moment represents an imposed, not a negotiated settlement. Therefore, its effectiveness is suspect.

Only with the creation of an independent viable Palestinian state in the region can there come a hope for peace. Only when the Palestinians can express themselves as equal, in human terms, to the Israelis will they achieve a modicum of respect.

With Israel seizing the moral high ground and exercising huge influence with the world's strongest superpower, the USA, the Palestinian leadership needs to get smart, and quick.

When the United Nations partitioned Palestine in 1948, David Ben-Gurion immediately announced that they had renamed their portion of the divide Israel. The Arabs should have countered by reiterating that their half was still called Palestine. The name of the land had not changed for 2000 years, but it is now no longer in use, having been literally wiped off the map. It is now referred to as the West Bank of the Jordan River, but why?

It seems that poor leadership, poor judgement, and poor decisions have cost the Palestinian people dear. Instead of moving to oust the new Jewish state in 1948, it is plain to see that the Arabs would have fared better by consolidating what they had, rather than attempting to wrest back the land that once was theirs.

Despite the defeat of the Arab armies, there have been numerous missed opportunities to restate their claim to the land historically referred to as Palestine.

303

Indeed, the PLO has long threatened to make just such an announcement. Why haven't they?

It appears that the Arabs, by stating what they know to be true, that the land they inhabit is called Palestine, fear the announcement would induce an Israeli response akin to that which greeted the Jewish state when it made its own profession of independence in 1948. Knowing that the Arabs can not defeat Israel in a conventional fight, they have been inclined to keep their mouths shut for fear of antagonising their powerful neighbour.

But neither the UN, the Arabs, nor the Israelis can deny that the land prior to 1948 was called Palestine. The only reason the name is no longer in use is just another case of bad Palestinian management.

So it may be that the two state solution will come about only with the creation of the separation wall, but I for one doubt peace will follow if that is to be the case.

THE STORY SO FAR.

The Patriarch of the Jewish people, Abraham, came from Ur in Mesopotamia, modern Iraq. He moved to Canaan, and then on to Egypt. His descendents later settled in the region of Goshen, where the Nile River divides into tributaries before joining the Mediterranean Sea.

The Pharaoh Akhenaten replaced the old order, doing away with the pantheon of Egyptian gods and installing monotheism in its place. This did not go down well in the corridors of power in the old capital, Thebes. Moses, who was either the Pharaoh himself in pseudonym, or at least his right hand man, took the children of the new religion and fled from the old guard.

The enigmatic leader and his faithful band of followers crossed the Red Sea and wandered in the Sinai Desert for 40 years, waiting for an opportunity to seize the Promised Land and fulfil their covenant with the Lord. However, the land of Canaan was already occupied, the Israelites were not strong enough to expel the residents, and so they patiently farmed the hills above instead while awaiting their opportunity.

The first mention of these people comes in the victory stele of the Pharaoh Merneptah, erected in 1207 BC.

The Egyptians were the dominant empire of the time, but they were soon confronted by the mysterious Sea-Peoples. Hailing from the Aegean, whose islands 'Poured out their people all together', this vagabond collective included the tribe of the Peleset, the first Palestinians.

The Sea-Peoples did battle with Raamses III, who ruled in Merneptah's wake between 1200 and 1170 BC.

Having been repelled by the Egyptians, these Pirates of the Aegean settled in the coastal city of Canaan that they had sacked on route. Although they had no historical ties to the area, the Peleset colonised the cities of Ashkelon, Ashdod, and Gaza on the Mediterranean and are still there today, more than 3000 years later.

Conversely, it was this military campaign that allowed the Israelites to leave their hilltop encampments and move into the terrain they so coveted.

The strangers from the sea and the religious community from the hills now shared the region of Canaan between them. A tense stand off, marred by occasional clashes, ensued. It would last for hundreds of years.

In 722 BC, the inhabitants of the northern kingdom of Israel and the Philistines on the coast, as the Peleset had become known, were carried off into slavery by the Babylonians. Only the undeveloped region of Judah, home to the practising religious Hebrew community, remained unscathed.

Then, in 586 BC, the people of Judah went the way of Israel, into exile. It was only with the arrival of the Persian Emperor, Cyrus the Mede, that freedom came to the Jewish people.

Israel was restored, her temple rebuilt, and the Philistine cities were repopulated on the coast.

Into the mix appeared Alexander the Great, a stunning young man who breezed through the region in 326 BC. His short-lived reign eventually gave way to the inexorable rise of the Roman Empire.

The Jews were seen as trouble makers, a difficult minority who posed problems for the ruling elite and kept themselves apart, answering only to their own religious rulers.

Something would have to be done about them, and the Romans had soon had enough. The Second Temple of Jerusalem was destroyed in AD70, and the Israelites were dispersed across the globe.

To complete the process of exclusion, the area, at the time referred to as Judea and Samaria was renamed Aelia Palestina, in honour of the other long term residents, the Philistines. For the next two thousand years, the name would stick.

Following the Romans, the birth of Islam and the Arabisation of the Fertile Crescent, through the Crusades, the Mongols, and the Ottoman Turks, the region of old Canaan kept the name of Palestine.

It is only with the adoption of the United Nations partition plan that the name Israel reappears. Having split the area into two separate states, one for the Jewish people and one for the Arabs, the Hebrews renamed their portion Israel. The area inhabited by the Arabs has, for the past two thousand years, been called Palestine. It still should be.

So who was here first? Who has the right to the land?

Israel was here first, claiming their ancestors had passed through here, but when they arrived after the Exodus, they were described as a people, not a place. So the Hebrew tribe were in the region by 1207 BC, but they did no more than loiter in the hills above and wait for an opportunity to seize the towns and villages below.

The Peleset came sweeping in from the Aegean. They arrived shortly after the Israelites, within a generation, and completed the military victory that the Hebrews could not. This benefited the Jews, who moved into many of the locations vacated in the rout.

This all took place 3200 years ago.

The Israelis then spent the next 1300 years there before disappearing into the Diaspora and only returning 1900 years later to recreate their state in 1948.

The Palestinians have enjoyed continued residence since their arrival more than 3000 years ago. That is until their nation mysteriously disappears in the aftermath of the UN partition plan.

The region has always been a magnet for the forces of Empire, owing to its unique location at the land bridge of Asia and Africa. Each invader has left their mark in the area, as conquest tends to do.

At present, the Palestinians have much in common with the Arabs who have been prominent in the region for 1300 years. They remain, though, the descendents of the Peleset, the people the Bible calls the Philistines.

To have been here within twenty years of each other, and so long ago, could be said to answer the question of who was here first. They both were.

307

Continued residence in the region would lend legitimacy to the Palestinians claim to the land, but Israel, now that it's back, is definitely here to stay and that should be acknowledged as fact.

They were both here then, they are both here now. They should learn once more to live side by side, just like they did in the good old days.

A PROPOSED SOLUTION.

A new start is required to bring peace to the Middle East. The United Nations Partition Plan of 1948 has not worked, that much is plain to see.

At present, Israel surrounds the West Bank, home of the Palestinians who have not fled the occupation and oppression, and is in a constant state of belligerence with the Arabs.

Either Israel seizes all of historic Palestine for herself and achieves Eretz Israel, or it completes the separation wall and retreats behind that self-imposed boundary.

If it is the former, Israel will have a border with Lebanon that she must contest with Hizbollah, a Syrian border that will also prove hostile, and several million Palestinians in Jordan refugeed for the third time since 1948.

Israel will be forced to secure and defend more than 200 kilometres of hostile border, tying up her armed forces and draining her economy. It would be a thankless, near impossible task.

The Separation Wall, as it stands, is an ugly scar on the landscape. It encircles the West Bank and hems in the Palestinians on three sides. It cuts through villages, separates farmers from their orchards and olive groves, and makes already difficult living conditions even harder. It does not bring complete security, and it adds to the sense of injustice.

The reason that the wall will not provide complete security for Israel is because of the pan-handle, the narrow strip of land between the West Bank and the Mediterranean, only about twelve miles wide, that accommodates Tel Aviv and other major Jewish population centres. These can be reached by mortar from the Palestinian side of the wall.

Although this unilateral disengagement could be said to end the occupation, which is the cause of much of the fighting and hostility between the two sides, it would not realise the Palestinian goal of an independent state, and

309

would still impact negatively on the lives of the Arab population, with Israel still controlling access and egress and maintaining her presence on the Jordan River, leaving the West Bank an open prison.

What is needed is a back to basics review. The division of the land in 1948 was nothing more than a recipe for disaster. This rectangular piece of land was split into quarters, with opposite quarters given to each side. That was never going to work.

The land should have been split half and half, so as to leave two twin states, side by side, and that is my proposal for peace.

Take a line starting at the present border between the two people in the middle of the Dead Sea coast line. From there, head towards Hebron, utilizing the road network, which will cede some land to the Israelis and allow access for both parties to the Biblical city.

From Hebron, the new border would proceed towards Bethlehem, cutting inwards so as to arrive at the eastern side of the birthplace of Jesus and of the capital of the new Jewish state: Jerusalem.

I think that, for now, we have to accept that each of the two nations, Israel and Palestine, should have their own capital.

Jewish communities have almost completely encircled Jerusalem with settlements, there is absolutely no chance that they will give them up, and Israel will not give up a portion of her northern territory without receiving something in return. What better prize to offer than the city of Zion itself.

The Palestinians, living in their own contiguous state, would do better to adopt Jericho or Ramallah as their capital city. They need this to compete, and move on. Access to Jerusalem, important because of the Al-Aqsa mosque, could be negotiated for Palestinian visitors.

The wall could then move towards Ramallah and continue along the road until it meets the present West Bank border. There, it would turn north, sweeping inland of Ariel to leave that major Jewish settlement on the Israeli side.

Then, the Wall could turn westwards towards the sea, to keep Nablus Palestinian, and join the river that runs from the West Bank town of Jit to the Mediterranean Sea between Netanya and Hadera. This would make for a far more beautiful, natural, and less aggravating border between the two sides.

A wall built along these lines would be less than half the length of the one currently being built, saving time and money, as well as reducing what is, in effect, a blight.

Israel will have extended her pan-handle border deep into Palestinian territory, fulfilling her security desires, there will be access for both sides to the contested cities, and the major cause of the conflict, the occupation, would no longer exist.

Although Israel would be ceding some northern territory, it has much to gain. At present, the Palestinians hold only 22 percent of the land that the UN divided 55/45 in favour of the Jewish people in 1948.

To return to something like these figures is a move in the right direction. Israel would also rid herself of the pending demographic time bomb, where Jews will soon be outnumbered by Arabs in her own country; a situation she does not want to happen.

There would then be an autonomous Palestinian state for the refugees to return to. Compensation packages have featured as part of previous Israeli/Palestinian negotiations, such as the Camp David Accords of 2000. These could be reactivated to ensure both parties go their separate ways with equanimity and a sense of justice.

The Arabs would be free to rename their state Palestine. It has been called that for 2000 years. When the land was partitioned into a Jewish half and an Arab half, the Jews chose to call theirs Israel. The Palestinians, through ineffective leadership, have failed to remind us that their region is still called Palestine. They have allowed this fact to become murky, then non-extant for fear reiteration might provoke an Israeli military response.

If enacted, Palestine would then become a buffer zone with Lebanon and Syria, leaving Israel with only one border, complete with wall, to defend.

The borders with Egypt and Jordan, with whom Israel enjoys normal relations, would not change in the slightest. Maybe, if Israel feels the need, she could always negotiate with Egypt for territory in the Sinai if the Jewish people need more room.

Most Arab states now accept Israel's right to exist, as recent Arab League statements testify, especially that announced in Beirut 2002 and in the words of Colonel Gadhaffi of Libya. They profess to be concerned primarily with obtaining justice for the Palestinians.

A recent survey by the American Peace Centre found that most Israelis and Palestinians want a two state solution. Peace should then follow because practically all the causes of dissatisfaction; the daily oppression, restriction of movement, ritual humiliation, close contact, would have been removed.

The only viable option is to trade land for peace. The Palestinians could then turn their back on Israel and look towards the Arab states that they are historically and ethnically related to: Lebanon and Syria.

The wall, as high as Israel wants it, would be half the length of the current border, and there could therefore be fewer checkpoints to man. Again, this represents a financial incentive for Israel to look at redrawing the map.

Finally, the border I have proposed, from north of Netanya to the current Dead Sea line, if drawn on a map would dissect Jerusalem. If only theoretically, it still provides for two states centred on the Holy City.

In practice, the wall follows sensible lines that give Israel security and the Palestinians a state. It could remove 60 years of hurt and 100 percent of the present injustice.

An Israeli state in the region could be an economic boon for all her neighbours, while a Palestinian state is the minimum requirement for the surrounding Arab countries to make peace with the Jewish people.

It is now time to tackle this difficult question, otherwise the problems will continue and this issue will remain an open wound. I believe the original partition plan has proved unworkable, and I think that my proposal is both practical and just.

To quote one young man interviewed in a book entitled 'Growing Up Palestinian', by Laetitia Bucaille:

'We're not against peace. If that's what Israel wants, let's do it. Peace would mean we could go wherever we wanted. We could go to Amman or Tel Aviv by car. But to go back to our grandparents villages, well that would be too difficult. We'll just forget about that.'

It sounds like the time is ripe to put down arms and to redraw the map, to create a contiguous state for the Palestinians, and to give the Israelis the security they need. Then, rather than interning her young people in the military, Israel might turn them to her own dividend.

The presence of Arab communities in Israel and Jewish in Palestine should not pose a problem. They will both be hostages of fortune for the other.

It is time to move forward in 21st Century style, out of this ancient quagmire.

There will be tough decisions ahead, and an ongoing process of negotiations as difficulties on the ground become evident when the theory is put into practice. But if there is the will, if this is followed by the requisite action, then there can be an end to the age-old conflict that has scarred the Middle East.

The cause of much of the fighting is land and not religion, and given that Judaism, Christianity, and Islam all believe in the same, omnipotent, omniscient and omnipresent God, I'd like to end on a quotation that I hope will cause offence to none but will give succour to those with difficult decisions ahead.

'Blessed are they that hunger and thirst for justice, for they shall have their fill. Blessed are the peacemakers, for they are the children of God.'

EPILOGUE.

The old guard of Fatah was ousted in democratic elections by Hamas, to the West's chagrin, in January of 2006. Both the US and the EU blocked the aid payments that the Palestinian Authority relies on to function. Unless Hamas were prepared to acknowledge the Jewish state's right to exist, the new government would be left to flounder.

In Gaza, Palestinian militants continued to fire rockets across the border into Israeli towns. The response was an economic blockade and the return of IDF soldiers into terrain they had abandoned, amid much soul-searching, less than a year before.

Then, on 25th June 2006, a group of guerrillas attacked an IDF outpost, killing two soldiers and capturing another, 19 year old Corporal Gilad Shalit.

'There will be no sleep in Gaza', Israeli Prime minister Ehud Olmert declared 'until Gilad Shalit is returned.'

Sound bombs exploded day and night, Hamas government officials were arrested, and militants were picked off with military precision from the air by fighter planes or unmanned drones. The main power station was destroyed by missile fire leaving 1.5 million people with limited access to water or electricity. The borders were closed.

Israel said it was simple. Return Gilad Shalit and their soldiers would return to their bases.

The Palestinians held out, despite the hardships. What they wanted, in order to release the young Corporal, was a prisoner exchange for some of the 10,000 political interns in Israeli jails. Hostage exchanges had taken place before. This time though, the Israelis preferred not to negotiate.

As the situation grew ever more desperate in the Gaza Strip, a new battlefront emerged when Hizbollah, the 'Party of God', attacked Israel at its northern border in the region of Southern Lebanon.

Two Israeli soldiers were taken hostage. A prisoner exchange was again demanded. Israel's response was the same. They would not deal with terrorists.

For the next 34 days, destruction rained down on the neighbourhoods on either side of the divide. Beirut, as in 1982, bore the brunt of Israeli aggression. The world watched aghast as the Mediterranean city that had risen from the ashes was reduced to rubble again. The airport was the first to feel the brunt of the Israeli air force. Western tourists fled the area by sea under the watchful eye of the United Nations. The Lebanese saw their escape routes, roads and bridges into Syria and Jordan, bombed from the sky.

A UN observation post was destroyed by a precision bomb with the loss of four international peacekeepers. It seemed Israel wanted no witnesses to the destruction being visited on the coastal towns of Tyre and Sidon and the villages of Southern Lebanon. Only with the deaths of more than forty civilians, twenty eight of them children, one only a day old, in the town of Qana did Israel acknowledge the growing outrage to her actions. Air strikes were suspended for thirty six hours.

A new tactic was employed, to send the IDF in on foot across the border, to establish a buffer zone to prevent Hizbollah rockets landing in Israel. Unfortunately, this was a situation the Party of God had long prepared for.

Established during the earlier Israeli incursion into Lebanon almost a quarter of a century ago, inspired by the Islamic revolution in Iran, and supported by the regime in Syria for broadening the front of resistance against the Jewish state, Hizbollah soldiers had dug into the territory of Southern Lebanon vacated by the Israelis in 2000. With the Lebanese guerrilla force employing a network of tunnels and cellars in abandoned houses, hilltop gun nests and well-appointed sniper positions, the IDF soldiers approaching on foot could not have anticipated the depth of welcome awaiting them. Powerless to prevent the Hizbollah rockets landing in Haifa and other towns in Northern Israel, the IDF found it virtually impossible to establish the foothold they required to bring security to the region, and their losses grew alarmingly, and raised uncomfortable questions back home.

Finally, having failed to pound the Lebanese into submission, despite the damage done, and with the world at last in unison on conditions for a ceasefire, Israel chose to accept UN Resolution 1701, and the sixth Arab-Israeli war, as the conflict came to be called, came to a close. It seemed Israel would have to negotiate the release of her captured soldiers after all.

In total, 150 Israelis died in the fighting, two thirds of them from the military. 1500 Lebanese died, two thirds of them civilians.

In Gaza, an area that has been termed the largest open prison in the world, the suffering continues. Hundreds of people have been killed or injured in the region since Gilad Shalit was seized, and there seems no end in sight to this tragedy unless Israel gives the Palestinians a state of their own, at which point this problem, and a lot of others in the region, would disappear.

I would like to go there, to see for myself the situation on the ground. I could fly to Cairo in Egypt and take the train south to Tel el-Amarna, the vision of Akhenaten, where Monotheism and the Exodus began. This, though, may prove too dangerous, as the area teems with activists opposed to Western visitors. If that's the case, I would fly to Hurghada on the Red Sea coast and turn westwards to face the desert and gaze upon the self-same sands.

Then, I'd take the ferry across the Red Sea to Sinai, and travel up the mountain to St Katherine's monastery, where the Lord first spoke to Moses from within the Burning Bush. Then, I'd take the road by bus or taxi to Taba and cross into the Promised Land. Traverse the undulating terrain, in turns barren and fertile, rocky, ravine, sandy or steppe, the snaking River Jordan and the Dead Sea down below, before finally reaching the ancient citadel of Jerusalem.

I'd cross the border into the West Bank at one of the Israeli checkpoints and witness for myself the discrepancies and differences between the two sides and then, at last, it might be possible to decide where Right truly lies.

It promises to be some journey.

NOTE ON SOURCES.

To have acknowledged every quote and source for this project would have rendered the text virtually unreadable and would have made the book twice as long as it is. Instead, I have endeavoured to find out what I could on this subject before regaling the reader with what I believe to be the facts. It does not aim to be an overly-academic work but rather a personal, subjective, yet informative account. Nonetheless, I am indebted to numerous books that I have read along the way, and the following is a list of some, most, if not all of the sources employed.

The Independent newspaper; the Bible (Douay version); The Bible Unearthed, by Israel Finkelstein and Neil Asher Silberman; A History of the Middle East, by Peter Mansfield; the Palestine/Israeli Conflict - A Beginner's Guide, by Cohn-Sherbok and El-Alami; The Middle East, by Bernard Lewis; the New Penguin History of the World, by J.M.Roberts; Moses and Akhenaten, by Ahmed Osman; Six Days, by Jeremy Bowen; From the Holy Mountain, by William Dalrymple; The New penguin Atlas of the Ancient World, by Colin McEvedy; Atlas of the Bible, by Luc.H.Grollenberg; Growing Up Palestinian, by Laetitia Bucaille; Moses and Monotheism, by Sigmund Freud, The Middle East, by Humphreys; Yasser Arafat, by Barry and Judith Rubin; Gaza First, by Jane Corbin; Pity The Nation, by Robert Fisk; Israel, by David Ben-Gurion; Herzl, by Desmond Stewart; The Jewish National Fund, by Walter Lehn and Uri Davis, as well as endless Internet research. Other sources appear within the text of the book. Apologies to any that I have employed and failed to acknowledge. This is, after all, my own subjective account. Above all, I have tried to be truthful. Peace through understanding. Thanks for listening.

THE END

Israel - Jewish
Palestine - Arabs
Suez Crisis P158